# The Friends of
# Richard Nixon

## Also by George V. Higgins

# The Friends of Richard Nixon

## by George V. Higgins

*An Atlantic Monthly Press Book*

Little, Brown and Company
Boston / Toronto

SECOND PRINTING
T   10/75
Portions of this work originally appeared in *The Atlantic* in slightly different form.


LIBRARY OF CONGRESS CATALOGING IN PUBLICATION DATA

Higgins, George V.      1939-
    The Friends of Richard Nixon.

    "An Atlantic Monthly Press book."
    Includes index.
    1. Watergate Affair, 1972-      I. Title.
E860.H53      364.1′32′0973      75-19269
ISBN 0-316-36080-5

ATLANTIC-LITTLE, BROWN BOOKS
ARE PUBLISHED BY
LITTLE, BROWN AND COMPANY
IN ASSOCIATION WITH
THE ATLANTIC MONTHLY PRESS


*Published simultaneously in Canada
by Little, Brown & Company (Canada) Limited*

PRINTED IN THE UNITED STATES OF AMERICA

# Acknowledgments

THIS BOOK is not Mike Janeway's fault, but it was largely his idea. At the outset. It was also Bob Manning's idea, to do it, but it was Bob's idea after it was my idea, and it was mine after it was Mike's.

Now it is nobody's idea but mine. That is not to say that I did it all by myself; when the Managing Editor of *The Atlantic* invests an idea in a writer, and the Editor in Chief of *The Atlantic* endorses it with that best evidence of enthusiasm (money), they do not, thereafter, fail to attend to its progress. Since May of 1973, when I started trying to figure out how come men and institutions, involved in Watergate, performed as they did, I have enjoyed that best variety of adult friendships with Mr. Manning and Mr. Janeway, the kind that begins with the cognition that matters proceed most satisfactorily when people say exactly what is on their minds. This was a long, expensive and arduous project. It was often frustrating, and neither Bob Manning nor I handles frustration well. But it was also very clearly work fit for a man to do, honest intellectual labor of genuine substance, arising out of what was certainly the biggest story that any newspaperman could ever ask. Bob Manning and Mike Janeway did not write this book for me, but they were resolute, vigorous and unstinting in their efforts to be sure that I write the best book I could, and because of those efforts, I have written, I think, a much better book than I would have otherwise.

I am, of course, disqualified by reason of interest, from entering that judgment. And, I suppose, the people who must make it ought to begin with the question of whether I was fair. There was, after all, no more that I could do about my biases, and my prejudices, than anyone else could do about theirs: recognize them, and try to prevent them from causing undesirable influence upon what I wrote.

In 1967, when I was one of several dozen new lawyers appointed by Elliot L. Richardson to serve in the Massachusetts Department of the

Attorney General, I was a Democrat. I had never been politically active; before I went to law school, I was an Associated Press reporter, and the AP forbade its reporters (wisely, I think) overt political behavior. When Mr. Richardson joined the Nixon Administration in 1969, he was succeeded as Attorney General by Robert H. Quinn, a Democrat. By then, I was a Republican, having changed registration in order to vote in a primary contest that interested me. Mr. Richardson had disapproved of political activity by his Assistant Attorneys General, and I never did any for Mr. Quinn, either. Nor, when I moved to the United States Attorney's Office in Boston in 1970, did I undertake any political work. I voted for Mr. Nixon in 1968 and, recidivistically, again in 1972. My commission as a federal prosecutor was signed by John N. Mitchell, as Attorney General of the United States; I never met the man. During 1970 and 1971, I was a consultant on organized crime for the National Institute of Criminal Justice, which is part of the Law Enforcement Assistance Administration; for several months I reported to Henry S. Ruth, then its Director. As a state prosecutor, I served under Charles H. Rogovin, the Chief of the Criminal Division under Richardson; Charlie, in 1973, assisted Hank Ruth, then Deputy Special Prosecutor, in selecting staff for Archibald Cox. I had known James S. Doyle, the Special Prosecutor's public information officer, when he was with the *Boston Globe* and I was with the AP. When I was a federal prosecutor, I was under the jurisdiction of Henry Petersen, both as Deputy Assistant Attorney General and as Assistant Attorney General and chief of the Criminal Division of the United States Department of Justice. I prosecuted several defendants who were represented by James D. St. Clair; none of the respect engendered by those rigorous experiences was diminished by what I saw of his work as attorney for President Nixon.

I recite all of that because Bob Manning, Mike Janeway and I decided very early in the project that I was going to try to call things by their right names. When the articles were published — two long pieces which were written in the first drafts of this book — in *The Atlantic*, some readers were very distressed. Sam Dash, for example, was quite upset by my suggestion that he did a lousy job as Counsel for the Ervin Committee, and there was a man who wrote from Abington, Massachusetts, to say he didn't think it proper to report coarse behavior of the late Lyndon B. Johnson.

Well, Mr. Dash will not find this extended report any better adapted to the service of his ego, and while I have not hesitated to correct, modify, and eliminate judgments and anecdotes appearing in the articles, the stories about President Johnson remain. I think it is serviceable to call reprehensible behavior *reprehensible*, and to keep in mind that Richard M. Nixon, while he certainly behaved reprehensibly, at most achieved only a new height of damnable arrogance; he did not invent the character defect any more than he was the first President to be more inquisitive than the Constitution permits, and no purpose is gained by blinking either fact.

Neither do I perceive any utility in undeserved tenderness of nomenclature in the characterization of villainous conduct; like Earl Silbert, I never dreamed that an Attorney General of the United States would lie to a grand jury, and I therefore think it quite appropriate to use harsh words about John Mitchell, in order to indicate responsive disapproval of his decision to do that. He took the same oath I had to take, to get that signed commission, and it contains something, as I recall, about upholding the Constitution and the laws of the United States. When he did what he did, he dishonored that oath, and I think that was contemptible, so I have said so.

But I also think that Judge John J. Sirica overstepped his boundaries, and that Earl Silbert did a fine job in prosecuting the first Watergate case, and that Leon Jaworski was forced by circumstances into making a mistake in bringing the case against Richard G. Kleindienst, and that the vaunted political judgment of Richard M. Nixon was at best intermittent: sometimes he was thoroughly stupid. I rather grew to like G. Gordon Liddy, whom I never met or spoke to: in the whole gallery, he was the only one with any integrity at all. If his view of life would scare the bejesus out of you, nevertheless, he had, literally, the courage of his convictions, and that's more than many of the rest of them had.

I formed the judgments in this book with the assistance (and to the more-than-occasional consternation) of a large number of people in the northeast megalopolitan corridor, most of whom had more pressing things to do than cure my ignorance or deflect my erroneous opinions. Of them generally I must say that they exemplify, to me, the best ideal of the thoughtful person: welcoming controversy, thriving on argument, constant through disagreement, questioning, disdainful of the pontifical mode, as generous to concede superiority of another man's idea as they were transparently delighted with the superiority of their own.

Mike Janeway told me I should get in touch with Walter Pincus at *The New Republic*, when I got to Washington, so I did, and there's another favor I owe Mike. Walter was much grouchier than I, in the Ervin summer, about the probable veracity of the witnesses before the Committee, and we used to spend the lunch hour doing as much wrangling as the lawyers had done in the morning session before. I don't know whether I like Walter better than his wife, Ann Terry Pincus, or the other way around; Ann's probably got more sense than Walter or I, and she's certainly better looking, but then, I don't have to choose.

Mike also recommended Harry McPherson, who was Counsel to LBJ. He did not tell me the story about the Secret Service man. He did arrange a luncheon with Clark Clifford, from which I took much profit. He did make himself available for drinks in the late afternoon, when he would probably have preferred to go home, and he took very special pains to make sure that I had the benefit of his numerous contacts with politicians and politician watchers who come from the South and the Southwest, and that was not a bad thing at all, for a fellow with my accent.

I met Marty Nolan in the freshman class at Boston College in 1957. By tending to business, he was Chief of the *Globe*'s Washington bureau considerably before 1973; Charlie Claffey was covering the hearings for the paper, and Sal Micciche was covering the court developments, and Cindy was running the office, I think, and I thank them all.

Louisa Crowe and Roy McGhee were running the Senate Periodical Press Gallery, which can be a sort of Seaman's Relief Home for your regular out-of-town journalist.

Leonard Garment was Special Counsel to the President. He plays the clarinet, speaks English as though it were his native tongue, somehow escaped the paranoia that afflicted so many in the Nixon White House, and in exchange for a straight question, gives a straight answer. Lovely man. Not a bad lawyer, either, I understand. Too bad his client didn't take his advice.

The thing about Art Buchwald is that he will not let you pick up a check for lunch at Sans Souci. He *insists* that you pick up the check. I beat Art Buchwald out of two lunches.

Dave Rosenbaum of the *New York Times* had the seat next to mine at the Ervin Committee hearings. That may have been his misfortune; it was my benefit.

Jane O'Reilly, of *New York*, is a friend of mine, a condition demonstrable from the fact that she suggested Sara Cooper as a research person. Sara can produce exactly what is requested by one impenetrable phone call, and, even better, volunteer what should have been requested, but wasn't.

When Tom Kennelly was Deputy Chief of the Organized Crime and Racketeering Section, at Justice, I was setting up seminars on organized crime for the Institute, and I roped him into speaking at Columbus, Nebraska. He got back at me: he made me speak in Columbus, Ohio. Tom was Gordon Liddy's local counsel. Mine, too.

I interviewed a lot of people, to find out what was going on and, more importantly, to find out what it meant. Some of their names appear in the text. A good many do not, some because they trusted me to keep their identities confidential, some because I just stole their ideas and let it go at that.

The best for last: Claffey introduced me to Loretta Cubberly, Dick Drayne's assistant in Ted Kennedy's office. That was a parley: Dick Loretta, Ed Cubberly, Carol Welch, Barney Patterson, Hunter Thompson, sundry others, but Loretta and Ed best of all.

It was all contained in my experience with Edward Bennett Williams, who was hard to reach, when I was trying to reach him, because he was trying a case in New Jersey. He called me, one day, from Trenton or some other godforsaken place, and wanted to know what he could do to help. A lot of people did that, reflecting an attitude that Richard M. Nixon had done well to have shared. After all, being President of the United States is not a bad job. The least you can do is be pleasant about it.

There were also people who were denied even the option to choose not to put up with me during almost two years of travel, long hours and weariness that often left me fit companion for neither man nor beast, but did it anyway, with regular grace. My children, John and Susan, somehow accepted the fact that there was nothing personal in my extended and repeated absences, nor in the occasional testiness that I displayed. My mother's only display of concern was the frequently repeated advice to be careful while flying in airplanes driven by pilots of commercial airlines. My friends, especially Marty Kelly, Judy Kelly, Jon Klarfeld, Patricia Klarfeld, Jay Goodman, Ellen Goodman, Mike Mone and Joe Tauro, must frequently have been profoundly bored, but never showed it, and were always patient. Undaunted by nearly two years as my secretary in the United States Attorney's Office, Mary L. Coughlin elected to leave a perfectly fine job in order to run my office, type this manuscript, retype this manuscript, retype the revised version, retype the revisions of the revised version, and then type the new drafts. While the experience afforded her, Mary McCormack, Frank Crowley, Mike Nigro and Ernie Finan, who also worked in that office, abundant opportunities to enrich their vocabularies of profanity and to learn more about Watergate than they probably desired to know, it was also trying and arduous, and punishing. She did it with extraordinary skill, and singular charity, and so did they.

To all of them, my deep gratitude.

George V. Higgins
Boston, Massachusetts
February 23, 1975

# Introduction

IN THE SUMMER of 1973, the United States Ambassador to Iran was relaxed. His credentials, as former Director of the Central Intelligence Agency, were as impeccable as his tailoring. His languor, nicely counterpointed by his faultless display of concealed high energy (conveyed by chain-smoking), was the perfect manner of delivery for his connoisseur's disdainful appraisal of a shoddy performance. The break-in at the Democratic National Committee Headquarters at the Watergate, said Richard Helms, was "amateurish in the extreme."

The Ervin Committee, which received that technical critique appreciatively (as it accepted, with pathetic gratitude, virtually anything that was proffered to it), was not thereby assisted overmuch in the performance of its principal mission. That objective was to find out if the President of the United States had put Gordon Liddy up to the burglary, and, if so, whether he had taken any measures to conceal his participation.

He had, of course, lots of them. And when those measures were discovered, his taking of them was his ruination. Good enough for him, too, the liar.

A careful, dispassionate, professional expert, with experience in plotting equivalent to Helms's — say, a prudent Mafia underboss in his occupational prime, or the perpetrator of frauds grossing at least two or three million without consequent service of a single subpoena — would have predicted that result. Anybody dumb enough to commission so feckless a project for people of such remarkable ineptitude would certainly lack the mother wit to think ahead, and plan for the contingency that he might get caught.

Thinking ahead, in criminal business, is of surpassing importance, even more so than in legitimate commerce and in politics, where it certainly does no harm. The professional outlaw seldom loses sight of the possibility that he, or someone working for him, may make a mistake, or suffer some bad luck, or succumb to overconfidence and get hooked for something big because he bungled something small. He is on guard from the instant he begins to make his operational plans (he does not cause his conferences to be tape-recorded, and he invites to those discussions only those with a pressing need to know, and he does not confide the agenda to the uninvited). If something goes wrong, and the cops come, he is not reduced to frantic, random foraging in the early morning hours, for a willing though sleepy attorney, and a bail bondsman. Nor does he negligently permit his operatives to carry his phone number in their belongings, helpfully annotated to show that, yes, it is his number. The practical crook is a man of provident humility, who sees to it, in advance, that investigation will be arduous, protracted, dispiritingly unproductive, and, in the long run, unsuccessful. By that foresight in frustrating the orderly procedures of American criminal justice (by leaving nothing to chance, and very little to be found), he exonerates himself from the alternative, more difficult, and vastly more dangerous obligation to obstruct the processes of American criminal justice. There is no substitute for knowing what you're doing.

President Nixon did not know what he was doing when he commenced to obstruct American justice. Neither did H. R. Haldeman, John Ehrlichman or John Mitchell, when they aspired to aid and abet him in that project. They knew what they needed, but they didn't know how to get it, right, the first time.

There, perhaps, was the hallmark of their self-hypnotic, delusive assurance that by some unspecified osmotic process they had, not taken, but been infused with all knowledge, as their province. Maybe that is what happens to you, when you once pull off some prodigy, such as getting elected President of the United States, with mirrors: if you can, and do, achieve the White House by passively allowing Hubert Humphrey to lose the election, without ever formulating (let alone committing yourself to) substantive programs, firm goals or intensely felt purposes (if, indeed, you become convinced that the resolute denial of such goals was the means of your success, because your vacuity offended no marginal supporter, and at last won over previously passive voters, who didn't like you much at first, because it let them believe what they wanted), then perhaps it is inevitable that you will come to embrace the view that in reaction, slow, delayed, restrained reaction, is contained the key to mastery of human events. "I can do anything," Annie Oakley sang fetchingly and without full understanding of the situation, "you can do, better," and so did Richard Nixon and his friends.

They could do that, and they did it, and it was wrong. John Wesley Dean III *was* a capable, diligent and obliging young man. He could draw up a simple trust with the best of them, and when it came to getting the President's tax returns done, by somebody else, well, there was simply no holding him. There wasn't any commotion around him. He wore his hair short and slicked down, and he was polite and a close student of the stock market. He did not make a lot of noise, and he was plainly impressed, himself, to be Counsel to the President while still in his early thirties. Good lad, John Dean; you asked him to do something, through channels, of course, and the first thing you knew, it was done. If there was going to be a bit of difficulty because John Mitchell had been inattentive to the plans that Gordon Liddy made, well, John Dean could handle it.

John Dean couldn't handle it. He didn't know what the hell he was doing. More than that, in justice to Dean, it's very likely that nobody with an overriding moral disinclination to use a revolver (Liddy had some notion of the gravity of the situation: he volunteered to be rubbed out, but nobody listened) could have handled it. Morally, ethically and legally it is of course to the credit of the President and his friends that they let no contracts to make hits, as the Mob does, to hasten the acceptance of hush money.

But, from a technical standpoint, that restraint was amateurish in the extreme. It made participation in the cover-up a volitional matter. Just another damned option that you had, if you'd been caught, flabbergasted, in the Watergate. Okay, so long as nobody came along with something that you feared more than you cherished what you had, e.g., twenty or thirty years in jail. The Mob's men don't take money for their families, and the prepaid services of counsel, just because they're so grateful for the largesse that they can cheerfully undertake to do five to seven as a spontaneous gesture of fraternal solidarity: they do it, and keep their mouths shut, because, if they don't, they'll wind up in the harbor with a couple in the head. That kind of certitude makes a man a whole lot more tractable, reliable and patient if the cash is late one month, or less than he'd been led to expect or had demanded.

Dean, devoid of managerial experience in the administration of conspiracies of silence, lacked also that means of keeping the boys in line.

Consequently they got out of line. Some, in fact, never actually got into line in the first place, although they pretended to, because it seemed useful. What Dean had, and it wasn't much, instead of the credible threat of grave bodily harm, was the variable reverence for the Presidency (and thus for the President) which Haldeman and Ehrlichman thought they felt, which Mitchell apparently did feel, and which the rest served more with their lips than with their hearts and minds. The Mob, trading on fear to maintain discipline, calls it *respect*; Richard Nixon and his friends mistook for respect, repeatedly, what was merely the strategic obsequiousness of rather limited men, who had espied in the paranoia of the Administration what certainly seemed to be windfall opportunities to redeem lost hopes of self-aggrandizement by doing dirty deeds.

Liddy, Jim McCord and Howard Hunt were disappointed men, whose lives had fallen short of their unrealistic expectations despite their protests to the contrary. The Cuban Americans were buoyed in their sad (because vainglorious) anti-Castroism because Hunt was able to invoke their earlier disastrous loyalties to get them to believe that a few B and Es, committed in the continental United States, would somehow start a chain reaction that would topple the Communist regime in Havana. Hunt's recruiting drive succeeded because he communicated an excited zeal that was genuine, but, like McCord's, almost entirely opportunistic. Only Liddy's passion, and the misguided fealty of the Cubans, survived the battering that the conspiracy of silence had to take, and that, of course, was not enough.

Unprepared, and undergunned, for his tasks, Dean found them further complicated by numerous changes in the rosters of his clients (whom he thought, in lawyerlike fashion, he was supposed to protect) and those other individuals whose protection was required, secondarily, for the protection of his clients. When he entered the case, he acted upon the premise that his list of clients was elastic, so that it could accommodate the addition or subtraction of any name, at any time, except that of Mr. Nixon (in April of 1973, Dean grew alarmed that he himself was about to undergo subtraction, and thereupon removed the exception). Realist that he was, Dean also perceived that when he had to lose one of those clients, he gained a potential enemy for his clients, who would have to be jollied along with as much assistance as possible in order to prevent disaster for those clients remaining.

He started with the welfare of the President, Haldeman, Ehrlichman and Mitchell in his hands. To further their interests, he essayed to influence, benignly, the subsidiary (to Dean) welfare of Liddy, Hunt, Mc-Cord and the Cubans. That effort simultaneously effected increase of the list of secondary clients (adding L. Patrick Gray III, Jeb Stuart Magruder, Herbert Porter, Hugh Sloan, Herbert Kalmbach, John Caulfield, Anthony Ulasewicz and Dorothy Hunt, at a minimum, between June 18, 1972, and September 15, 1972), reduction, by one, of the list of primary clients (John Mitchell had to come up with a little perjury to flesh out the efforts of the added starters to limit indictment to Liddy and subordinates), and the confusion of those whose bungling had caused the difficulty in the first place.

Dean, it is hard to remember, spent only ten months in the supervision of the cover-up; what makes it difficult is the amount of frenetic activity that he crammed into those months: in the course of them he had to scramble to invent several conspiracies of his own design, and to implement a few more which others pressed upon him. He had been designated *beekeeper*, but he spent most of his time fighting the swarm. Instead of one, smooth-running conspiracy to obstruct justice (which would have been superfluous in a well-run gang), hard enough for a novice to control, Dean had a congeries of conspiracies, some at odds with others; instead of a little band of felonious brothers, scheming unanimously with due regard for their interdependency, he presided over a veritable hospitality suite of vacillating independent contractors, as unschooled as he in the necessity for united action, and regularly fractious in strident profession of their individual interests. James McCord was nothing short of impertinent.

Dean wasn't stupid. He knew bad management when he saw it, even when he was the manager himself. When the President congratulated him, September 15, 1972, for limiting defendants to *Liddy, et al.*, Dean exhibited poise remarkable for a man accepting the gratitude of a President of the United States: he warned Mr. Nixon that his personal security was precarious, and that it would have to be shored up with something a lot stronger than he'd been able to construct, if it were to last. Mr. Nixon was euphoric; if he listened, he did not take heed.

That was very poor judgment on Mr. Nixon's part. It manifested the flaw that was fatal to him. Dean's jerry-built, haphazard, ad hoc, improvised and tottering series of conspiracies would have collapsed in a week if fabricated by a group of crooked bankers to avert a major fraud prosecution. At best it was a stall, and it wasn't a very good stall. Its effectiveness was temporary, the consequence of the advantage which its participants passively enjoyed, did not value highly enough (because they did not respect it enough, and that was how they had been able so to demean it), and thereby failed to cherish as resolutely as they should: a President of the United States, whatever the experience of lesser mortals in negotiation of the constitutional promise, gets the full benefit, and then some, of the presumption of innocence. And so do those minions of his, whose actions invite the assertion of guilt which suggests his own.

That concept, for the majority of Americans, rebutted the mounting evidence of presidential culpability well into the spring of 1974, perhaps into the summer. Its strength overrode Dean's defection, Sam Ervin's plain suspicions, Elliot Richardson's resignation, Archibald Cox's dismissal, Leon Jaworski's ominous silence, Peter Rodino's responsible caution, the appropriate anger of wrathful commentators, and disclosure after disclosure of facts which established, then demanded, then importuned the dismaying verdict that the President, indeed, was as guilty as hell. And when at last it was refuted in his case (shortly to be revived in a more modest disguise by Gerald R. Ford's presidential decree that because Mr. Nixon had disgraced himself, he did not deserve to be found guilty of the acts which had merited the disgrace), John Dean was in jail, doing one to four for obstructing the justice that his master had eluded, in large part by Dean's efforts.

That was not entirely satisfactory, but it was the best, in the circumstances, that could be managed, and it was fully bad enough to suit Dean. Unlike his clients, he did not underestimate their pursuers. Earl Silbert's reticence, as the Assistant U.S. Attorney in charge of the *Liddy* case, did not lull Dean (as it did some commentators) into false confidence of eternal safety, because he knew what Silbert had in mind to do after he got the convictions he would surely get. And Dean, if he had had access to the President when Henry Ruth, another quiet man, took office as Archie Cox's deputy, would not have been encouraging about the President's consequential prospects. Dean was an amateur, but Ruth and John Doar and the others were not, and before they ever arrived, he saw them coming, and despaired. He was an amateur, but he knew it, and he was not a fool. Not as much can be said for his clients.

# The Cast

RICHARD M. NIXON

Scoundrel, in Chief. Also: President of the United States; Oath-taker; Coconspirator (unindicted); Accessory after the fact; Client; Recording Artist.

H. R. HALDEMAN

First Henchman. Also: chief of White House staff (Lord High Executioner); Liar; Coconspirator (indicted and convicted); Accessory after the fact; Client; Scoundrel-tamer; German Shepherd; Recording Angel.

JOHN D. EHRLICHMAN

Second Henchman. Also: Domestic Council chief; Liar; Coconspirator (indicted and convicted); Accessory after the fact; Client; Scoundrel-tamer; German Shepherd; Recording Artist (inadvertent).

JOHN W. DEAN III

Memorybank. Also: Sometime henchman; Counsel to the President of the United States (same thing); Plotter (apprentice); Unindentured servant; Recording Artist (inadvertent); Television personality; Defendant; Convict; former attorney.

SAM DASH

Trial lawyer (ret.).

| | |
|---|---|
| SAM J. ERVIN, JR. | Moralist. Also: member of the United States Senate; Chairman, Senate Select Committee on Presidential Campaign Activities. |
| KING TIMAHOE | Dog (blameless; will not appear). |
| L. PATRICK GRAY III | Jerk. Also: Acting Director, FBI (in the unavoidable absence of J. Edgar Hoover). |
| HENRY ROTHBLATT | Unretired trial lawyer. |
| BERNARD L. BARKER<br>FRANK A. FIORINI (STURGIS)<br>EUGENIO R. MARTINEZ<br>VIRGILIO R. GONZALEZ | Clients of Rothblatt. Also: Burglars; Photographers; Go-through guys. |
| JAMES W. McCORD, JR. | "Stool pigeon." Also: Locksmith (incompetent); Wireman (incompetent); Spy (ret.). |
| EVERETTE HOWARD HUNT, JR. | Spy (ret.). Also: Author; Liar; Burglar. |
| G. GORDON LIDDY | Stand-up guy. Also: Burglar; Wiretapper; Coconspirator; Contemner (convicted); Exemplar (per judgment, Sirica, C.J.). |
| HENRY S. PETERSEN | Assistant Attorney General, Chief, Criminal Division, United States Department of Justice. Also: Dupe. |
| EARL J. SILBERT | Principal Assistant U.S. Attorney, District of Columbia. Also: Victim. |

| | |
|---|---|
| HOWARD BAKER | Second Moralist; Entertainer. Also: Member of the United States Senate; Senate Select Committee on Presidential Campaign Activities. |
| RUFUS EDMISTEN | Protégé. Also: Deputy Counsel, Senate Select Committee on Presidential Campaign Activities. |
| FRED THOMPSON | Former Assistant U.S. Attorney, Tennessee. Also: Minority Chief Counsel, Senate Select Committee on Presidential Campaign Activities; Source, usually "well informed." |
| JOHN J. SIRICA | Maximum John. Also: Chief Judge, United States District Court, District of Columbia (ret.); Senior Judge, United States District Court, District of Columbia; Man of the Year. |
| HERBERT W. KALMBACH | Private Counsel to the President of the United States. Also: Bagman. |
| JEB STUART MAGRUDER | Adolescent. Also: Perjuror. |
| JOHN J. CAULFIELD | Acting Director, Enforcement, Alcohol, Tobacco & Firearms Division, Internal Revenue Service, United States Department of Justice. Also: Frightened Meddler and Message-bearer; Liar. |

| | |
|---|---|
| Archibald Cox | Professor of Law, Harvard Law School (on leave). Also: Special Prosecutor (fired). |
| Leon Jaworski | Texas lawyer. Also: Special Prosecutor (resigned). |
| Henry S. Ruth, Jr. | Shane. Also: Deputy Special Prosecutor. Special Prosecutor. |
| Hugh W. ("Duke") Sloan, Jr. Herbert ("Bart") Porter | Friends of Magruder. |
| Gerhard Gesell George S. Hart | Friends of John J. Sirica. Also: Judges, United States District Court, District of Columbia. |
| Richard G. Kleindienst | Former Attorney General of the United States. Also: Golfer; Liar. |
| John N. Mitchell | Former Attorney General of the United States. Also: Coconspirator (indicted, convicted, appealed); Liar. |
| Maurice W. Stans | Big-game hunter. Also: Former Secretary, United States Department of Commerce; Expert witness; Misdemeanant. |
| Anthony Ulasewicz | Comic relief. Also: Bagman. |
| William O. Bittman | Attorney-at-Law, cash fees preferred; leave at elevator (very expensive). Also: Counsel to E. Howard Hunt, Jr.; former Special Attorney, United States Department of Justice. |
| Elliot L. Richardson | Man of Probity. Also: Attorney General of Massachusetts; Undersecretary, United States Department of State; Secretary, United States Department of Health, Education and |

Welfare; Secretary, United States Department of Defense; Attorney General of the United States.

THE MAN            Designated observer (replaces Well-informed Sources, Senior Officials, Highly Placed Authorities, and Top Officials). Each remark attributed to The Man was uttered by a living human being; only tenses have been changed. Contributors included, but were not limited to, four cops, three lawyers, four journalists, and some others.

# Part I

*Dean worked for the Government, but he had private clients too; among them was the President of the United States.*

# 1

EARL J. SILBERT, then thirty-six, had not lived a sheltered life, but, in June of 1972, he was just as unprepared and undergunned as Dean. He was not prepared to accept, without reservation, the premise that the President of the United States would go ahead and order a goddamned sneak attack upon the political opposition. His power to investigate that unthinkable possibility was limited by the Constitution and the laws of the United States.

Like his mentor, Henry S. Petersen, Chief of the Criminal Division of the United States Department of Justice, he was not a grandstanding prosecutor. Twelve years in the job, in one disguise or other, he had built upon his Exeter and Harvard education an attitude which left civility of manner and toughness of mind nicely balanced in a realistic cynicism about human nature that was rarely disappointed, but gave short shrift to fantasy.

As principal Assistant United States Attorney for the District of Columbia, he applied energetically the no-knock and preventive detention clauses which he had helped to insert in the 1971 D.C. Crime Bill. He did that in the office of Deputy Attorney General Richard G. Kleindienst; he installed his experience of criminal violence and trickiness in the stead of ACLU constitutional arguments bottomed on the brotherhood of man and the fatherhood of God.

Earl Silbert knew that felons flush the heroin away as the cops arrive politely with their warrants, and he knew that vicious bastards out on bail will shoot another druggist while awaiting trial on charges of robbing the first. He lived in a nice townhouse made of brick and painted white, in Southwest Washington, and he was not deceived by its daylight calm. There children are sunned in their carriages by day, but the adults come home at night with enough milk, beer and cigarettes to last until breakfast, because predatory men emerge after dark from the slums unrenewed nearby, and prowl around the townhouses with knives and blunt instruments. Silbert went to work early and he got home late, because those prowlers, and others, committed enough crime in the District to keep a hundred and fifty prosecutors overworked in his office, trying to imprison enough to diminish the inexhaustible legions ready to do anything they can get away with. Because he was good at it, respected in the District as a fair, highly intelligent, fearsomely thorough and unrelentingly tenacious adversary, Silbert found his work exhilarating. But at the same time, he found it frustrating.

Frustration comes with the American prosecutor's territory. Elected or appointed, local, county, state or federal, he must minister convincingly to two congregations, one of which believes there ain't no Hell, or shouldn't be, the other of which declares: "The hell there ain't," and tends to become upset when official prosecutorial action seems limply to imply the opposite heresy.

The legacy of the Warren Court, although wasted somewhat by the occasionally prodigal conservatism of the Burger Court, descended to the rhetorical enrichment of the liberal minority; previously highly articulate in the expression of opinions about the mandates of the Constitution, the liberals became vocal in utter disproportion to their numbers once they got *Miranda, Mapp* and *Escobedo* off, and went too far. They (by "they" I mean the partisans of the American Civil Liberties Union positions on criminal law and procedure) were so emboldened by what Warren had wrought that they came to demand a nicety of statute and procedure so extreme as to refute, in practice, Mr. Justice Cardozo's maxim that each defendant is entitled only to a fair trial, not a perfect one. Sometimes, regrettably often, they prevailed in demands for perfection, so that acknowledged murderers, rapists, robbers, muggers, burglars, child molesters and smut peddlers were delivered from the jails, absolved — perhaps, in effect, even pardoned — of their sins and not even open to admonition that they sin no more. Silbert understood that. He didn't like it, but he understood it.

To those bereaved by the works of murderers; to those raped, robbed, mugged, dispirited by the loss of their possessions, or enraged by violation of their children, or unalterably convinced that untrammeled traffic in dirty books, pictures and films will certainly proliferate rapists and child molesters: to that vast popular majority which fears that legal cession of a monopoly on the use of force, to the government, under the social contract, is not in fact a matter of unanimous consent, too — sedulous attention to the rights of those accused is not a welcome course of conduct. To the cops — who have to see the corpses; console the next of kin; assist to the hospitals those who have been raped, robbed, and mugged; endure the abuse of those who have been ripped off and who believe, rightly, that the police will probably not be able to retrieve what they have lost; stand helplessly in the presence of parents beside themselves in grief about a damaged child; and equally impotent in contemplation of people they call merchants of filth — to the cops, the popular distaste for the taking of infinite pains in the arrest, trial and conviction of vicious bastards is wholesome, manly, healthy and reasonable. Silbert recognized that. He did not buckle to it, but he understood it.

The cops believe that the victims of crime are their clients. They feel a sense of responsibility toward those clients, to make it as sure as cops can that the victims receive whatever meager solace there may be in the visitation of lawful punishment upon the offenders. They also have a personal stake in the outcomes of prosecutions: catching criminals is hard work, and it is dangerous work, too, and there is no fun in doing all that work, and exhausting yourself, only to see the bastard get off because you forgot one or two of the magic phrases that the Supreme Court says you have to recite over him before you put him in the cell. Particularly when you start to think about how stupid, careless, ineffectual and useless his escape will make you look in front of your clients. Silbert's defendants rarely got off. The cops appreciated that.

Cops are not lawyers. They used to be treated as lawyers, in lower local courts where they presented the evidence themselves, but one of the effects of Warren Court decisions was to make the law, in the eyes of the lawyers, too sophisticated, arcane and abstruse for administration by mere cops, and so they were obliged to relinquish prosecutorial control of all cases (not just the serious ones) to that bunch of hairsplitters whose very own hairsplitting was advanced to justify the insult. That left them totally dependent upon the diligence and effectiveness of prosecutors for the vindication of the clients that they found standing stunned around the scenes of crimes committed against them.

In that dependency, cops are insistent upon regular reaffirmations of their lawyers' (the prosecutors') unswerving dedication to the long-term incarceration of the thugs that they have managed to catch. Because they have a symbiotic relationship with their prosecutors, they have the means to enforce their demands: if the prosecutor presents their evidence in a desultory fashion, and the defendant is consequently acquitted, the prosecutor will soon find himself bad-mouthed around the department, rejected when it comes time to try an important case, and repeatedly embarrassed by recalcitrance, forgetfulness and carelessness in the testimony of the officers. If, in the alternative, the prosecutor is dutiful, well prepared, vigilant of the dignity of his witnesses, and as forceful in court as defense counsel, he will get 'round-the-clock, ass-busting effort out of his investigators, and that will make him look good. Silbert's investigators worked very hard for him.

"Always remember," the Detective Lieutenant Inspector instructs his novice prosecutors in Boston, "that you represent five and a half million people of this goddamned Commonwealth, and they ought to get the same kind of service from their lawyer that this rotten son of a bitch is going to get from his. When he hollers, you holler back. Don't let them give you any shit about their poor clients; you've got poor clients too."

Ramsey Clark infuriated cops. It was all right with them if Ramsey Clark wanted to take what they considered to be mushy liberal positions about electronic surveillance, and searches and seizures, and imprisonment and rehabilitation and all the rest of it. It was also all right with them if he wanted to be Attorney General of the United States, the chief law enforcement lawyer in the country, the man who supposedly set the tone for the lawyers who represented cops. But it was not all right with them if he was going to do both at the same time. As far as the cops were concerned, Ramsey Clark running the United States Department of Justice gave the bastards one lawyer, on their side, and another lawyer who was supposed to be on the cops' side, before a Supreme Court of the United States that was loaded in favor of the bastards anyway, and that left the people and the cops with no lawyer at all, after they had been assured that nobody could count on his rights unless he had a lawyer. Ramsey Clark couldn't have raised carfare in a stadium full of cops, when he was Attorney General. Earl Silbert did much better with the cops who worked with him. They did anything he asked, because they trusted him never to ask for anything that was improper, or would get them in trouble, and he didn't. He restrained them when they might have done so on their own.

Silbert had thus trod a fine line between professionally debilitating zealotry and the sort of exaggerated concern for defendants' welfare which destroyed Clark's credibility as a prosecutor. He was resigned to frustration. He did not back timidly away from a fight, and he did not foam at the mouth when a fight was offered. He did not expect to be able to land every suspect in the can, and he hated to lose — or to wipe out a case which he knew he would lose — even though he knew the guy did it. Frustrated as it made him to dump a defective case, and refuse to seek an indictment, he choked it down.

He saw himself as functioning in a system. The system says that there is a difference between "We know he did it" and "Guilty." *Guilty* means not only that he did it, but that the Government has evidence, obtained by means which the Constitution and the laws allow, which to the satisfaction of a jury of reasonable men will *prove* that he did it, and prove it beyond a reasonable doubt.

It was that nice sense of balance which had made Earl Silbert the logical choice for second-in-command of the United States Attorney's Office for the District of Columbia. It was that deserved eminence which moved U.S. Attorney Harold Titus to designate Earl Silbert to supervise the prosecution of James W. McCord, E. Howard Hunt, and some Americans of Cuban origin caught bugging and ransacking the offices of the Democratic National Committee around 2:00 A.M. on June 17, 1972.

For Silbert, the case was something of a comedown. It did not constitute a very serious offense. But the victims were Democrats of considerable status. It was an election year, and Harold Titus was an appointee of a Republican President who was running for reelection. To Earl J. Silbert, the importance of justice done is recapitulated by the importance of the appearance that justice has been done. The case needed a precise hand. It needed supervision and preparation by someone capable of controlling the eagerness to grab everyone in sight; it also needed resolute determination to let no provably guilty defendant escape. It needed unremitting realism, tempered perhaps with a near-cynicism, acquirable only by direct and theoretical experience in the criminal justice system.

Earl Silbert thought he had that. He knew what the system allowed him to do, and he knew its limitations, though he did not especially like them, and he had been denounced by the liberals when they inferred that dislike from his willingness to install as many teeth as possible in the D.C. Crime Bill. It did not occur to him that he might be excoriated from the same pulpits for going easy on suspects. Nor did it occur to him that he might have become too trusting, or that his career and fine reputation were going into hazard. He was not prepared for John Dean, who looked like a Government lawyer, but was in fact representing private clients who happened to work for the Government. Who ran it, in fact, and who needed to make it malfunction. Dean did not confide that circumstance to Silbert, or to Henry Petersen. Neither of them suspected it, and neither had any means of discovering it.

# 2

THE FIRST AND most exposed of Dean's clients, on June 17, 1972, was John North Mitchell, former Attorney General of the United States. Dean, assigned to the cover-up on June 19 (when he returned from Manila where he had made a speech to some new federal narcotics agents), was not fully cognizant of that. Acting upon Ehrlichman's instructions to find out what was going on, Dean did not know that Mitchell was one of his clients, and did not know that he was in potentially grave danger. Ehrlichman didn't know it, either; Haldeman probably did, but he didn't talk to Dean, and he didn't confide in Ehrlichman. The President kept mum.

Dean therefore commenced the arrangement of a conspiracy (it is doubtful that he was aware, at the time, of doing so) to protect John Mitchell, without knowing that it was John Mitchell whom he was protecting, or why. Dean's instructions from Ehrlichman were vague, and implied that Ehrlichman was as ignorant as Dean about the causation for the Watergate burglary. Dean was totally ignorant about actual commissions to commit felonies: on January 27, 1972, he had approached the limit of permissible behavior in Attorney General Mitchell's office, filially admonishing Mr. Mitchell not to countenance criminal proposals by Gordon Liddy within the confines of the Department of Justice. Mr. Mitchell had taken it pretty well, then, and what Mr. Liddy and his accessories had been caught doing in June was not one of the proposals that had been horrifyingly made, back in January. Dean may have been suspicious, but he wasn't informed. In his own sweet way, he was as much, initially, the victim of the concept of presumed innocence of government officials, as he was the manipulator of others by means of that concept. He rather liked John Mitchell. John Mitchell had seen to his appointment as Counsel to the President. He respected John Mitchell. Any man can make a mistake. Dean persisted in his error for about two days, at the very least.

Mitchell, then fifty-nine, had experienced turbulence only during World War II. A Fordham graduate, he went to work for the law firm of Caldwell & Raymond while still attending Fordham Law School at night: "I could work during the day and use my time better that way." In the service he commanded the torpedo boat squadron that included John F. Kennedy's PT 109. Then he went back to Caldwell, Trimble & Mitchell, as a partner.

John Mitchell was a specialist in the legal aspects of floating municipal bonds. That is a very quiet kind of legal practice. Municipal bonds, rated by Moody's, and Standard & Poor's, return rates of interest which are governed by market conditions. Their placement returns standard fees to the lawyer who places them. In the abstract, it is difficult to perceive why one municipal-bond lawyer gets business, and another does not. Municipal-bond lawyers who get business make prodigious amounts of money.

In 1967, Caldwell, Trimble & Mitchell merged with Mudge, Rose & Guthrie, by then more recently known as Nixon, Mudge, Rose & Guthrie.

In 1962, probably too soon after the punishment of the 1960 campaign, certainly before the seething anger of the loss, and the manner of it, had subsided, Richard M. Nixon went back to California and tackled Pat Brown. He had not changed his style. H. ("Harry") R. ("Bob") Haldeman was on leave again from his vice-presidency of J. Walter Thompson Company and his job as manager of its Los Angeles staff, laboring in ways that the California Supreme Court on November 4, 1964, found tricky and dirty, not to mention falsified by Haldeman when he was deposed about them. And Nixon, considering that he would win because a former Congressman, Senator, Vice-President, and presidential nominee — moral titleholder of the presidency itself, he thought — *ought* to win the minor prize of the governorship of California, lost.

It was a bad loss. It was probably worse for him than 1960 had been, and 1960 had been bad enough.

Kennedy, to Nixon, was all flash and no preparation. Everything had been given to JFK. He had earned nothing. He was rich. He chased women, and women chased him. He rode around West Palm Beach in a white Continental convertible with his sunglasses up on his goddamned hairdo, and he smiled, and he never had to kiss Ike's ass. All he ever was was lucky. He did not *deserve* what he had gotten. He got it by smiling, and being funny, and beguiling the dumb sons of bitches in the press into helping him to mislead the people whom he had not served. He distracted them from the solid merit of the man who had worked, *worked* his way up from Whittier. And then, when the magic spell was not quite complete enough to razzle-dazzle victory all by itself, he went the rest of the way, Nixon thought, and he stole it.

John F. Kennedy drove politicians nuts; he did the same things they did, and made it look easy. LBJ looked at Bobby with the kind of vigilance that an eighty-year-old virgin would confer upon a convicted rapist, and in 1972 Richard Nixon scoffed at predictions that Ed Muskie or George McGovern would be nominated to run against him; he knew what Larry O'Brien and the rest of them were up to: when they got to Miami Beach they were going to put three quick moves on the field and hand the nomination to Teddy. When Teddy said he didn't want it, and wouldn't take it, and had no intention of even going to the convention until after somebody else was nominated, Nixon did not believe him. But he was President then, and maybe he could have somebody do something about it.

In 1962 he wasn't anything but broke. Nearly fifty, he had spent his adult life fooling around in politics, presumably living on salaries which John N. Mitchell would have deemed barely adequate as fees. Sufficient to maintain life in that era of comparatively modest inflation, those wages did not provide enough surplus for the convenient accumulation of a substantial estate. His net worth was reported at approximately $60,000. The limousines and the aircraft, the comfortable offices and attentive staffs which he had enjoyed, and become accustomed to, had been provided by the Government. Not by the fruits of a flourishing private law practice like John Mitchell's, which would have produced, along with the money for those perquisites, a comfortingly sizable personal fortune. When Nixon lost, not once but twice, the salary ended and the emoluments passed to his conquerors. All that remained to him was his ticket to practice law, and the speculative currency of his former celebrity as a politician.

As much as any man, Mitchell, starting in 1966, made him rich. Well, perhaps not rich, although his share of firm profits was calculated in the neighborhood of $250,000 a year. (To be rich, he would need Charles G. "Bebe" Rebozo, and some questionable income tax deductions. To stay rich, he would need to finish two terms in office, quietly. He got Rebozo and the deductions, but not the other.) Solvent, maybe, well enough to do so that the nagging fear of ending up not only a loser, but broke, was exorcised, and repair of the psychological damage from 1962 accelerated accordingly. For that assistance, John Mitchell was rewarded with that position of trust which for Nixon has seldom had more than one occupant, at any one point in time. Or for very many points in time, for that matter; he uses them up.

John N. Mitchell didn't know that. Feral in his grasp of the main chance, he thought there was such a thing as loyalty. He thought it was loyalty that inspired Richard Nixon to designate him Attorney General of the United States, and he knew it was loyalty that made him take it.

On January 14, 1969, Mitchell appeared for confirmation hearings before the Senate Judiciary Committee. Senator Philip A. Hart of Michigan was concerned about Mitchell's views on electronic surveillance; Hart thought Ramsey Clark's horrific attitude toward bugs had made him "a superb Attorney General."

Lyndon Johnson, reduced to a diet of Fresca on doctor's orders, visited Chicago briefly one night while Clark was in office. The press bus was late getting back to O'Hare, and LBJ invited, among others, the new U.S. Attorney for the Northern District of Illinois to come aboard Air Force One for a drink. He said he didn't know how the hell a man was supposed to run the country on Fresca, and then he asked the new prosecutor what he thought of Ramsey Clark. The prosecutor waffled.

"Tom," the President said, "Tom's an old friend of mine. And Ramsey, Ramsey's a nice boy, a *fine* boy. But he's as soft as shit."

Clark was an issue in Nixon's 1968 campaign. The candidate had promised a tough-minded prosecutor.

"Senator," John Mitchell said to Hart, "I don't know as I can answer that in full. I believe that I can point out one difference that has been discussed here this morning, and that is perhaps the extent to which electronic surveillance may be used, particularly in the area of organized crime."

The area of organized crime is dimly lit territory, for decades believed populated chiefly by the Mafia. But Joseph Colombo's Italian American Civil Rights League convinced the new Attorney General that the word implied an ethnic monopoly of systematic criminal behavior which did not in fact exist. John Mitchell directed his employees at the United States Department of Justice, and the Assistant U.S. Attorneys who served at his pleasure in the nation's ninety-four districts, to call the Mob *organized crime*. At the time we thought he was talking about hoods.

The hallmark of organized crime is delegation of responsibility. The head man — the *capo di tutti capo* — makes policy. He decides what shall be done. He does this with the advice of his *sotto capos*, or underbosses. He confers with his *consiglieri*, who are sometimes retired chieftains electing elder-statesman status in preference to interment, sometimes unscrupulous lawyers, and sometimes upwardly mobile, younger thugs who think, correctly, that they can exercise the substance of the old man's power by manipulating the old man. The Boss then transmits, through layers of underlings, the strategy which he has devised. Perhaps it dictates that someone be hit.

It very seldom happens that a competent hit man is caught in the act. It very seldom happens that he is caught after the fact. Almost never does such a man revise his loyalties to testify against the fellow who relayed the order. That fellow, if so embroiled, will usually keep silence. The *capo di tutti capo* acts decisively, in contravention of the law, because with good reason he considers that it will be extremely difficult to catch him.

Henry Petersen knew that, in 1972. By then he was an Assistant Attorney General of the United States, Chief of the Criminal Division. In 1961 he had been designated Chief of the Organized Crime & Racketeering Section. He agreed with John Mitchell about ethnic monopolies, and the nonexistence thereof. He was not quite cognizant of the political possibilities of condign strategies. He was the kind of man who would trust the President of the United States. He did not mistrust the Attorney General, either.

At the conference of January 27, 1972, Gordon Liddy had commended to Attorney General Mitchell, in his imposing office at Justice, additional prospects for inclusion in "the area of organized crime." He did it by implication, and probably without intention. Soliciting a million dollars to finance kidnappings of radical leaders, and to transport women and girls in interstate commerce for the purpose of prostitution and debauchery, Liddy also had it in mind to use electronic, mechanical, and other devices, to intercept wire and oral communications, all in violation of Title 18, United States Code, Sections 1201, 2421, and 2518. The organization targeted for this proposal was the Democratic National Committee

*13*

and its underlings, associates and fellow travelers, bent upon the sinister purpose of nominating a presidential candidate implacably inimical to the possessor of John N. Mitchell's loyalty.

Mitchell rejected Liddy's plan; he thought it was too expensive.

Later he called it "unproductive."

John Mitchell used that word to manifest reservations about the strategic and tactical aspects of proposals which to a man of less experience with the Mammon of unrighteousness might seem profoundly outrageous on moral, ethical and legal grounds alone. Such as, for example, clandestine approaches to Judge Charles R. Richey of the United States District Court for the District of Columbia. Judge Richey was proposed, despite his complete unlikeliness as a candidate for such shoddy work, as amenable to sneaky influence in his capacity as trial judge of the civil litigation brought against the Committee to Re-elect the President by the Democratic National Committee.

Mitchell also applied that word to Liddy's felonious solicitations, when he was before the Senate Select Committee on Presidential Campaign Activities in 1973, driving the pin of his watch-strap buckle into the quick beneath his thumbnail, in lieu of gnashing his teeth. But by then he had been apprised, by the hindsight of a man indicted and under a drumfire of unremitting public criticism, that many of his countrymen were angrily hostile to a concept of organized crime inclusive of millions of citizens whose offense was that they were Democrats, or might turn out to be if Senator Edward M. Kennedy were dangled seductively before them as a nominee for President of the United States.

Mitchell was in a rage by then, as he had not discernibly been the previous summer when he used that word in greater privacy to describe his response to the Liddy plan. In his wrath he did not see that he had vastly misconceived the claims of loyalty; he felt his loyalty had been maliciously misconstrued. Darkly he permitted himself to wonder if there might not be a plot afoot to inveigle even Nixon into repudiation of him; he thought they might be setting him up to take the fall. And he was right: they were.

The decision had been passively made (if bowing to necessity constitutes the making of a decision, as it probably does not) no earlier than March of 1973, when the menacing prospect of McCord before the Ervin Committee at last registered upon Dean's principal clients, Mr. Nixon, Mr. Haldeman and Mr. Ehrlichman. With great delicacy, Mr. Ehrlichman had proposed to Mr. Mitchell that he might like to dive over the side. Mr. Mitchell, no fool, plainly held the opinion that there wasn't anybody around who could push him over, then, and declined to jump. Besides, he was loyal, and probably did not fully credit the possibility that his President thought of him as the big enchilada, whose apprehension would divert the President's pursuers.

It is difficult to pinpoint the day when President Nixon, like the driver of a troika kicking passengers off to deflect pursuing wolves, began to sacrifice his henchmen to the perpetuation of his presidency. Publicly, at least, they obdurately persisted, most of the time, in submitting to the fact that they had been sacrificed, by refusing to concede that they had been jettisoned, and thus precluded specific inquiry about when it occurred. Most of them, anyway: John Dean was an exception, but by and large they were stand-up guys for Nixon, who screwed them in return.

Notwithstanding that difficulty, it seems likely that John N. Mitchell became excess baggage between 9:00 A.M. and 6:12 P.M. on June 20, 1972. On the evening of the nineteenth, Mitchell received John Dean, Jeb Stuart Magruder, Robert Mardian and Fred LaRue at his apartment. That was when Dean found out, for sure, that he had Mitchell for a client: they discussed the break-in.

The next morning, at 9:00, Mitchell met with Haldeman and Ehrlichman at the White House. Attorney General Richard G. Kleindienst came in fifty-five minutes later; John Dean arrived ten minutes before Kleindienst. It was that meeting which led to Haldeman's 11:26–12:45 meeting with the President; the tape of the conference was marred by eighteen-and-one-half minutes of buzzing. At 6:08 P.M., the President and Mitchell had a telephone chat about the break-in: the President's Dictabelt recording for the day quoted Mitchell as apologizing for not controlling unnamed personnel at the Committee to Re-elect the President. No questions asked, none answered: that was Mitchell's story, and the President's too. But by June 23, 1972, Mr. Nixon was giving Haldeman very detailed, knowledgeable instructions about using the CIA–Bay of Pigs gambit to divert the FBI from full investigation of the DNC burglary, and Haldeman was being very precise about Mitchell's foreknowledge of that breaking and entering. Either Haldeman got his information on the twentieth, or else he got it by the twenty-third, and in either event he got it from Mitchell, for relay to the President.

Dean took his orders from Ehrlichman. He was in the White House, to take orders from Ehrlichman, because Mitchell had gotten him there. Dean was not unappreciative of that patronage. If he did not desire eagerly (as eagerly as he could, anyway) to complete successfully any task which Ehrlichman might set for him, and he did, he at very least owed Mitchell the most diligent representation he could give. He went to see the Acting Director of the FBI.

Retired from command of U.S. Navy submarines, daily communicant, Connecticut lawyer laboring by political activity to compensate for entry into practice three decades after his competition, Pat Gray was used to thinking about the occupant of the White House as the Commander in Chief. "Knowing at least what I know now," Gray told the Committee, "and knowing that in the service of my country I withstood hours and hours of depth-charging, shelling and bombing, but I never expected to run into a Watergate in the service of a President of the United States, and I ran into a buzzsaw, obviously."

He did not think of himself as a loyalist; he thought of himself as a patriot. They should have called him Patsy. What he knew, the White House knew, and that was where the crooks were.

"I believe," Dean said, "that it was on June twenty-first that I first met with Gray in his office in the late morning, regarding the FBI's investigation. At that meeting he told me he fully realized the sensitive nature of the investigation they were pursuing, and that he had placed his most trusted senior people in charge of the investigation. I told Gray that I had been asked to be kept informed about the investigation. Mr. Gray told me that he had been visiting a number of regional offices and would be doing so in the future. Thus, if I needed any information, I should call Mr. Mark Felt in his absence. I might note at this point that indeed Gray was frequently absent from the city during the course of the investigation, and this irritated Ehrlichman greatly when he asked me to get information from Gray and Gray was out of the city. On several occasions, in fact, Ehrlichman instructed me to tell Gray to return to the city and mind the store. I passed this message to Gray, but I cannot recall what prompted Ehrlichman to have me do so, at this time."

J. Edgar Hoover died May 2, 1972, an action of uncharacteristic submissiveness to the will of a superior deity. The Special Agents in Charge of the FBI's regional offices mourned him much more sincerely than did the Special Agents who work in those offices. Hoover was as difficult to work for as he was to manage from a seemingly higher office; the Bureau was regulated down to the shoe tops of the agents, and those were required to be brilliantly shined. When Gray came in, he at first greatly pleased the younger agents, who were released from dress codes so extreme that button-down shirts were banned in the 1960s. His tours persuaded many that the Bureau could move into the 1970s without losing its special quality; one agent said that Gray's accession had relaxed regulations to the point at which married agents were then permitted to have conjugal relations with their wives.

Later discontent began to filter through the Bureau. In Washington — the Seat of Government, in Bureau-speak — he became known as "Two-day Gray," a capsule summary of his weekly attendance at work. His attitude toward administration, initially deemed welcome and fresh by those who had chafed under Hoover, was soon perceived as dangerously slack. Gray overlooked, in his efforts to fuel the self-esteem of his agents, the acquired characteristic which makes the Special Agent's self-esteem a direct variant of his pride in being a Special Agent. It became evident, early on, that Gray was too much the opposite of Hoover; though there was limited nostalgia for Hoover himself, there was genuine concern for the manner in which Gray wanted the Bureau to do business.

His problem, as the agents saw it, was that he did not know what he was doing. And they were correct. Gray professed himself aware of the fact that "the FBI occupies a peculiar position with reference to the President of the United States, and that the President of the United States looks to the Federal Bureau of Investigation in a little different manner than he does the other departments of government." But he didn't know Word One about law enforcement, which is what the FBI is mostly engaged in, and his ignorance was plain the first week he put in on the job; it took just about a month for the Bureau's grapevine to get the word around the country.

Felt, a Hoover holdover, and the rest, began to resist Gray's aimlessness. Ehrlichman complained to Dean, and Dean to Gray, because when Gray was out the phone was off the hook at the FBI. There is nothing more talkative, nor less informative in response to questions than a Special Agent of the FBI who doesn't want to tell you what you want to know. That is something which was learned under Hoover. And when, in the estimation of the agents, aimlessness degenerated into the recklessness of tolerating political meddling, another lesson learned from Hoover came to light: the calculated use of publicity. Sandy Smith, of *Time*, by reason of long years of specializing in organized crime news a known and trusted newsman at the Bureau, got information every time somebody went to the bathroom after the Fourth of July in 1972. There was an unremitting fusillade of source stories out of the Bureau, and its Wash-

*17*

ington Field Office, for a solid year, and when Ehrlichman griped to the Committee about the work of those unhappy agents, he declared nothing more than an angry grasp of the truth.

Gray, bemused by his own apparent eminence, failed to appreciate the gravity of his situation. "Mr. Dean called me, as I recollect, called me on the telephone on a Sunday morning, and said that he wanted to meet with me and wanted to talk to me, and I said: 'Well fine. We can meet in my office in the Department.' And he stated that this would not be practical, because of the fact that there are not too many people present at the Department on Sunday, and that it would be easily noticed that he would be coming into the Department of Justice and there would be another leak. And I suggested: 'All right, we can meet over here, my apartment is very small,'" curious, that explanation: an apartment too small for two people? or didn't Pat Gray want his wife to hear? "'We cannot meet in the apartment, but we can meet over here.' And we agreed to meet over at the apartment and I met him outside the apartment, and we walked around the apartment building and sat down and chatted on a bench overlooking the channel, there. This is in Southwest Washington, in Harbour Square Apartments."

Gray wasn't quite sure what he discussed with Dean that Sunday. "I know that one of the first remarks he made was that this was a heck of a note, when the Acting Director of the FBI and the Counsel to the President have to meet on a park bench to avoid leaks. We could have discussed on that particular Sunday afternoon the various theories of the case that the FBI had been considering, and that he and I had already discussed. We could have discussed the leaks that were rampant in that first two-week period, and it is entirely possible that he could have raised with me the question of making available to him the FBI materials available to me for his use in the conduct of his inquiry. I cannot state it with any kind of certainty, but I can say that it is entirely possible."

During the next week, at least, Dean put it on him. "To the best of my recollection, following this meeting, on the bench there at the Harbour Square Apartments, a phone call ensued following that, during the week, and it was in that phone call that Mr. Dean raised the question of making available to him the materials, FBI file materials that were available to me."

Gray was questioned by Rufus Edmisten, a large young man with a secure purchase upon Sam Ervin's coattails and a design to win election as Governor of North Carolina, first parlaying his role as Deputy Counsel to the Committee into the job of Attorney General of that state. In 1974, he won that job. Edmisten had an arrangement with Bob Daugherty, of AP: Daugherty hung out by the columns on the southerly side of the Caucus Room, and Edmisten responded to his hand signals by leaning up close to Ervin for one of those tight little three-head conference photos, Baker to the left in the picture. From time to time, a research assistant to the Committee interrupted her enraptured all-day attendance at the hearings to fetch Rufus a couple more packs of Carter Hall; she had to wedge herself back into space on the staff bench behind the Committee, the crowdedness of which perhaps offered at least partial explanation for the fact that the staff work broke down completely before the hearings were three weeks old: nobody on the staff was doing any work at the office.

"Now, Mr. Gray," Edmisten said, "did you consult with Mr. Petersen and Mr. Kleindienst about the advisability of giving the FBI data to Mr. Dean?"

"No, sir," Gray said. "I did not."

"Why did you not?" Edmisten said.

"I didn't do it," Gray said, "because I thought I was the Acting Director of the Federal Bureau of Investigation, and when I have a request from the Counsel to the President of the United States, I don't have to go run around to the Attorney General and to the Assistant Attorney General in charge of the Criminal Division and ask him to hold my hand and help me to respond in making a decision. I did not do that and I would not do that."

"To the best of my recollection," Dean said, "it was during this June twenty-first meeting, with Gray, that he informed me that the FBI had uncovered a number of major banking transactions that had transpired in the account of one of the arrested Cubans, Mr. Barker. He informed me that they had traced a $25,000 check to Mr. Kenneth Dahlberg, and four checks totaling $89,000 to a bank in Mexico City.

"I do not recall," Dean said, "whether I first learned about the Dahlberg check from Mr. Gray, or whether I learned about it in a meeting in Mitchell's office, by reason of the fact that the FBI was trying to contact Mr. Dahlberg about the matter, and Mr. Dahlberg had called Mr. Stans. At any rate, the fact that the FBI was investigating these matters was of utmost concern to Mr. Stans when he learned of it. Stans was concerned about the Dahlberg check, I was informed, because it was in fact a contribution from Mr. Dwayne Andreas, whom I did not know, but I was told, was a long-time backer of Senator Hubert Humphrey. Neither Stans nor Mitchell wanted Mr. Andreas to be embarrassed by disclosure of the contribution. The concern about the Mexican money was made a little less clear to me. I was told it was a contribution from a group of Texans who had used an intermediary in Mexico to make the contribution. Although I had not been told, I assumed at that time that they were concerned because it sounded to me as if it might have been a corporate contribution and clearly a violation of the law."

Stans had been scuttering around the country shaking down, among others, airlines which had new route requests pending before the Civil Aeronautics Board, Government-regulated industries, and Government contractors. Several thought it seemly to make five-figure contributions to the Finance Committee. All of that, of course, was prohibited by statute.

"Mr. Stans also explained," Dean said, "that he had checked with Sloan to find out how this money had ended up in Mr. Barker's bank account, and Sloan reported that he had given the checks to Liddy and requested that he cash them. He said he had no idea how Liddy had cashed them, but surmised that he had obviously used Barker to cash them. I was also told — and I do not recall specifically who told me this — that the money had absolutely nothing to do with the Watergate; it was unrelated and it was merely a coincidence of fact that Liddy had used Barker to cash the checks and Liddy had returned the money to Sloan.

"I was told," Dean said, "that the investigation of this matter, which appeared to be connected to the Watergate but wasn't, was unfounded, and would merely result in an unnecessary embarrassment to the contributors. Accordingly, Mitchell and Stans asked me to see if there was anything the White House could do to prevent this unnecessary embarrassment."

A large part of the potential for embarrassment lay in the fact that the money represented secret contributions made after April 7, 1972, when secret contributions became illegal.

"I, in turn," Dean said, "related these facts to both Haldeman and Ehrlichman. On June twenty-second, at the request of Ehrlichman and Haldeman, I went to see Mr. Gray at his office in the early evening, to discuss the Dahlberg and Mexican checks, and determine how the FBI was proceeding in these matters. Mr. Gray told me that they were pursuing it by seeking to interview the persons who had drawn checks. It was during my meeting with Mr. Gray on June twenty-second that we also talked about his theories of the case, as it was beginning to unfold. I remember well that he drew a diagram for me, showing his theories. At that time, Mr. Gray had the following theories: It was a set-up job by a double agent; it was a CIA operation because of the number of former CIA people involved; or it was someone in the reelection committee who was responsible."

From that, Dean developed his first conspiracy to obstruct justice. His clients were Mitchell, Nixon, Haldeman and Ehrlichman; he didn't know Haldeman was in it, but he certainly assumed it. Five days had passed since the burglary (there had been a conspiracy in that, too, and the purpose of Dean's first conspiracy was to prevent detection of its participants: Mitchell, Liddy, Magruder, Hunt, McCord, the Cubans). Dean reported to his other clients, and the machinery was started to convince Mr. Gray, and thus Mr. Silbert, that what Mr. Gray feared to be true (it was false) was in fact true. The trouble with Dean's choice of rationales was that it was false. It is much better to start an obstructive conspiracy with something that is true.

# 3

IT IS BETTER to start with something true, as Dean painfully discovered, because there's a lot less heavy lifting involved in the salesmanship of a misleading rationale which seems to be based upon actual facts. But Dean's inexperience was showing: he had not, with the chilly precision he would later demonstrate, learned to limit his bite to what could be conveniently chewed. He was, by the CIA ploy, attempting too much, far more than he could expect to accomplish, and considerably more than was needed. That was because Dean, in the summer of 1972, did not himself know all the facts.

Dean's general purpose was to keep the burglars out of White House ranks, when the roll was called down yonder in the U.S. District Court. The best way to do that was to leave the investigation alone and let Silbert and the Bureau find out who did what, and on whose orders, and prosecute them. In other words, let all the facts come out, and then, when they did, perform a public presidential headshaking on the question of what in the name of God had gotten into John Mitchell's head.

That (the option of telling only the truth and keeping your mouth shut, where the truth was uncertain, or unknown) was not a popular stratagem in the Administration which Dean served. There were philosophical reasons for that behavior, but there were also practical considerations which seemed to require it; they stemmed from the organizational pattern of compartmentalization, of which the Administration's proponents were, at first, so inordinately proud.

The President was compulsively secretive. His preference for sneakiness was perceptible, and perplexing, to men like Elliot Richardson, in existence though not in extent. His suspicion of the press and his ill-concealed hostility toward the Congress baffled them; his furtiveness, in the execution of those suspicions and hostilities, impressed them, too mildly, as curiously aberrant behavior. They did not apprehend its pervasiveness.

Dean, later, did. So did we all, honorable and dishonorable alike. But, in the summer of 1972, Dean was fettered in his work by the fact that he was kept in ignorance of salient facts. The men who kept him ignorant — Ehrlichman and, by extension, Haldeman — did not necessarily do so by design; as was demonstrated when the tapes were played at the trial of Haldeman, Ehrlichman, Mitchell, Mardian and Parkinson in the autumn of 1974, the President always kept a little information back. Even from his closest henchmen. In January of 1973, it turned out, he had ruminated with Chuck Colson about a pardon for Hunt; in the spring of that year, he evaded Ehrlichman's inquiries about such a discussion (when, for the purposes of his own survival, and Ehrlichman's as well, it was desperately important for Ehrlichman to know about such a discussion), and permitted Ehrlichman to blunder, to his own detriment, as a result. Dean was not the kind of man who went scouting around for adventures, as Uncle Wiggily and Gordon Liddy were inclined to do; if he set out to put an umbrella over the entire Administration, as he did, it was certainly because he could not eliminate the frightening possibility that the entire Administration — not just John Mitchell — was potentially culpable. Or, more precisely: since Dean did not really know who was responsible, he was constrained to assume that everybody was responsible, and to act accordingly.

That imposed upon Dean, as far as Dean was concerned, the obligation to cover Chuck Colson, for example, with the same vigor that he devoted to the protection of John Mitchell; he didn't know that Colson, in the summer of 1972, was clean, and Mitchell was not. To cover Mitchell, Dean needed only that perjury which would seem to prove that Liddy deceived everybody he worked for. But to cover Colson, Ehrlichman, Haldeman, the President, and everybody else who might possibly have had something to do with the DNC burglary, Dean had to derail the whole investigation. That was why he floated the CIA balloon: if he could halt the investigation, dead in the water, everybody would be covered, and he'd no longer need to worry about discriminating between the sheep and the goats. Besides, it was, to a beginner at obstruction, a promising gambit: Gray half-believed it anyway and wanted to believe it, and if the mines of evidence could be salted to support his surmise, the likelihood of his wholehearted acceptance of the fabricated explanation was extreme. If Gray believed it, Silbert would believe it, and if Silbert believed it, well, Dean would have made a hat trick, rescuing not only the innocent, but the guilty as well, whoever the hell they were.

That is the kind of breathtaking coup which beguiles the minds of the uninstructed, in every field. In law, industry, sales and brokerage, they generally get fired for their excesses. In medicine and commercial aviation, they are usually deflected from the management of serious matters. In politics they are humiliated; in government (as Liddy was), transferred; in teaching, promoted and given tenure; and in crime, convicted and imprisoned. Dean, like Liddy, was committing crimes, under the erroneous impression that he was committing government.

To advance his cause (Ehrlichman, as inexpert as he, proposed the measure), Dean approached Major General Vernon A. Walters of the CIA, and blandished him to see to it that Pat Gray heard what he really wanted to hear. General Walters was cuter than that, and so were Helms and General Robert Cushman of the CIA: they would do what the White House wanted, only if the White House ordered it, in writing. Dean was disposed to take that for: "No." So disposed, in fact, that when Ehrlichman told him to go back and try again, Dean somehow never got around to it.

He was learning. By the close of business on June 23, 1972, Dean had scuttled his first conspiratorial program, because he was sure it would not work, and set about the accomplishment of more practicable objectives. He did not overtly repudiate the CIA gambit, leaving it out there to distract any harriers who might find it intriguing (the mark of a promising obstructor, who will accept any benefit he can get), but he spent his time on less ambitious (and more convenient) projects. The first Dean conspiracy had died aborning, but the second improvisation would be much better, utilizing, as it would, liars that he knew he had, not liars (or cagey bureaucrats) that he wot not of. Dean was learning to use what advantages lay at hand, and to shun intemperate fantasies.

# 4

SILBERT HAD NO inkling of Gray's loquacity, or of Dean's anxious receptivity toward suggestions that would hinder and torpedo Silbert's probe. Nor did Silbert divine the possibility that the Career Justice Chief of the Criminal Division was being snookered by the Counsel to the President. In 1972 that was not a particularly untoward species of credulity; it was the cornerstone of Dean's temporary, unmerited prosperity as a conspirator. It was a reliable means, and it was handy.

Each of them — Petersen directly, Silbert at one remove — had been a Government lawyer for all of his professional life. That does not condition an intelligent man into the sort of autonomically reflexive behavior that Gray showed, but it does develop a habit of reference to what is known in the law as the presumption of administrative regularity.

Government lawyers correctly perceive of themselves as an embattled lot. Of course all trial lawyers are embattled, but Government lawyers are on salary, and get no better pay for days spent fending off irascible defense lawyers in criminal cases, or scattergunning private lawyers representing plaintiffs in civil cases against the Government, than they get for placid hours spent reviewing files. Government lawyers think many of the motions brought in criminal cases, and much of what is filed in civil cases against the Government, to be absolute dogshit, harassment, foolishness and melodrama, intended to impress private clients and not to advance the cases in question. They are correct often enough to make contradiction careful.

The customary response to a civil claim (for example: that the Secretary of HEW, Defense or State, has maliciously and willfully discriminated against the plaintiff by refusal to issue a grant, contract or passport by reference to the plaintiff's age, race, creed or sex) is to assert that the Secretary (who is, of course, blissfully ignorant of the plaintiff, his or her case, and all the rest of it) directed his or her subordinates to follow the law and the Code of Federal Regulations, and that, as far as is known, they did. That leaves the plaintiff to prove either that the CFR was not followed, or, in the alternative, that the regulation or statute in question is unconstitutional.

Most plaintiffs can't do that. Most criminal defendants can't prove that the federal cops whacked them around, failed to advise them of their rights, or refused them the assistance of counsel. The courts know it. The Government's lawyers become accustomed to believing that assertions of governmental misfeasance are duplicitous, or weightless, or both. Then they get blindsided with a case of genuine misfeasance, but it takes a hell of a lot of proof to make them concede that the procedures employed were very much irregular.

Henry Petersen, fifty, had trusted all his life to the precepts of a stern Roman Catholic upbringing to keep himself from harm's way. In 1974, describing his ordeal to the media, he compared his handling of Watergate to a progress through a minefield; then, shifting similes abruptly, he said: "I am not a whore." That evening, at home, his youngest daughter asked him why he said that. Miserably, he said: "I don't know."

But he did know, if he thought about it: his gimlet-eyed scrutiny of all actions, for occasions of sin lurking beneath their tranquil surfaces, had been too limited, and the discovery of its insufficiency all but grieved him in the manner of it. Ambitious himself, and rewarded in his ambitiousness, he did not think to include the darker variants of his own virtuous striving as potential warning signals of corruption.

Sex, money and laxity in the practice of traditional morals: those he understood, and accorded to them the profound respect he believed them to deserve as engines of personal destruction. Appointed Deputy Chief of OCRS by Robert Kennedy, after nine years with Justice in the Antitrust and Criminal divisions, he recruited a willing corps of nomads for the Field Offices (informally known as Strike Forces). It was plain to him that temptations would lie in the paths of those starting out to bedevil the Mob, because the Mob has done rather well, over the years, catering to human weaknesses. Familiarity, he reasoned, breeds more familiarity, and a man who knows his town too well may be too well known in his town to be ruthless in pursuit of his prosecution target. Concomitantly, a prosecutor in his hometown may be bent upon becoming well known, but only in that good-fellow configuration that attracts business to a private practice established after three or four years of publicity-generating Mafia-chasing, or beguiles the electorate into ardent consent to political aspirations.

Henry Petersen wanted none of his prosecutors going easy on somebody who did not deserve easiness by reason of his virtue. He wanted gunslingers whose sole loyalty was to Justice (John Doar, an RFK contemporary of Petersen's, in the Civil Rights Section, devastating to the President in his 1973 disguise as Majority Counsel to the House Judiciary impeachment inquiry, perhaps expressed Petersen's attitude, along with his own — and what made him work so hard, much later, for Peter Rodino's Committee — when he said at Medgar Evers's funeral: "I'm from Justice, and you know what that means").

Henry Petersen thought Justice was important. He measured the applicant's dedication to that view by his submissiveness to the rule, relaxed only much later, that long residence in New York absolutely disqualified him from service in any Strike Force in the neighborhood. It was a United States Marines sort of attitude, perhaps explicable by reference to Petersen's three years as a Marine sergeant in the Central Pacific during World War II.

He thought Justice was important, too, because Justice had been good to him. After a year at Georgetown University, Petersen worked his way through law school as an FBI clerk at Justice. Except for his Marine service, Petersen never held a full-time job anywhere but at the United States Department of Justice. He was Career Justice.

In that practice his prosperity was most remarkable. Career Justice employees, lacking political clout, seldom come to savor the satisfaction of bossing the divisions which they, in fact, operate. About the best they can hope for is promotion to Deputy Assistant Attorney General, where they get to do the work of running the operation while the politically connected Assistant Attorney General goes posturing around the country as Chief of whatever Division, making a big fool of himself.

In 1969, the new Nixon Administration had selected Will Wilson to be Assistant Attorney General, Chief of the Criminal Division. Mr. Wilson is a very personable man, polite and nice, and, in the grand tradition of political appointees to high Justice slots, knew not a damned thing about what the Criminal Division of Justice is supposed to do, and what it means to the people who work in it. The Texas lawyer buffooned his way around the Republic, making a great many speeches devoid of content, but full of sound and fury, and, on October 15, 1971, stepped down in apparent bafflement that his departure should be dictated by his habit of accepting loans from bankers under investigation by his own Division for fraud in the Sharpstown Bank scandals.

That made Henry Petersen Acting Assistant Attorney General, by virtue of his 1969 designation as Deputy to Wilson, which appointment Petersen accepted avidly, and discharged impeccably. It also middled the Administration very nicely: hot in public for law and order, its principals were significantly embarrassed, also in public, by Mr. Wilson's clumsiness in the management of his financial affairs. While Congress was in recess, the President escaped the bind by appointing Petersen to take Wilson's place. On January 11, 1972, sixteen days before Gordon Liddy visited the Department to broach call girls, wiretaps and kidnappings to Attorney General Mitchell, Henry Edward Petersen became an Assistant Attorney General of the United States.

It pleased him, and it delighted also the federal prosecutors who had chafed under Wilson's aimless direction. There was a lot of ridicule for federal prosecutors in 1972, and I must say that we bore it with very limited charity. The Wilson imbroglio, which few found surprising — he was seldom mentioned without prefix or suffix of "that asshole" — was precisely not what was indicated to stifle the criticism. But if Henry Petersen, stuffed to the bursting with integrity, was to run the operation, well, that would be fine, because nobody in the world could question Henry Petersen's integrity.

And nobody has since, either. It's his intelligence that's been questioned, and that not justifiably, though certainly understandably. Henry Petersen, to widespread astonishment, turned out not to have been savvy enough to suspect the President. He proved to be the kind of man, who, when asked by the President of the United States "to do something," would do it. He trusted the man who was President, because he was President, and the President's lawyer, John Dean, because he was the President's lawyer. Thus he undid himself: What Silbert told Petersen (they conferred just about every day during the summer of 1972, Silbert dutifully keeping his supervisor briefed on this important case), Petersen promptly told Dean.

That was Dean's second unique advantage as a beginner in obstruction, to go along with his marvelous disguise as a Government lawyer: first he got useful inspiration from the principal cop, and devised from it tactics that would mislead the investigators. Then he took the indicated steps. Then he monitored, through Petersen, the results which his tactics had brought. He was putting on a play, but the people he directed did not know it. With those advantages, a thoughtful baboon could obstruct justice. For a while.

Earl Silbert drove a blue Plymouth compact to work, with an infant seat in the back and the rugs littered with the detritus of family transportation. It started with some hesitation, even in warm weather, but there was nothing serious that anyone could do to the exterior in the tight quarters of the assigned-space parking lot at the District courthouse, and he was used to it. He was used to it in the same way that he was accustomed to the balkiness of the criminal justice system: while he might have preferred, and could have afforded, a more efficient car, he was resigned to the conditions which made the Plymouth preferable to something better, because they were conditions about which he could do nothing. At least within the rules, and that is the only territory where Silbert permits himself to range. He drove his blue car, and he did not cultivate nightmares. He called John Mitchell before the grand jury, and expected him to tell the truth.

Moving party to an agreement to "volunteer nothing" that might damage the President's chances of reelection, Mitchell in the summer of 1972 had been joined by numerous men in impressive places who feared erosion of Nixon's majority. He disguised his purposes with a cooperativeness that was very nearly affable. Maurice Stans, former Secretary of Commerce and member of the Accounting Hall of Fame, or something, extorted deference to his eminence, by means of a tantrum catalyzed by the prospect of being jostled about by a grand jury appearance; he was interviewed in Henry Petersen's office at Justice. But Mitchell traveled docilely from his New York apartment to the Watergate grand jury room in Washington, waiving such courtesies and effectuating his continuing loyalty with a spurious humility as false as it was disarming, and also as successful.

Earl Silbert put the questions. He asked John Mitchell about Gordon Liddy and Howard Hunt and Jeb Magruder and Herbert Porter and Hugh Sloan, and all the money that had gone to James McCord and his Cuban American assistants. Mitchell answered politely, disappointing expectations that he would prove as intractable as a witness as he had been severe in his calls for law and order.

He took an oath and he kept a third of it. He told the truth, but he did not tell the whole truth, and he did not restrict himself to narration of only the truth, but willfully and contrary to his oath, stated and subscribed material matters which he did not believe to be true (because the election was yet to come and he wasn't volunteering anything) in violation of Title 18, United States Code, Section 1623. He made false declarations.

John Mitchell told Earl Silbert and the grand jury that his first inkling of Liddy's frolicsome approach to politics reached him in the middle of the morning of June 17, 1972, when someone in his party at the Beverly Hills Hotel relayed a radio news item about five burglars who had been caught in the Democratic National Committee headquarters in the Watergate Office Building. Before that, Mitchell said under oath, he had no knowledge whatsoever about Liddy's excursions, which would have been true if he had not participated in a second meeting, when Liddy cut the rate to $500,000, and a third, when the tag was reduced to $250,000, and if he had not presided at the first meeting. Mitchell pronounced himself, if not shocked and appalled by Liddy's behavior, at least strongly disapproving of it. He would never have sanctioned such a scheme, he assured the grand jury and Earl Silbert in two appearances as a witness; anyone could have seen that it would be "unproductive."

That word was the only one that disturbed Silbert in receiving Mitchell's testimony. "I couldn't understand why he said that." The disturbance was fleeting. "I never dreamed," he said, "it never occurred to me, that a former Attorney General of the United States would lie to the grand jury." Nor did he seriously believe that the President of the United States was procuring the obstruction of its justice. That was how Dean managed, for a while, to protect his first client, by means of a poor conspiracy.

# 5

THE CONSPIRATORIAL LOVELINESS of the scheme, that Mitchell's lies advanced, was its modesty. That was the way Dean saw it, at least, in the exercise of his increasing expertise. He was considering only the number of cooperatives it would require. The scope, which he unsophisticatedly ignored, was enormous.

All you had to do was to recruit a few liars, from a pool of spineless but ambitious men, to corroborate the falsehoods that the chief suspect would tell. With luck (Dean's plots, all of them, invariably depended for longevity on luck, which reflects poor planning and exaggerates risk, but he had no choice), their bland mendacity would synergize with the presumption of presidential innocence and the presumption of administrative regularity, and set the guilty free. It damned near did.

There were, in addition to the perfidy of a former Attorney General of the United States, other things that Silbert did not dream.

He thought he was dealing with a criminal case. The way you deal with a given criminal case is the way you have dealt with every previous criminal case of comparable magnitude and complexity. You review what your investigators have found. You interview witnesses. You apply as much pressure as the Constitution permits. You take your witnesses before the grand jury, and interrogate them. And if it is an important case, you keep your superiors informed. Silbert's immediate superior was Har-

31

old Titus. But beyond him was the Chief of the Criminal Division of the United States Department of Justice, Henry Petersen.

None of them suspected Mr. Nixon of obstructing justice. Consequently, they did not suspect his lawyer, Mr. Dean.

There were, as a matter of fact, plenty of people who said, or strongly implied, that the President was doing exactly that. And he was. But the people who said it could not prove it, and the people who could have proven it were busy helping him do it, thus being understandably disinclined to prove it.

Dean (and thus the President) had two kinds of helpers: those who worked actively to sabotage Silbert's case, and those who listened, passively, to collect information useful to the saboteurs. Dean shuttled between them.

Silbert, in the summer of 1972, apprehended the existence of neither group. He spent the whole summer, while John Mitchell and the others were plausibly lying to him, trying to belt (plea-bargain) the burglary cases out.

In cases involving multiple defendants, standard prosecuting procedure calls for private negotiation between the Assistant and each defense lawyer, until one of the defendants caves in and pleads guilty in exchange for a recommendation of lenience in sentencing, conditioned upon coming coco (his agreement to testify fully) against his codefendants. The rule is that the first to crack gets the only deal; the rest, firmly hooked, may plead a hopeless case if they choose, but get no consideration for their tractability unless they can make (convict) somebody new. The pressure upon them, to waive trial, comes from the judge, who is assumed — correctly, in most instances — to prefer cop-outs to useless trials, and to sentence less harshly the fellow who does the right thing. Judges are reticent about this, because the idealism of the system says that there shall be no additional penalty imposed for exertion of the constitutional right to a trial; they practice it because the idealism doesn't take into account the fact that the system erected upon it would break down in short order if everyone insisted upon that privilege.

Silbert, under stern pressure himself to ferret out all parties to the Watergate break-in — the sources of that stress being precisely that sector of the community ordinarily most vehement about the rights of the accused: the liberal press and the people who read it — by the close of business on July 6, 1972, had seven birds in hand. McCord and the four Cubans had been caught, stupefied, in the DNC headquarters, their pockets and luggage crammed with burglary tools and hundred-dollar bills. Hunt's room and Liddy's stuff had yielded other hundred-dollar bills, numerically sequential with the burglars' cash. Alfred W. Baldwin, the lookout who divided his attention between the break-in and the late show on television, had spilled his guts in a reasonable desire to avoid jail. "We let him sit down out there in the corridor," Silbert said, "and he thought about it, and then he came in. It took him over five hours, but he came in."

Liddy by any measure was the most puissant of the birds in hand. He was also an attorney, and attorneys enmeshed in criminal investigations are assumed to think about the threat to their livelihoods, not to mention their liberties, which is posed by conviction of felony. Silbert therefore unloaded on Liddy's attorney, Peter Maroulis, confronting him with the profound hopelessness of Liddy's position and pledging his best efforts to obtain life plus twenty on and after for Liddy, if he refused to talk.

Maroulis certainly communicated those sentiments to Liddy.

Liddy refused to talk.

At first Silbert was incredulous. Then, by the first of August, he was convinced. He went to work on Hunt and McCord. Hunt, sincerely believing that his lawyer was going to get him off, stood fast and would not talk. McCord budged a little; when Silbert and the other prosecutors threatened to indict McCord's wife as an accessory after the fact of the burglary, McCord saw to the delivery of the bugging transmitters and receivers to the U.S. Attorney's Office. But he, too, refused to talk, and so did the Cubans.

That brought Silbert, Seymour Glanzer and Donald Campbell, assigned to assist him in the prosecution, to the extreme verge of stratagems permissible to extract guilty pleas and evidence from prospective defendants. Tactically, at least, the bind they contrived for McCord went beyond the verge. Still they came up empty; on September 7, 1972, the Watergate grand jury indicted Liddy, Hunt, McCord, Barker, Gonzalez, Martinez and Sturgis. Silbert was perplexed. "I couldn't understand it," he said. "If they were going to have to plead, and they were, there should have been at least one of them who'd make a deal before he got indicted."

Perplexed, but not finished. A suspect intransigent under the pressure of the threat of jail occasionally proves more cooperative as a convicted defendant facing the fact of jail. The prosecuting team surmised that motives powerful enough to insure silence before indictment might erode between indictment and trial, and if not then, after trial and conviction. Silbert resignedly set about the successful performance of what he regarded as a needless task, with no information of any substance to indicate its enormity.

The maintenance of an ongoing conspiracy depends upon convergence of the interests of the conspirators. When the interests of some diverge from the interests of the rest, people start talking, and then people start going to jail. In simple terms, the prosecutor's job is to hasten and worsen such divisions, obtaining his leverage upon the conspiracy by the application of constitutionally permissible force to the conspirators, one by one.

During the summer those efforts failed because Liddy, amenable to his own assassination after the burglars were caught, was a stand-up guy; because Hunt thought he had a legal defense; because McCord thought, with good reason, that he had the fix in; and because the Cubans, who didn't know much of anything anyway, thought they had been working for the CIA. They failed also because the people who conspired to have Liddy and the rest break into the Watergate had conspired among themselves, afterward, to volunteer nothing. Or, more formally, to obstruct justice, by willfully endeavoring by means of bribery, misrepresentation, intimidation, and force and threats thereof, to delay and prevent the communication of information relating to a violation of criminal statutes of the United States, by any person, to a criminal investigator, in violation of Title 18, United States Code, Section 1510(a).

Silbert's experience was heavily weighted with the investigation and prosecution of comparatively unsophisticated crimes. From law school he went to the Tax Division of the Department of Justice, spending four years on appeals of convictions of tax-evasion cases. The facts in such cases are the petrified evidence introduced at trial; the lawyers on appeal seek progress only on the law, and the defendant's case is set in amber. In 1964 he began five years in the U.S. Attorney's Office in the District, where he was conditioned by its singularity among the ninety-four U.S. Attorney's Offices in the United States: in other districts, a federal prosecutor seldom encounters a murder case or a drugstore holdup, because such matters are handled by local and State prosecutors; in the District of Columbia, the U.S. Attorney runs the only game in town, and his Assistants lack the leisure to forage through the jurisdiction for secret crimes gone unreported because both criminal and victim are quite content with the results. In Silbert's second tour at Justice he worked in Deputy Assistant Attorney General Richard Kleindienst's office, on what amounted to a legislative recapitulation of his first hitch as prosecutor. Then he went back to the U.S. Attorney's Office, because "the D.C. Bill had passed and was going to have a significant impact on the U.S. Attorney's Office. Implementing it was going to take a lot of work. They were generally familiar with it, but not specifically, so far as it would affect the office. I was involved with developing policy guidelines on how to implement it. Trying to develop a consistent approach. There were so many changes all at one time."

That kind of background, coupled with Earl Silbert's impressive abilities, had made him, on June 18, 1972, the perfect choice as prosecutor for what then seemed to be a common burglary made uncommon by the identities of its victims and the peculiar characteristics of its apparent perpetrators. Hidden, then, were the ramifications which made it more like a white-collar crime.

There is a significant difference between breaches of the peace and white-collar crimes, a difference conceded by Titus when he created a special unit in his office to deal with that kind of offense, and put Seymour Glanzer in charge of it. A breach of the peace, no matter how atrocious, is complete when committed; the burglars take the color TV and screw. But a good fraud, committed upon a bank, brokerage house or the taxpaying and usury-paying public, is never really complete. In the expectation of the crooks, it is temporally infinite. Often the victims don't know they've been cheated. Frequently, too, they're agreeable to the fraud; customers of loansharks can't get credit from banks, and will pay any price to get it. Then there are the members of the honest populace, who pay higher taxes to cover the cost of bribes in Government contracts, higher utility rates fixed by energy companies, and bankers shut out of business by competitors illegally blandishing investors with returns in excess of statutory limits. That kind of crime has to be ferreted out; it does not surface because a twenty-four-year-old private security guard spots tape on the locks of garage doors late at night in a high-rent office building.

The ferreting is delicate work. To succeed, it demands initial and continuing recognition that the initiative never passes totally to the Government, as it does when the burglars have finished, and left with the goods. Or when they are caught before they have finished. The objective for the investigator of white-collar crime is to determine where the criminals were, and whether they left anything behind to show they did it, and how to prevent them from going back and getting it, and how to prove that they were there in the first place. The difference is the difference between an entirely offensive exercise, and one that is at least fifty percent defensive.

When Titus pulled Glanzer out of the white-collar unit, and Campbell off supervision of District organized-crime investigations, he acknowledged the dimension to the Watergate burglary which was completely concealed until Alfred W. Baldwin turned around and tipped Liddy in, along with Hunt. That was fair enough, because it was as prompt as it could have been. It constituted recognition that the existence of additional defendants, one of them placed fairly high in ostensibly respectable circles, implied the possibility that one or more unidentified people might have it in mind to balk the orderly processes of justice.

Impossible to gauge was the number or the location of those anonymous people. McCord, passive in the cover-up during the summer of 1972, was exchanging notes with John Caulfield, and keeping that secret from his attorney, Gerald Alch. There was another hallmark of the Watergate cases: very often none of the lawyers involved really knew what was going on.

Dean, after his preliminary stumbles, generally did. Of course he had the benefit of virtually everybody else's information, but that was because everybody, on both sides of the case, thought he was the Lone Ranger, told him everything, and did not perceive that his serenity was a mask.

It was a mask for cautiousness that indicated an appropriate respect for the hazard implied in expecting too much of one's overly ambitious, first conspiracy. Dean was scared, not as scared as he would get, but scared enough. He settled for a conservative game: the thing to do was to ask no more than the coconspirator was willing to deliver, and then make sure he did it very well. He had his willing pupils.

# 6

SOME YEARS AGO, on a college campus in a New England state which prohibits Sunday liquor sales, a teenaged townie with a terrible thirst and a girlfriend of fifteen pulled up at a frat house where some of the brothers were enjoying a Sabbath beer on the front porch. The kid said he was on his way to a party, and had promised to bring the beer. He asked if the brothers would sell him some. They at first refused, secure in their confidence that among rightful privileges congenitally acquired was the franchise to maintain and ingest supplies of beer in Sunday monopolies.

The kid, desperate in the autumn sunlight under the maple trees, permitted his fear of being ridiculed to overcome his judgment, if he had any. He pleaded with the brothers, and they at last made him a counter-offer: they would trade him a case of beer for the use of his girlfriend. The little rat accepted, carried his beer to the car, and assisted his benefactors in overcoming the girl's reservations about the bargain. She was escorted into the house and taken upstairs and violated by ten or a dozen of the brothers. She was allowed to arrange her clothing in the parlor after the agreement was consummated, and sent upon her way.

Returning somewhat later, accompanied this time by a parent and some cops, the girl found the fraternity house all but unoccupied. The few brothers on the premises included none that she recognized. Loyal to the others, who had scattered out the back, those then present were unable to give the cops much help in the conduct of their investigation. No, there was no one else around, hadn't been all day, in fact. Yes, they understood that the girl was upset; they could see, in fact, that she was hysterical. Most assuredly, there had been some harm done there, a thoroughly reprehensible kind of behavior, in fact. But they were loyal: nobody like the people she described had been around all day. Or ever, for that matter.

That was Jeb Stuart Magruder's kind of loyalty. Dean tutored him in its testimonial practice. It differed from the species which addled the brains of the Cubans. It was nastier. It was grounded in a clear-eyed, fresh-faced, well-barbered, naïve and mean assurance that by birth, education, or the whim of the electorate, those who worked for Richard Nixon had been dispensed from all obligations and responsibilities imposed by law, ethics or scruples, upon the sole condition precedent that they vow always to act in a higher order of patriotism: loyalty to each other, for the greater honor and glory of Richard M. Nixon.

It was that which made them such devastatingly effective saboteurs of the governmental system: they were not conscious of doing wrong, because, like the corrupt scavengers who succeeded the original Knights of Malta, they thought they had a deed in perpetuity to this country, and an absolutist's right to do anything they pleased with it. When outrage was the product of their behavior, it was nothing to fuel concern; Ron Ziegler was calm in receipt of angry, and correct, assertions that he had lied to the press, because he thought he had a right — indeed, an occupational duty — to lie to the press. (Ziegler, encountering a Senator's press secretary one evening at a reception, remarked the identity of their jobs, which, he said, consisted of "lying to the reporters." The Senator's man was both irritated and incredulous, and replied, rather shortly, that he did no such thing. "Oh, come on," Ziegler said, smiling, "of course you do. We all do." No point in saying: "No comment," when you have the option of a deliberate falsehood.)

Magruder, in the performance of his fraternal duty, went forward smugly. On June 19, two days after the break-in, he propounded his cheerful amorality to Hugh Sloan. "We had two meetings on Monday," Magruder told the Committee. "The first meeting was when I determined from him that the money" — found on the burglars — "was our money, and we discussed that in his office. And he came up to my office, and in attempting to allay his concerns, or to help him in some sense, give him some advice, I think, we talked about what would he do about the money. My understanding of the new election law indicated that he would be personally liable for cash funds that were not reported. These were not reported funds. So I indicated," Magruder said earnestly, perceiving no genuine issue to argue, "that I thought he had a problem and might have to do something about it."

The Committee probed for the truth as gingerly as a man using a short stick to coax a long rattlesnake out of a deep crevice. Its members, vainly striving to attend to regular Senate business, interrupting lines of questioning to hustle off for roll-call votes, unprepared for Tuesday's session because exhausted by Monday's all-day session, in some instances timorous and in all legitimately concerned about the actual effect of their television exposure upon their future chances of reelection, understandably accepted volubility in lieu of candor.

Their formal mandate from the full Senate was the acquisition of facts which might illuminate legislative deliberations on the improvement of election reporting laws. Their actual task, as they manifestly conceived of it, was to get the truth out. That was what the journalists clamored for, that, and a restoration of some unspecified Augustan Age, when politicians told the truth, and did not steal. But their practice was embarrassingly shallow, often consisting only of the kind of posturing with which Senator Ervin demeaned himself — when the *New York Times* published an Alan Lelchuk piece fawning on Ervin as "My Uncle Sam" in a virtual ecstasy attributed to the Senator's use of the Scriptures as a substitute for inquiry, Ervin spent the day in an orgy of Bible-belting. Senator Weicker's eruptions of virtue outraged usually coincided with the best times of day for television newscasters, who were seldom unprepared for them, it seemed.

The consequence of fatigue, combined with political apprehensiveness and exacerbated by the toll of extraordinary public idolatry, was a hospitality almost pathetic in its receptiveness toward any sound that the current witness might deign to utter.

Duke Sloan, as Ehrlichman called him, came before the Committee to acknowledge that he had declined to lie quite as Magruder wished, although he certainly lied some, because he was afraid. And he quit the Finance Committee on July 14, 1972, because, as he told Judge Sirica — well, he didn't actually *tell* Sirica; Sirica, still hunting for money as the explanation for questionable behavior, wormed it out of him — he was scared of getting caught at something that might, ah, well . . . he thought it was risky. But he went back to work for Stans in January of 1973, as a consultant, because he'd been out of work for five months, and Stans asked him and all, and Maury was a nice guy and everything, and besides, he thought the heat was off. For that profession of cold feet, he received this reward:

"Senator ERVIN: 'Mr. Sloan, I want to thank you on behalf of the committee for your appearance here. I want to thank you for the intellectual integrity which you have displayed throughout your examination, and for the very forthright manner in which you have testified.' "

Sloan, before the Committee, did not precisely agree with Magruder's recollection of the conversations about Sloan's problem, and what he might have to do about it. "I forget all of the circumstances surrounding it," he said. "I am not positive on the dates, but, to the best of my recollection, this would be the general time frame, the time period. I forget. I believe he called me to his office."

The statute which proscribes perjury before grand juries and courts also provides for perjury before congressional committees, and every other body conducting proceedings in which the law authorizes the taking of testimony under oath. You can't commit perjury by accident. The statute says the liar has to do it on purpose. He must hear a question which asks for subject matter, as Mitchell might say, material to the investigation underway. He must swear to the contrary, and know he is swearing to the contrary, and intend to swear to the contrary, and sit there (it's not necessary for the offense, but it's sure as hell necessary for the fellow who plans to prove the offense was committed) barefaced, hoping to goodness that the interrogator swallows the whopper, because the witness or some buddy of his will be in serious trouble if the questioner starts laughing.

It's not statutory perjury, at least provably, to forget something. Nor is it provable perjury to say something that isn't so, if memory misled. And while it's perjury in the abstract to say that you believe something, when you don't, that's the kind of perjury that's impossible to prove. Mr. Sloan was well advised by his two attorneys. His professions of vagrant memory, prefacing his hesitant report of discussions with Magruder, suggest very strongly that he was amenable to assisting readily in the degradation of Magruder, so long as the Committee would let him keep his own skirts clear. The Committee let him.

"He indicated to me," Sloan said of Magruder, "that we are going to have . . . or suggested to me, a figure of what I had given to Mr. Liddy, in the range of, somewhere, $75,000 to $80,000. I do not believe, at that point in time, I had prepared a summary of figures, so I did not know the precise amount of money that I had given to Mr. Liddy at that point. However, I did know that the sum was considerably larger than that, because Mr. Magruder himself had authorized a payment for $83,000 in one single installment.

"I must have indicated to him," Sloan said thoughtfully, in the exercise of his intellectual integrity, " 'Well, that just is not the right figure.' " Jeb, for God's sake, you know better'n that. "I did not have the right figure, 'But that is too low.' He indicated to me, at that time, that I said to him . . . he must have been insistent, because I remember making to him, on that occasion, a statement: 'I have no intention of perjuring myself.' "

"He said," Magruder said, " 'You mean, commit perjury?' I said: 'You might have to do something like that,' and, very honestly, was doing that in good faith, to assist Mr. Sloan at that time." Nothing like a good faith, honest effort to persuade a friend to commit perjury.

Dash said to Sloan: "What did he say to you when you said that?"

Sloan said: "He said: 'You may have to.' "

That, of course, contravened all of Sloan's ethical precepts. He was determined to tell the truth. Not the whole truth. Just the truth, some of it. He went before the grand jury prepared to agree to any figure proposed to him by the prosecutors. The whole truth was $199,000. But he was prepared to agree to $45,000, $55,000, $90,000 and, as it turned out, $104,000. Because, of course, he had disbursed each of the lesser amounts to Liddy, as part of the total amount — if, of course, $199,000 *was* the total amount; it's difficult, even now, to be sure — and thus by acquiescing to those sums he wasn't really, well, *lying*. He even murmured to the prosecutors that Magruder was lying, which further eased his mind. Duke Sloan got a lot less credit for obstruction than he deserved.

Bart Porter also gratified the Committee.

"Senator ERVIN: 'The Bible bestows blessing upon him who swears to his own work, and changeth it not. I want to commend you on the forthrightness of your testimony before this committee. Thank you very much.'

"Senator BAKER: 'Mr. Chairman, before the witness is dismissed, I want to join in that expression to the witness. I must say that he and I trod on delicate and painful ground on Thursday.

" 'And I think you were very manly in the way you reacted to probing and searching questions. It is not an easy job you have undertaken. And the committee is not here to sit in judgment on your guilt or innocence. But the committee is privileged. I would like to comment on your forthcoming testimony and spirit.' "

I think *forthcoming*, in Watergatese, meant *forthright*, but I can't be sure; it may be a word which was employed to convey the impression that a witness had been satisfactorily forthright, when in fact he had not been, but the exigencies of national television demanded the perfunctory assertion of the contrary.

" 'So while we have used your testimony to prove and explore the atmosphere of campaigning, I hope we have not left the impression that we have done so with an absence of sensibility for your own situation, and you are to be commended for appearing and testifying, and the committee is grateful, and I am grateful.' "

Silbert, Glanzer and Campbell probably weren't. Porter appeared before the Committee to be shriven on June 7 and 12, 1973. He had testified before Sirica on January 23. He backed Magruder right down the line, just as he had done when Silbert, troubled during the summer by Sloan's Delphic hints of Magruder's mendacity, had called Porter before the grand jury.

"Following the break-in at the Watergate," Committee Assistant Chief Counsel David Dorsen said to Porter, "did you have a conversation with Mr. Jeb Magruder concerning any statements you might make to the Federal Bureau of Investigation?"

"Yes, sir," Porter said, "I did."

"When and where," Dorsen said, "did this conversation occur?"

"I would say," Porter said, "that approximately ten or eleven days, I am not sure of the exact date, whether it was June twenty-eighth or the twenty-ninth, but in that time frame, Mr. Magruder asked me to come into his office, which I did. He shut the door, and he told me that he had just come from a meeting with Mr. Mitchell, Mr. LaRue, himself, and a fourth party whose name I cannot remember, where my name had been brought up as someone who could be, what was the term he used? 'Counted on in a pinch,' or 'a team player,' or words to that effect."

"I do not know," Dean told the Committee, "when I first learned of Magruder's proposed testimony, but I did not know it had already been formulated when I first heard it. I informed Haldeman and Ehrlichman of the story. We discussed it, and no one was sure it would hold up."

It wouldn't have, without the support it got from the stories of Porter and Sloan, and, if it hadn't, Mitchell's would have collapsed next. Dean would have been very upset.

"He said," Porter said, referring to Magruder, "that, I believe, at that time, Mr. Liddy had been fired from the campaign, he said it was, *apparent* was the word he used, that Mr. Liddy and others had, on their own, illegally participated in the break-in of the Democratic National Committee, and Mr. Magruder swore to me that neither he nor anybody higher than Mr. Liddy in the campaign organization, or at the White House, had any involvement whatsoever in Watergate, at the Watergate break-in, and reinforced that by saying: 'Doesn't that sound like something stupid that Gordon would do?' And, you have to know Mr. Liddy, I agreed with that." Old Jeb was a barrel of laughs.

"He said," Porter said, " 'I want to assure you now that no one did.' He said, however: 'There is a problem with some of the money. Now, Gordon was authorized money for some dirty tricks. Nothing illegal, but nonetheless, things that could be very embarrassing to the President of the United States, and to Mr. Mitchell and Mr. Haldeman and others. Now, your name was brought up as someone who we can count on to help in this situation.' And I asked: 'What is it you are asking me to do?' And he said: 'Would you corroborate a story' " — i.e., lie to the investigators, so they won't know the rest of us are lying — " 'that the money was authorized for something a little bit more legitimate-sounding than dirty tricks?' Even though dirty tricks were legal, it could still be very embarrassing. 'You are aware that the Democrats have filed a suit against this committee.'

"I said," Porter said, " 'yes, I read that in the paper.' He said: 'Do you know what immediate discovery is?' I said: 'I do not.'

" 'They may get immediate discovery,' " Porter said, apparently quoting Magruder, " 'which means they can come in at any moment and swoop in on our committee and take all of the files and subpoena all of the records, and you know what would happen if they did that.'

"I conjured up in my mind that scene, and became rather excitable," Porter said, "and knew I didn't want to see that. So I said: 'Well, be specific.' And he said: 'Well, you were in charge of the surrogate campaign, you were very concerned about radical elements disrupting rallies and so forth,' and I said: 'Yes,' and he said: 'Suppose that we had authorized Liddy, instead of the dirty tricks, we had authorized him to infiltrate some of the radical groups? How could such a program have cost $100,000?"

"I thought very quickly," Porter said, presumably utilizing his training as an officer in the United States Marines as well as "seven and one-half years in the marketing of data-processing computers and software," but omitting to think very deeply, "of a conversation I had with a young man in California in December, as a matter of fact, and I said: 'Jeb, that is very easy. You could get ten college-age students or twenty-four- or twenty-five-year-old students, people' " — students, after all, are a lot like people — " 'over a period of ten months.' Mr. Magruder had prefaced his remark by saying: 'From December on.' And I said: 'You can pay them $1,000 a month, which they would take their expenses out of that, and that is $100,000. That is not very much for a $45 million campaign.' "

Not very much at all, considering that Stans had raised more than $60 million.

"And he said," Porter said, still quoting Magruder, " 'Now, that is right. Would you be willing, if I made that statement to the FBI, would you be willing to corroborate, that when I came to you in December, and asked you how much it would cost, that that is what you said?' "

In other words: are you willing to lie to the FBI and everybody?

There are varieties of software, and among them was Porter's conscience. "I thought for a moment and I said: 'Yes, I would probably do that.' I don't remember saying: Yes, but I am sure I gave Mr. Magruder the impression I would probably do that, and that was the end of the conversation." And he did it. He lied to the FBI, to the grand jury, and to the petit jury. From the halls of Montezuma, to the shores of Tripoli, fighting his master's battles, keeping the Democrats out of the files.

"Following Magruder's appearance before the grand jury," Dean said, "I received a call from Higby" — Lawrence Higby, a White House assistant — "requesting information for Haldeman as to how Magruder had done before the grand jury."

"I subsequently called Mr. Petersen," Dean said, "who said he would find out and call me back. Petersen called back and said he had made it through by the skin of his teeth," that very articulate young man. "I called Haldeman, and so informed him, and subsequently informed Mitchell and Magruder. I recall that Haldeman was very pleased, because this, of course, meant that the investigation would not go beyond Liddy."

The cops in that New England town were inclined, when the taxpayers alleged excesses to have been committed by the college boys, to scrutinize the responses which the boys made in denial. Well then, said the cops, this girl here must be making it all up. The fraternity brothers agreed. So in that event, the cops suggested, there'd be no harm in letting her and the cops go through the house, just to make sure there was no one inside that she recognized. No harm at all, said the brothers, because, of course, there wasn't anyone inside. All there was, in the parlor, was a group portrait, taken the previous June, and the girl picked about eight of her attackers out of it. Among them was one whose loyalty did not surpass his fear, and he betrayed the rest. There's one in every group.

# Part II

*For Dean, and his clients,
McCord's impertinence was
dangerous, and so was Hunt's
anxiety; they were not
permanently joined up.*

# 7

In Dean's original group of secondary clients, there were two such men. One was E. Howard Hunt. The other was James W. McCord, Jr.

McCord baffled Silbert. He puzzled Dean a good deal, too, but Dean did not have a contemplative mind, and soon grew bored with McCord's posturings. Hunt grew to loathe McCord. Liddy didn't talk. McCord kept his own counsel, in the summer of 1972, and he kept it *from* his own counsel.

McCord's counsel was Gerry Alch.

He fought off penury in law school with his earnings as a cabaret comedian in Catskills resorts. He has a high-speed mind, which is not a handicap for a trial lawyer. He has developed a sure sense of the impression he makes upon his listeners, which does not impede his efforts to persuade jurors of his view of the evidence. And he makes a good appearance, although the roots of his charcoal black hair are yellowed at the temples and forehead by the artificial suntan lotion which he lavishes on his face.

"In July of 1972," Alch told the Committee, "my office received a telephone call from Mr. McCord, requesting an appointment. On a Saturday morning during that month, I met with him for the very first time. He identified himself as one of those arrested in the Watergate building on June 17, 1972. He told me that he had taken a calculated risk in doing what he did, and was prepared to face the consequences. Within that

49

framework, however, he indicated he wanted the most effective legal representation possible, and asked whether or not my partner, Attorney F. Lee Bailey, would be interested in representing him. I told him that I had advised Mr. Bailey of my appointment with him, and that he, Mr. Bailey, was not interested in representing any defendants in this particular case."

On March 22, 1973, Dean testified to the Committee, "Mr. Mitchell raised the fact that F. Lee Bailey, who had been very helpful in dealing with McCord, had a problem that he would like to bring up. He said that Mr. Bailey had a client who had an enormous amount of gold in his possession, and would like to make an arrangement with the Government, whereby the gold could be turned over to the Government without the individual being prosecuted for holding the gold. Mitchell was addressing his request for assistance to Haldeman, but Haldeman was nonresponsive and the matter was dropped."

Bailey's clients, according to Wayne J. Smith, associated with Bailey, consisted of thirty-five to forty people who had discovered 292 bars of gold worth $26.5 million, in a cave on the Missile Range at White Sands, New Mexico.

"Mr. McCord," Alch said, "told me, as a result of his impression of me, he desired my counsel. A fee of $25,000, plus expenses, was quoted, and agreed upon by Mr. McCord. Arrangements were made for the payment of this fee over a period of time, which arrangements were ultimately met by Mr. McCord, although over a longer period of time than originally agreed upon.

"I asked Mr. McCord to give me specific details attending the Watergate break-in, but he specifically declined to do so, except to state his personal motivation for so acting. That is, as he told me at the first meeting, the protection of others. I explained to him that since he had been physically apprehended in the Watergate complex, he could obviously not deny that fact, and inquired as to his motivation in so acting. He told me that as Chief of Security for the Committee to Re-elect the President, he had received information to the effect that various antiwar demonstrations, by groups which he described as 'radical,' were being planned for the upcoming presidential election, and that these demonstrations had, in the past, and would invariably in the future, lead to violence or the threat thereof, to various prominent Republican officials, including, but not limited to, the President of the United States. I told him that I would explore whether or not this motivation could, in any way, be embraced by a recognized legal defense. He told me that he wished me to come to Washington, D.C., and meet with an attorney by the name of Paul O'Brien, whom he described as one of the counsel to his employer, the Committee to Re-elect the President. He desired that I contact Mr. O'Brien and advise him of this — Mr. McCord's — position."

The first demand of the defense attorney to his client is that the client come coco with him. Alch waived that right, permitting McCord to limit his disclosures under the attorney-client privilege strictly to McCord's motivation in committing the burglary. The inescapable inference from McCord's conduct was that somebody had put him up to it. That inference is useful, to a defendant, only if the putter-upper is in some position to improve the situation of the man who has been caught, either by refraining from killing him, which is the boon assertedly guaranteed by the Mob, or by doing something positive for him. Alch plainly concluded that McCord was wired in somewhere, which gave their relationship a nice symmetry. McCord, designing to employ Mitchell's liberty as his own ransom, retained Alch to demonstrate his determination. Alch, tacitly conceding McCord's tacit assertion that he was well connected, permitted McCord a wide and unusual latitude. The effect of their unspoken agreement was that Alch would act as the front man, while McCord did the best he could behind the scenery.

It is not common, though not by any means unknown, for a defendant to negotiate sub rosa with the Government, unbeknownst to his attorney of record. But that seldom happens unless the defendant's attorney is beholden to someone other than the defendant, and then the defendant takes elaborate precautions to keep his lawyer in the dark; he certainly doesn't deliver hints to him about personal connections. It happens, ordinarily, only in Mob cases, when the defendant's lawyer is under retainer to the Mob, and the defendant is skulking around to make a deal that will endanger his employers, who in fact are the real parties in interest for his lawyer. Its occurrence is *prima facie* proof that there is a divergence in interests between the defendant and the people who are paying his lawyer, which, *mutatis mutandis*, means that the defendant is not the man who is paying his lawyer, and that means somebody else is worried. Worried enough to pay.

Alch received from McCord "periodic payments in cash, with the exception of the last two installments, which were in the form of cashier's checks in relatively smaller amounts of seventeen hundred dollars. The bulk of the money received was in cash, in one-hundred-dollar bills." He began his representation of McCord by traveling to "the Capitol," and he telephoned "Mr. O'Brien for an appointment. Mr. McCord drove me to Mr. O'Brien's office, whereupon I met with Mr. O'Brien and a gentleman introduced to me as Mr. Kenneth Parkinson. I introduced myself, told Mr. O'Brien I had been retained to represent Mr. McCord, and was here at Mr. McCord's direction to inform him, as a representative of Mr. McCord's employer, the Committee to Re-elect the President, that Mr. McCord was, as he told me, prepared to face the consequences of his acts."

Like hell he was. McCord thought he had the fix in, and it was easy for him to think that, because he expected to get the fix in.

"I worked first," McCord said, "for the Federal Bureau of Investigation in 1942, 1943, in Washington, in New York City. I, subsequently from 1943 to 1945, was an Army Air Corps officer. From 1948 to 1951, I worked as a special agent for the Federal Bureau of Investigation in San Diego and San Francisco, California. I worked from 1951 to 1970 with the Central Intelligence Agency as a security officer. I retired from that agency in August 1970, after twenty-five years' federal service." The Ervin Committee was attentive.

"Between our original meeting in September of 1971," Jack Caulfield told the Committee, "and June 1972, Mr. McCord and I grew to be personal friends, even though we did not physically see each other frequently with the exception of March 1972, when I saw him on a daily basis at the Committee to Re-elect the President. During this period we casually discussed on some occasions the possibility of going into business together after the election campaign was over, and Mr. McCord felt quite beholden to me, since he felt that I had been responsible for placing him at the national committee, and the Committee to Re-elect the President."

Caulfield had latched on to Ehrlichman's office when Ehrlichman was General Counsel to the President, capitalizing on relationships developed during the 1968 campaign when he was assigned as a New York police officer to security details for the candidate in Manhattan. He had proposed Operation Sandwedge, a security plan for the 1972 campaign which would not have omitted an important position for himself; Dean let that "die a natural death," having succeeded Ehrlichman, because

Mitchell and the rest didn't go for it. Then Caulfield, with Dean's intercession, sought from Mitchell "a position similar to that occupied by Dwight Chapin in relation to the President, and that in addition to handling the kinds of activities that Chapin handled for the President, I could be of value to Mr. Mitchell as a bodyguard." Mitchell didn't hear that part about making Caulfield into a major domo: "Ultimately, on the first of March, 1972, I went to the reelection committee to commence my duties there. It soon became clear to me that Mr. Mitchell regarded me only as a bodyguard, which was not what I had in mind at all."

Maneuvering nicely, Caulfield then fetched up at Treasury, running the Enforcement Branch of the Alcohol, Tobacco & Firearms Division, and that was where he was when McCord got caught in the Watergate, ready to be active in the cover-up with Parkinson and O'Brien. "In July of 1972," Caulfield said, "and that date may well be wrong, and I don't know, but my recollection of the date was July of 1972, in July of 1972, after his arrest, I had Mr. Ulasewicz call his home and tell him to go to a designated public telephone booth near his house where I would be calling him."

Caulfield had met Ulasewicz during their simultaneous tenure in the radical-chasing Bureau of Special Services of the NYPD. Ulasewicz left the Department in 1969. Caulfield got him a job which had him taking orders from the White House — primary among them snooping around after Teddy Kennedy, posing as a newspaperman putting insulting questions at press conferences dealing with the Chappaquiddick incident — but getting paid $22,000 per year as a putatively private investigator for Herb Kalmbach's San Diego law firm, the one with the presidential seal on the wall. It was, of course, only natural that the Acting Assistant Director for AT&F would experience a poignant interest in his old friend McCord, who had been arrested, and spontaneously set about to convey his personal concern.

"Now," said Dash to Tony Ulasewicz, "in July of 1972, did you receive a call from Mr. McCord?"

"In June of 1972," Ulasewicz said. His diction, though colorful, may have distracted from the precision of his memory.

"In June of 1972," Dash said. "Can you just briefly tell us what the nature of that call was?"

"Yes," Ulasewicz said. "Mr. Caulfield called me somewhere around the twenty-fifth or twenty-sixth of June, and asked me to come to see him in

Washington, D.C." Ulasewicz was a rover back for the Nixon Administration; while he did what the White House told him, and got paid by a California law firm, he retained his home in Day, Saratoga County, New York. Later, in 1975, he got indicted for not paying federal taxes on that California income.

Caulfield said he wanted to see Tony "on a personal matter. I met with him around noontime. He mentioned he was thinking of contacting Mr. McCord, a friend of his, that he did not have his telephone number. It was unlisted. It had been changed. And he said: would I assist him in arranging for an appointment, so that he may speak, not me, but speak with Mr. McCord."

"Then what did you do?" Dash asked.

"I said all right," Ulasewicz said. " 'If you do not know any other, if you want my help, I will do it.' I did not question him in any way. He asked me: could I do it as soon as possible? I said: 'I will do it right now.' I said: 'Number one, you will have to give me some identifying information. How will Mr. McCord know that it is you that is contacting him?'

"What I did," Ulasewicz said, "was, I wrote a note on a plain piece of paper, and told Jack I would deliver that to Mr. McCord, setting up a telephone, and then he can have his conversation. The purpose of this call, he said, he wanted to help Mr. McCord, express his sympathy, et cetera. They had been such good friends in the past.

"I wrote a note," Ulasewicz said, "arranged, I told Jack I must have some identifying information, so that this thing, that Mr. McCord would believe it is he. He said: 'Well, there was an incident recently,' in which Mr. Caulfield left his raincoat somewhere, and I put that, that was the identifying information, that 'I am a mutual friend for whom you recovered a raincoat.' "

"Did you," Dash said, "in fact, take that note?"

"Yes," Ulasewicz said.

"Where did you deliver it?" Dash said.

"I proceeded immediately to the area where Mr. McCord resides," Ulasewicz said, which is the kind of syntax that cops develop from writing reports and testifying in court for years and years and years. It meant: "I went where he lived."

"Mr. Caulfield had given me the address," Ulasewicz said. "I looked around through the area, located a place, a Blue Inn or something, which has a large parking lot, two telephone booths isolated by themselves. I took the two telephone numbers of the booths, put them on the note, put two different times, like 2:30 and 4:30, and then wrote on the note about a mutual friend wishes to speak to you, or words to that effect. 'You recently recovered a raincoat of his.' It was not signed.

"I then proceeded," Ulasewicz said, "this telephone booth is within the vicinity, of course, of Mr. McCord's residence. I then took the note. I went to Mr. McCord's residence, placed it in the letter box, and walked away. I then called from some area not too far. I called Mr. Caulfield and informed him that it was done."

"I called him at that public telephone," Caulfield said, "and simply asked him if there was anything I could do for him or his family at this time of personal difficulty. No one had asked me to make this call, and I was motivated entirely by my own personal concern for his condition and that of his family."

Caulfield and Ulasewicz, when they testified, had not been charged with any offenses, let alone convicted before Maximum John Sirica and promised forever in prison unless they talked; McCord had been. All of them, before the Committee, thus had cognizable motives to embroider the facts, McCord to make the story worse than the truth, Caulfield and Ulasewicz to make it better. Their stories agreed in substance, but not in detail.

"Sometime in July 1972," McCord said, "shortly after I got out of jail, which was in June 1972, about midday there was a note in my mailbox at my residence, and when I opened the letter, which had not been stamped nor sent through the mails, it was a note from Jack Caulfield, signed: 'Jack,' which said: 'Go to the phone booth on Route 355 near your home,' and he gave three alternate times at which I could appear at the phone booth for a telephone call from him.

"To the best of my recollection," McCord said, "one of those times was very shortly thereafter, an hour or two later, and another time was the next day, and that seems to me that the third time was the following evening. I went to the telephone, to that telephone booth on Route 355 that afternoon, the same afternoon, as I best recall, and I heard the voice that I have referred to in the memorandum of today. I do not know the individual's identity, he had an accent that I would refer to as a New York accent. He said that he had formerly worked for Jack Caulfield. He said: 'I am a friend of Jack's. I formerly worked with him. Jack will want to talk with you shortly. He will be in touch with you soon.'

"I received a telephone call subsequently from Mr. Caulfield," McCord said. "To the best of my recollection it came to my home first, and it said: 'Go to the same phone booth on Route 355,' which I did, and there Mr. Caulfield told me that he was going overseas in a few days. He said: 'If you have any problems,'" McCord said, perhaps reflecting for a moment upon Judge Sirica's more than desultory interest in his activities on behalf of CREEP, "'if you have any problems, call my home,'" not Caulfield's office, where he too made a modest living off a promise to uphold the Constitution and the laws of the United States, "'and leave word, and I will call you back from overseas to your residence.' He said: 'When you call my home, ask for Mr. Watson.'"

"Mr. Watson?" Senator Gurney asked.

"Watson," McCord said. "He said, also: 'After my return, if you ever need to call me at my office,' he gave a number, the office number, and he said: 'Simply leave word that Mr. Watson is calling.'"

McCord, at least on a par with Hunt, and recruited as the wireman for the Watergate jobs by Liddy (Ulasewicz sneered at the "army" dispatched to tap the DNC phones, which shows that Tony knew little about the enterprise; the Cubans went in to photograph Larry O'Brien's files, and McCord went along as the wireman, all by his lonesome), was the only technician in a group of ideologues. He never believed that the burglary was a CIA enterprise. He didn't think it was an FBI enterprise. He did think it was approved by John N. Mitchell, the Attorney General of the United States, because Liddy recruited him for the wirework while Mitchell was still in office, and asserted that Mitchell had approved. Therefore, when caught, McCord thought he would get it fixed like a traffic ticket. He was a Liddy without illusions: he thought the Attorney General of the United States could do any damned thing he pleased, including retaining Jim McCord to bug the opposition, and if Jim McCord got hooked installing the bugs, John N. Mitchell or somebody else would get him off.

McCord's interest, then, by June 19 had begun to diverge from the interests of Liddy and Hunt and the Cubans. He was not interested in philosophical niceties: he had gone into that office, and been caught, and he wanted to get off. Executive clemency was not on his mind then; he wanted a little help from his friends in getting his case dismissed. And he didn't intend to do time, either.

Until September, McCord, with some reservations, acted charily upon a tentative confidence in his expectations. Raked fore and aft by the same broadsides that Silbert was firing at the rest of the defendants, he stood fast against everything but the prosecutor's firmly credible threat that McCord's wife would find herself indicted if certain electronics equipment did not turn up in the U.S. Attorney's Office. Caulfield, after all, remained in power, and had pledged some kind of assistance upon short notice, and McCord would trust that until it was invoked and came up short.

Silbert on the one side, Alch on the other, Dean in the middle, spent the humid Washington summer of 1972 in mutual confusion. Each lacked at least one essential fact (Silbert lacked two), which McCord was keeping from him.

Dean thought McCord, and the other suspects, were fungible. Later he would change his mind. But what he was getting from Mardian, Gray, Petersen, LaRue, Parkinson, O'Brien, and others made him think that if you took care of Liddy, and if you took care of Hunt, McCord would string along. No such thing.

Alch thought McCord was probably nuts. He dismissed McCord's ravings about having the fix in, tried to formulate a defense, and found none.

Silbert did not know that McCord thought he had the fix in, and did not know that McCord was talking to Caulfield. Neither did he know that Gray was talking to Dean, who was talking to White House people as well as to Caulfield. Silbert was sure that McCord was nuts.

McCord, who knew everything except that Dean was dancing him along, by means of Caulfield's agency, thought they were all crazy. He did not plead, though his case was hopeless. He bided his time. That led to the further confusion of the people actively engaged in the cover-up. Dean, though a novice, handled it well.

In the long run, though, that mattered very little to Silbert, only temporarily to Alch, very slightly to Hunt and not at all to Liddy. But it was a serious concern to Mitchell, and that was why McCord's behavior was of more than transient interest to Dean. Not because Dean had to save Mitchell: because Dean had to save the President, and that, in the summer and the fall before the 1972 elections, seemed to Dean to require the salvation of Mitchell.

McCord had been signaled by Caulfield. He was signaling back. His selection of Bailey's firm was intended as a declaration of independence; he considered that Bailey was wired in to the Administration, a connection which served the same purpose for him, vis-à-vis CREEP, as Caulfield's raincoat served for Ulasewicz, vis-à-vis McCord. His purpose was to be taken seriously, and the message which he wanted seriously considered was what he told Alch: in substance, that he had acted upon orders of the top man in CREEP, John N. Mitchell. Dean probably understood that, but he was a neophyte with a bad hand. That was a matter of comparative indifference; a sage with a good hand could have done no better.

# 8

THE PRESIDENT, OH best beloved, was most 'sclusively — though non-committally — pleased by Mr. Silbert's choice of candidates for prison terms for breaking into Larry O'Brien's office. More pleased, Dean thought, than he realistically ought to have been. He tried to warn the guy, and failed.

When the indictments were handed up on September 15, 1972, Richard M. Nixon congratulated Dean on his containment of the investigation, and, by extension, on his second conspiracy. Dean was underwhelmed.

Silbert was patient. Dean knew what that meant, better than the President did. If things worked right, Silbert would get convictions which not even the rampantly idealistic J. Skelly Wright–David Bazelon school of the Court of Appeals for the District of Columbia Circuit would find reason to overturn, notwithstanding the fact that to get them he would have to check Judge Sirica's habitual preference for the prosecution's case, short of demonstrable bias, prejudice and error in the record. Then, with the birds firmly in hand, he would approach them again, still within the rules of the idealistic system, and invite them to tell what they knew, in hope of lenience on sentencing. He didn't think the system worked well, but he thought he could make it work the best it could, and that, he thought, was what he was supposed to do.

Dean had seen Ehrlichman the afternoon of June 19, 1972, after his morning conference with Liddy, Mardian and LaRue, reporting what Liddy had said. Liddy had said that he himself should be killed, for clumsiness. Then he said why. Dean had therefore plainly believed, then, that the interests of the suspects would keep them in line.

"I recall Ehrlichman asking where Hunt was," Dean said. "I said I had no idea, and Colson made a similar statement. At that point, before the meeting started, Ehrlichman instructed me to call Liddy and to have him tell Hunt to get out of the country. I did this, without even thinking. Shortly after I made the call, however, I realized that no one in the White House should give such an instruction, and raised the matter. A brief discussion ensued between Ehrlichman and myself. As I recall, Ehrlichman said that he was not a fugitive from justice, so why not? I said that I did not think it was very wise. At this point, Colson chimed in, that he also thought it was unwise, and Ehrlichman agreed. I immediately called Liddy again, to retract the request, but informed me that he had already passed the message and it might be too late to retract." It was: Hunt had fled to California, where he would commence scouting up a Mexican hideout.

Sirica would be far less trusting. "It was obvious," the man said, "the man" being a composite of lawyers, cops, and reporters who watched the *Liddy* trial: "You can't belt a man with the maximum unless you get the jury to find him guilty first, and from the day that trial started, anybody who'd ever been in a courtroom in his life before, knew that something like that was going to happen."

That was in January 1973, when everybody had more facts. It wasn't so right after Labor Day of 1972, when almost everybody was in the dark, one way or the other.

McCord had whiled away the summer in unshakable confidence that he'd never be tried, and if tried, that his friends in high places would not permit him to be convicted. E. Howard Hunt, for differing reasons, had similar confidence: he thought he would beat the case on legal grounds. Silbert, as wanting in significant facts about Hunt as he was about McCord, was as confounded by one as he was about the other. In neither instance was there a blessed thing he could have done about it. Dean could have helped him to solve Hunt, but he didn't want to.

On CIA assignment in Paris soon after World War II, E. Howard Hunt bought some black notebooks that he used for the rest of his useful life. In them he logged names, real and alias, addresses, code words and telephone numbers acquired in the course of his sneaky trade. When he went to work as a Plumber, he put them in his safe in his office at the Executive Office Building. That's where they were when he was caught. The contents of Hunt's safe worried Chuck Colson. At Colson's direction, Dean had the safe jimmied by the Secret Service on June 20, parceling out the contents between himself and Bruce Kherli. No inventory, so far as is known, was made of what came out of that safe and went into the boxes; only Hunt knows for certain what was in there, and only Dean knows where it went. Some of it went to Gray. Dean kept the rest. Then he dissembled.

Dean was responsible for the existence of at least four understandings about what happened to the notebooks. He did not narrate all of them; some were deduced from his actions and the facts which appeared implied in them. All were erroneous, and each was the basis for actions later greatly regretted.

*The Gray version*: Pat Gray said he didn't examine what Dean gave him, except to glance at some of the State Department cables which Hunt forged to implicate John F. Kennedy in the assassination of Ngo Dinh Diem. So horrified was he that he pitched the whole bundle into his furnace. Once he said he did that in July; later he said it was December. Gray acceded to the notion that he must have burned the notebooks along with the other stuff.

*The first Dean version*: Agreeing with Ehrlichman and Colson that the contents of Hunt's safe were political dynamite, he got Ehrlichman's permission to turn the materials over to the Director, with the instruction that they should never see the light of day; he was startled to learn that Gray had burned the stuff, or else he was not startled. He did not directly mention the notebooks, when he told that to the Committee in June of 1973.

*The Silbert version*: Dean, Colson and Gray responded to FBI inquiries about Hunt, and Silbert, along with the investigators, believed they got everything that the White House had to offer on the subject. No notebooks surfaced in the course of those inquiries. Silbert and the FBI did not know that Hunt kept notebooks. Consequently, the absence of the notebooks inspired no suspicion.

*The Bittman-Hunt version*: Hunt told his lawyer, William O. Bittman, about the notebooks. Bittman, from conferences with Silbert, deduced Silbert's confidence: that the White House had disgorged all of Hunt's stuff. That, of course, would include the notebooks. The notebooks would connect Hunt nicely with the rest of the defendants, and with some who were not suspects, but should have been.

Bittman reasoned that Silbert had made his case against Hunt and the others by means of the notebooks. Bittman and Hunt had not given the FBI or anyone else permission to crack Hunt's safe, and Hunt had not abandoned the property: it was his. Neither the FBI nor the Secret Service nor anyone else had secured a search warrant for that safe. Bittman therefore concluded that he had a very fine argument to suppress the evidence acquired from the notebooks, together with everything which, he believed, Silbert had acquired as a result of having the notebooks. That, Bittman thought, would demolish the Government's case against Hunt; though it would have no effect whatsoever upon the admissibility of notebook evidence against the others, it would spring Hunt. And, he and Hunt reasoned, Silbert sooner or later would be obliged to confront the fact that what was in those notebooks would not assist the reelection of the President in November, if it came out in the papers.

In that mood, confirmed by the mysterious deliveries of cash on window ledges in Bittman's building, and in Hunt's mailbox, Bittman expected only token opposition by Silbert. He filed his motion to suppress, counseled Hunt to ignore Silbert's energetic efforts to plead him out, and was greatly pleased when Chief Judge John J. Sirica marked the motion for hearing on October 26, less than two weeks before election day.

Nobody in court that day really knew what the hell was going on. Silbert *was* relatively indifferent about the Government's position; while he did have material from Hunt's safe, it had been worthless as evidence, or as a source for investigative leads. If it had been suppressed, very little damage would have resulted to his case, and he couldn't understand why Bittman was so lathered up about the whole thing. He concluded that Bittman was showing off for his client, a practice not uncommon among defense lawyers seeking to justify large fees by creating a worthless fuss in open court.

Bittman, on the other hand, had been bewildered from the outset by Silbert's apparent insensitivity both to constitutional issues of search and seizure and to political dynamite. Thus both attorneys, in court to enlighten the Judge about the issues before him, were almost completely in the dark themselves. With the consent of both sides, Sirica suspended the matter so that Bittman and Silbert could get together and talk. Their conference in Silbert's office was his first inkling of the existence of the notebooks. It rendered inoperative both the Silbert version and the Bittman-Hunt version.

For Bittman and Hunt, the discovery was more immediately distressing than it was for Silbert. If Silbert's case against Hunt was not built upon the notebooks, then the evidence against Hunt would be admitted, and Hunt was in trouble. But Bittman and Hunt retreated from that conclusion, adopting the rationalization that while *Silbert* might not know about the notebooks, and what was in them, *somebody* in the Executive Branch knew, and if they could prove that at trial, the knowledge would be imputed to Silbert as an executive officer, though a dupe, and he would be barred from introducing the evidence against Hunt.

The money kept coming, which consoled them.

Silbert did not admit it to Bittman, but he was troubled by the same possibility. There is an underground custom among cops whose legal sophistication exceeds their principles, and from time to time it is indulged: aware that a confession obtained by threats or physical coercion will be suppressed, unable to solve the case without a confession, and frustrated by a suspect who will not confess unless threatened or coerced, the cops do what they have to do, get the confession, and present it to the prosecutor as motivated only by the suspect's remorse.

The prosecutor offers it in evidence. The defense lawyer says it was coerced. The judge orders a *voir dire* on the issue of voluntariness, and the cops lie and say it was remorse. Then the defendant says it was threats, and besides, they kept him falling up and down this flight of stairs they had down in the basement.

When the cops succeed, it is because virtually all defendants say that, including those (the enormous majority) who never had a hand laid on them, were AORed to death, and blabbered out their statements notwithstanding the Advice of Rights because they were relieved to have been caught, or thought they'd been caught better than they had been. No prosecutor of any quality disputes the possibility that the idealism of the system may gripe a tough cop in a mean case severely enough to make him cut corners — steal evidence, roust a guy on a bad charge just to search him, or improve what he's got for probable cause for a warrant until at last he's got enough. And all of them — there are some who plainly encourage such cheating, but nowhere as many as defense lawyers of shabby ethics are inclined to suggest — concede the attendant possibility that a smart tough cop could do it to a suspect, and then blow the product past the prosecutor and the court.

Silbert is a prosecutor of very high quality. He checked out the possibility and satisfied himself that there had been no unreported winnowing of Hunt's notebooks; none of his people had ever seen them. He reported that to Bittman.

Now all were very curious indeed. Bittman's perplexity was greater than Silbert's, paradoxically, because he still knew a lot more than Silbert did about what was going on behind the prosecutor's back. He had the benefit of what the attorneys for CREEP, Kenneth Parkinson and Paul O'Brien, got from sitting in on Silbert's interviews with CREEP personnel, and that was a big advantage. It had been created by the Democrats, and the Common Cause liberals.

Being very annoyed, and anxious to capitalize on whatever political opportunity might have been created by McCord's shortcomings as burglar and eavesdropper, the Democratic National Committee, Larry O'Brien, and in piggyback fashion, Common Cause, had promptly sued CREEP for the intrusion at the Watergate. In 1974, O'Brien collected $400,000 in settlement of his case, and immediately turned it over to the DNC. But that didn't help George McGovern much, and the pendency of the suits in 1972 seriously disrupted Earl Silbert's management of the criminal cases, which might have helped McGovern more.

The DNC and Common Cause lawsuits raised in civil disguise the same sort of issues implied in the pending criminal matters. If Hunt and Liddy had been provably incited by someone in authority at CREEP, the poor fellow's criminal liability would be recapitulated by hopeless civil liability for CREEP itself.

Silbert and his agents, probing CREEP employees for evidence that would enlarge the number of criminal defendants, simultaneously presented for Kenneth Parkinson and Paul O'Brien a colorable cause for apprehension that could be legitimately propounded to any judge: a business entity, and the people who administer it, cannot be attacked in a lawsuit with evidence obtained from second-echelon employees, unless it is first proven that the employees were within the scope of their duties when they acted, and authorized by the administrators to make damaging admissions when they made them.

Wresting full advantage from this narrow commonality of interest with the prosecutors, the CREEP attorneys insisted upon attending all prosecution interviews of CREEP employees.

Dean, cuddling up to Petersen and blowing smoke at Pat Gray, performed a similar function for the protection of people who worked at the

White House. The result was that the investigation commenced with Silbert in much the same position as the gentleman in the Gillette ad, who saw his neighbor each time he opened the cabinet to reach for the Right Guard: every time his agents went out to interview someone, another guy showed up to take notes.

The Bureau doesn't like that. Special Agents recite the litany of *Miranda* warnings to all potentially suspect, but when a suspect declines to waive his right to have counsel present, the agents are by policy obliged to terminate the interview.

To get the evidence, the prosecutor in such cases has to conduct the interviews himself. The agents sit in and take notes, and sometimes they even ask questions. But as far as the Bureau is concerned, the enterprise is that of the prosecutor: if you want to have your lawyer talk to the Government, it will be the Government's lawyer who talks to you.

In ordinary cases, the effect upon the prosecution is minimal. But in those requiring defensive action by the Government, the full-dress interview presents obvious hazards. It confides to another person, perhaps totally guileless, the direction of the investigation, and that sort of information can be devastating in the mind of a blabbermouth incautious of his company in his choice of a forum for conversational self-importance. It invariably makes an already-guarded witness more guarded still, so that valuable hearsay, fruitful as a source of leads to admissible evidence, never sees the light of day. And when the lawyer, putatively defensive of the witness, in fact cherishes other interests inimical to those of the witness, the stakes are raised out of sight.

Parkinson and O'Brien severely inhibited the CREEP and Finance Committee witnesses who appeared for interrogation by Silbert, Glanzer and Campbell. Those interrogations formed the basis for the evidence which the witnesses delivered, without the supervision of Parkinson and O'Brien, before the grand jury.

It is safe to say that the witnesses had been apprised, before they entered the grand jury room, of the hazards that lurked in the perjury and obstruction statutes, not to mention in the hiring and firing offices at CREEP and the Finance Committee, for those whose memories suddenly improved in the absence of their benevolent attorneys.

Some, like Judith Hoback, comptroller of the Finance Committee, were sufficiently irked by the shepherding, and strong enough of character, to obtain secret conferenees with the prosecutors. But she went and told Hugh Sloan about her visit, and Sloan told Bart Porter, who told

Magruder, and that disposed of the secrecy nicely. Most elected discretion, and said little that was not obvious before they started talking.

Knowing what was going on, and knowing that nobody else did, Dean kept his mouth shut about those notebooks. When Silbert, concerned about the very possibility that Bittman propounded, wheeled up Henry Petersen to aid in the pummeling of Dean (and his ignorant associates, Bruce Kherli and Fred Fielding) about the notebooks in December, Dean lied again, and stood firm. He left those notebooks out of his testimony before the Ervin Committee, the following summer. He did not say what he had done with them until December of 1973. That was a year after Dean's second conspiracy had failed.

The fight had gone out of Hunt back in December of 1972, when his wife was killed in a Chicago airplane crash. He went all to pieces, and had to be taken home and nursed by Bittman, who would need some nursing himself before the whole thing was over, at least professionally. On January 10, 1973, Earl Silbert, before John J. Sirica, moved for trial on the case of *United States of America* v. *George Gordon Liddy, et al.,* no. 1827–72. Liddy, when his name was called, gave Sirica a military salute. "I'm going down there," Alch said in Boston, in December, "I'm going down there and shut up." Alch does not say that about cases he expects to win. He was more candid than Dean, but then, he had fewer responsibilities.

# 9

SILBERT HAD STARTED out planning to keep the trial neat, which is hard to fault, and, to that end, initially decided to omit evidence about the hundred-dollar bills. Then, in December of 1972, preparing his case, he changed his mind, reasoning that neither court nor public would permit trial of the *Liddy* case without presentation of everything that could be proven about the sources of that heavy cash, and, preferring to enter the case ready to make that proof instead of being forced to it later, included it in his preparation.

In part, too, Silbert shifted his ground to protect his flank against a defense strategy appealing to the jury for the acquittal of those caught, on the ground that there were plainly others who had not been caught, a thrust which surely would have come if Silbert had left to the defense the option of triumphantly brandishing all that currency, "which the Government, members of the jury, didn't want you to know about."

He took that course reluctantly. It obliged him to call Magruder and Porter as Government witnesses. It is a rule of evidence and procedure that the proponent of the testimony adopts it as his version of the truth; the Government, in effect, silently endorses the veracity of each of its witnesses, unless the prosecutor is enabled by the stupidity or anger of an unfriendly witness to persuade the court to declare him hostile and turn the prosecutor loose to savage him as a cross-examiner.

In common with all of the contrite who later groveled before the

Committee, Magruder and Porter were mannerly, well-groomed and not given to snarling. If called by the Government, as proof about the cash would require, they would answer Silbert's questions with a civility leavened only by their shared regret of the actions of their subordinates. And precisely because each corroborated the testimony of the other, Silbert could entertain no serious expectation that mendacity would be so obvious, in the testimony of either, to ignite an explosive reaction from the bench resulting in a declaration that this or that polite fellow was hostile, and could be tackled.

Magruder, impeccably dressed but by then known ethically peccable, from his Committee appearance, encountered Charles Bartlett at lunch in the Federal City Club at the Sheraton Carleton, and acknowledged as a compliment from one club member to another Bartlett's critical evaluation of Magruder's *mea culpas*: "The trouble with you, Jeb," Bartlett said, "is, you're too good a liar." Magruder smiled.

He was a good liar. But the excellence of his falsity was limited by its ambitiousness: what was impressive was not the internal coherence of his story, the usual hallmark of good perjury, nor its complexity, which usually diminishes the quality of the perjury because it demands considerable alertness to keep the false details arranged; Magruder's disgusting accomplishment was the frustration of an investigation, and thus the obstruction of justice, in a case of surpassing importance to the Nation, by stoical, bland persistence in the simple statement of events that never happened.

That, in John J. Sirica's courtroom, was not such a hot idea.

" 'First,' " the man said, imputing unuttered statements to the Chief Judge, as denominative of his presumed attitudes, " 'we're going to nail them, and then one of them'll start talking, and then we're going to find out what really went on in that damned office building. So, let's get started, all right? Now, Mister Foreman and members of the jury, these here defendants enjoy the presumption of innocence. That means you can't convict them for a few days. We got these formalities to go through. But you just be patient, there, keep your shirts on, and we'll get right back to you.' So, maybe Liddy was right. Maybe he didn't have anything to lose, because it was all gone when he started.

"I'll tell you what I think," the man said. "I think Liddy's probably been right two or three times in his whole life, just like any other stopped clock. And this was one of those times. He's always had this attitude, the system's just a story we tell to the people that aren't running it, and they're supposed to just mind their own business and believe it. And as long as they do that, they're fine. But if they're not running it, and they come around and start interfering with it, getting in the way, boy, then you're going to find out what the real facts are, and you better watch your ass, because that's when all that due process stuff gets put up there on the shelf with the Easter Bunny."

Fascinating as the press, the public and Sirica himself found the question ("Who put Liddy up to it, and where did he get the money?"), the issue was not before Sirica in the *Liddy* trial. Under the rules, he should not have messed with it.

The defendants were accused of conspiracy, second-degree burglary, interception of wire communications and interception of oral communications. There was a jury. Sirica's job was to decide whether the Government introduced evidence which, if taken in the light most favorable to the Government, would warrant a reasonable man in finding, beyond a reasonable doubt, that the defendants were guilty of the charges against them. The jury was to decide whether, in fact, as reasonable men and women, they so found. In some counties of Massachusetts today, the clerk admonishes juries in the Superior Courts with a maxim that Sirica himself might have kept in mind: "To this indictment the defendant has said that he is not guilty, and for his trial has put himself upon the country, which country you are, and you are sworn to try the issue. If he is guilty, you are to say so; if he is not guilty, you are to say so; *and nothing more.* Jurors, hearken to the evidence." Sirica wanted something more.

So did others; most of the country, it was later to seem, and with damned good reason, too. The problem was not with what was wanted (except, perhaps, for John Mitchell, and his ilk): the truth, the whole truth, and nothing but the truth; we are, after all, supposed to get that from our public officials, at least, without resort to the rack and the wheel, which we are not supposed to resort to anyway, and they, of all people, ought to be estopped from making us do it. The problem lay in how to get what was wanted: the evidence, if any, that the system had been tampered with, distorted, and debased, if it had been, without tampering with the system, distorting or debasing it, to get what was needed.

"On January 11," John Dean reminded the Committee, "the Senate

Democrats formally voted that Senator Ervin would head the inquiry into the Watergate and related matters, and I must add, much to the displeasure of the White House."

Hunt was staggered by his wife's death on December 10, 1972. By the end of the year, convinced that he had neither stomach for trial nor chance of acquittal, Hunt instructed Bittman to make a deal with Silbert. On January 11, the second day of trial, Silbert stood up to spring it.

"Liddy's face never changed," the man said. "Everybody in the courtroom sneaked a look at him and the rest of them when Bittman stood up to throw him in. If Liddy did anything, he only smiled a little."

Hunt made his deal on the weekend of January 8 and 9. Named in six counts of the indictment, Hunt essayed to plead to three of them. That would have convicted him of conspiracy to break and enter, intercepting a telephone communication, and of intercepting an oral communication.

Silbert considered that a reasonable offer, and reported it to Chief Judge John J. Sirica by telephone over the weekend. Sirica, mindful of the chastening effect of a codefendant's plea upon those accused still obdurate before the court, pronounced it a fair bargain. Three days later, he had changed his mind.

"In the matter now before the Court," Sirica said, "the Defendant, Mr. Everette Howard Hunt, Jr., who is charged in six counts of the eight-count indictment herein, requests leave of the Court to withdraw his earlier plea of not guilty and to instead plead guilty to the offenses charged in Counts One, Two and Eight.

"Pursuant to this request," the Judge said, "the other three counts in which Mr. Hunt is named would be dismissed as to him after sentencing. The United States acquiesces in this request."

That was not enough to seal the bargain. Rule 11 of the Federal Rules of Criminal Procedure gives the Judge a certain latitude in oversight of guilty pleas. Jake Jacobsen, in September of 1974, would learn that when he took a Special Prosecutor's deal back to the Northern District of Texas where he faced charges totaling thirty-five years. The Texas judge didn't care how much Jake planned to say about John Connally. Neither, in the spring of 1975, would the Connally trial jury, which heard Jake's testimony and acquitted Big John. He refused to dismiss the Texas case. Sirica exercised his discretion.

"In arriving at its present decision," Sirica said, "this Court has considered several matters. Some relate to the apparent strength of the Government's case against the Defendant, Mr. Hunt. Exhibits in the record indicate that the Grand Jury investigation leading to the indictment herein was extensive and thorough, lasting some three months. Also in the record are statements by Department of Justice officials to the effect that the investigation in this case was one of the most complete ever conducted. In argument on pretrial motions, counsel for the Defendant made frequent references to the Government's long and wide-ranging investigation. Counsel for the United States had also characterized the Government's case as an exceptionally strong one against all Defendants.

"Turning to a further consideration," Sirica said, "the Court sees as an element of its discretion and as part of its duty proper representation of the public interest in justice. The Court and the public have an interest in the just administration of criminal law and the Court believes that such interest encompasses not only the substance of justice, but also the appearance of justice. Given the nature of this case, the Court is compelled to the conclusion that both the substance and the appearance of justice require that the tendered plea be refused. The Court in this case is unwilling to accept a plea of guilty by a Defendant other than to all the counts in which he is charged."

Ordinarily there is no substantial difference, on sentencing, between a Change of Plea to all counts and copping out on a few counts. The working rule is one tail per donkey. Bittman, throughout his negotiations with Silbert, had treated the issue as whether Hunt would plead guilty to anything, or go to trial on everything, seeing the likely difference as between five years on a trial and two years on a plea. Silbert agreed with him. Judge Sirica's actual private views were known to neither of them. Bittman thought: three counts or six, what's the difference?

"In view of your Honor's ruling," Bittman said, "Mr. Hunt at this time respectfully asks leave of the Court to withdraw his plea of not guilty, and plead guilty to Counts One, Two, Three, Four, Five and Eight."

"Those are all the counts he is charged in?" Sirica said.

"Yes, sir," Bittman said.

Hunt was now to get the treatment. Reduced to terms, the defendant, changing his plea, must acknowledge that he is a rotten son of a bitch who did everything he's charged with, and more besides, in all likelihood, and that he agrees that the Judge can land all over him for being it and doing it.

"Now I advise you," Sirica said, "that you are charged in this indictment, and I am going to read these charges to you, in six different counts. I will refer to them briefly first before I read them to you.

"Now, Count One is known as a conspiracy count, in violation of Title 18, United States Code, Section 371.

"Count Two is burglary in the second degree in violation of 22 D.C. Code, Section 101(b).

"The third count, burglary in the second degree. Count Three, as I indicated, is under the same Code Section.

"Count Four, endeavoring to illegally intercept oral communications in violation of Title 18, United States Code, Section 2511.

"Count Five, endeavoring to illegally intercept wire communications under Count Five.

"Under Count Six, unlawful interception of wire communications in violation of 18 United States Code, 2511.

"These are briefly the charges against you in the indictment," Sirica said. "Do you understand that?"

Fred Thompson, Minority Counsel to the Committee, professed difficulty understanding Hunt's behavior. "You state in your opening statement that in your opinion the Watergate break-in was an unfortunate use of executive power. What executive power are you referring to?"

"I am referring," Hunt said, "to the power delegated to the Attorney General of the United States by the President of the United States."

Hunt told Judge Sirica that he understood. "I do, your Honor."

"'In furtherance of the aforesaid conspiracy,'" Sirica said, having read it all, "'and to effect the objects thereof, the Defendants did commit, among others, the following overt acts in the District of Columbia. . . .' I believe, alleged here, I won't go through them all with you, there are twenty, I believe, all in violation of Title 18, United States Code, Section 371. I have already identified briefly to you the nature of the other counts." To Bittman, Sirica said: "Do you concede your client is familiar with all of the elements in the other counts besides the conspiracy count?"

Silbert had drawn his indictment cautiously, taking no risks. What was alleged, he could prove, beyond a reasonable doubt. Maybe there was more; he rather suspected there was. But what was charged could be proven, and that is what a prosecutor is supposed to do.

"Your Honor," Bittman said, "I know that he is familiar with the elements."

"You have gone over them carefully?" Sirica said.

"I have," Bittman said.

"He understands," Sirica said, "what the elements are, that must be proven by the Government beyond a reasonable doubt as to each count that he is indicted under?"

"Yes, your Honor," Hunt said.

Bittman had struggled through the autumn to sever Hunt's trial from that of the other defendants. Initially his purpose was strategic, connected with his motion to suppress the evidence against Hunt; had that motion succeeded, the evidence would probably have remained admissible against the others. After Dorothy Hunt was killed, Bittman renewed his motion for severance on new grounds: he said Hunt was emotionally distressed, and might not be able to assist in his own defense. Silbert had Hunt examined by doctors working for the Government; they agreed that Hunt was distraught, but said he was fit enough to stand trial.

"Now, in connection with the elements of the offense which the Government must prove beyond a reasonable doubt," Sirica said, "as to each one of the counts in which you are charged, did you commit each one of those elements of those crimes, Mr. Hunt?"

There has probably never been a defendant in his right mind who subjectively believed himself to be a criminal. There is an intellectual space where dignity survives the shock of being accused. Defendants daily admit that they have done the acts they're charged with doing; others are informed by jury verdicts that their protestations of innocence have been rejected. Still none of them ever completely surrenders in his mind to the external fact that he has been proven guilty of a crime, and thus shunted from the community of citizens into the society of criminals.

"I did, your Honor," Hunt said.

In relentless if tacit acknowledgment of that self-concept of innocence reserved, the courts demand that the defendant accede to his position between the rock and the hard place, and opt for less punishment because failure to opt will bring more. When jail brings the leisure of reflection, and pride recovers from the humiliation of admitting guilt, resentment develops, resentment which can motivate the prisoner to recant his plea in order to get out, and in order to repair his image of himself. Judicial doggedness in the pleading process is designed to preclude such recantation, establishing in cold type that the defendant knew what he was doing when he pleaded.

"Knowingly," Sirica said, "and intentionally and unlawfully: did you do that?"

Knowingly: well, certainly. Hunt had to know what he was doing. As he told the Committee: "I was an intelligence officer, a spy, for the government for the United States," for more than twenty years. And intentionally, too: he had meant to do what he had done. But not unlawfully; he had never meant to do anything unlawfully. He had meant to do what he was directed to do by the Attorney General of the United States. For him, employment with the special unit was a deeper and higher-level cover for the same kind of work he had been paid to do for the CIA. Knowingly and intentionally. "Yes, your Honor," Hunt said, miserably.

It is customary, upon presentation of a guilty plea, to call upon the defendant to participate in his own obsequies, again to cut off a possible recantation later on. "Now, in your own words," Sirica said. "I would like you to tell me from the beginning just how you got into this conspiracy, what you did, various things that you did so I can decide whether you are knowingly and intentionally entering this plea voluntarily with full knowledge of the consequences."

When the presiding judge alludes to "full knowledge of the consequences," he intends to remind the defendant that no man has a deal he can count on until sentence has actually been pronounced. The negotiations between the prosecutor and the defense lawyer are not binding on the judge. Silbert and Bittman had bargained with the expectation that Hunt could get a sixty percent discount from a five-year sentence if he did the right thing and pleaded out. Bittman told this to Hunt. Sirica was now telling Hunt that he didn't care what Bittman had worked out with Silbert; as the sentencing judge he might honor the expectations of the attorneys, and then again he might not. Hunt, like every other defendant, was going to have trouble hearing that; when a man gives in and pleads guilty, he does it to get a deal, and he never quite comprehends the admonition that he doesn't have a deal he can enforce.

"Now," Sirica said, "as to the possible penalties in this case. I am not indicating at this time, because I don't know myself, what sentence I will impose in this case, or sentences, do you understand? But I think he should know this, this is provided by statute: as to the counts under which you have pleaded guilty, because first of all I am going to refer the case to the Probation Officer, naturally, for a presentence investigation and report. We do that in practically every case, and that might take some time. But, I want you to know what the sentences are as to each count.

"Under Count One," Sirica said, "Title 18, United States Code, Section 371, the conspiracy count, you could be fined not more than ten thousand dollars or imprisoned for not more than five years, or both. Do you understand that?"

Hunt understood no such thing. He was going to get two years and he was going to debase himself, by ratting to the grand jury. "Yes, sir," he said, because that is what his lawyer had told him to say.

"Under Count Two," said Sirica, allowing Hunt as he would allow any other defendant in the same straits to misrepresent his own state of mind, "which charges second-degree burglary, under Title 22, D.C. Code, Section 1801(b), you could be imprisoned for not less than two years nor more than fifteen years. Do you understand?" Then he went through the rest. It came to more than fifty years.

Hunt said: "Yes, sir."

The only defendant who knew what was going on was Liddy. He had been an Assistant District Attorney in Dutchess County, New York, and he made deals with defendants who gave in, and tried those who did not, in Poughkeepsie for three years, from 1966 through 1969.

"Yes, your Honor," Hunt said.

"Do you understand these sentences could run concurrently?" Sirica said.

Hunt, along with Bittman and Silbert, perhaps understood that Sirica could add them all up, but each of them understood it as a hypothetical possibility, not an actual threat. "I do, your Honor," Hunt said.

Silbert harbored, behind the perfectly expressionless face which the prosecutor presents when the opposition starts to fold, a feeling of satisfaction and anticipation. He had been wrestling with these curiously unreasonable people for months, attacking his Watergate problems with the same method employed by Richard A. Sprague, the Philadelphia Assistant District Attorney who brought Jock Yablonski's killers to justice by working his way up the ladder of the conspiracy. Now at last Silbert had one of his cats in the basket; what he had been denied by process of reasonable pretrial negotiation he was going to get by means of the permissible duress of the threat of a recommendation of severity in sentencing. It gave him pleasure to observe the development of events as he expected them to be; he believed in the rules in the book, and as an officer of the Executive Branch, took the best care he could that the laws were faithfully enforced.

"Has your guilty plea," Sirica said, "to the six counts that I have mentioned been induced by promises or representations by anyone as to what the sentence will be, imposed by this Court?"

Of course it had been. "No, your Honor," said Hunt.

"Has anyone threatened or coerced you into making this plea of guilty," Sirica said, "the plea of guilty to these counts?"

Silbert had assured Bittman that Hunt would probably get considerably more time if he demanded a needless trial, and Bittman, cognizant of Sirica's reputation as Maximum John, earned by the imposition of heavy sentences, agreed with him. Bittman certainly told Hunt.

"No, your Honor," Hunt said.

"Has any promise, of any kind been made to induce your plea of guilty?" Sirica said.

Silbert had promised to recommend lenience if Hunt cooperated and pleaded guilty. Bittman certainly reported that promise to Hunt. "No, your Honor," Hunt said.

"Are you entering this plea voluntarily," Sirica said, "of your own free will, because you are guilty, and for no other reason?"

Perhaps. "Yes, your Honor," Hunt said.

The pleas were changed. From among seven previously implacable defendants, each staring down the barrel of a hopeless case without blinking, adamantly refusing all but the most perfunctory cooperation with authorities who believed, at least, that full cooperation was extremely desirable to the Republic, and that they and their superiors represented that Republic, one now stood apart.

Ordinarily, the man who cracks, expects, and gets, fairly considerate treatment. His public undertaking to scuttle his codefendants is unlikely to charm inmates of correctional institutions where he might be lodged; he is therefore commonly admitted to bail, if at all possible, or else stored in facilities away from the jail, where living conditions are better and no one within reach has a shiv. This tends to reinforce his decision to switch sides, by confirming his good judgment in pleading guilty, and that makes him happy, and that in turn makes him a better witness. Only when the prosecutor, or the judge, suspects a propensity for mendacity, intent to run away, or a disposition to commit crimes of violence, is an apparently cooperative witness deprived of such comforts.

Silbert was willing to take Hunt at his word until such time as Hunt might furnish reason to mistrust it. Bittman knew that. Hunt knew it, too.

"Do you want to make a statement," Sirica asked Bittman, "before I say anything about commitment?"

"Your Honor," Bittman said, "of course. I would respectfully request, for all the reasons I outlined yesterday and other reasons I am prepared to bring to your Honor's attention, ask that Mr. Hunt be continued on his present bond. I do not believe in any way the interests of the public, the interest of the prosecution in this case, the interest of anyone, would in any way be prejudiced if Mr. Hunt is continued on his present bond. If the Court would give the opportunity, if the Court desired it, if there is any question in your Honor's mind about the fact Mr. Hunt may flee or may be a menace to any individual or society, I would respectfully ask the opportunity for a short hearing so I could sustain the burden that is required on the Defendant pursuant to Rule 46." Bittman was floundering.

"I explained to you yesterday," Sirica said, "I think, Mr. Hunt was present, what my usual practice is in cases after conviction or plea of guilty. Now, Mr. Hunt stands before this Court, convicted by virtue of his plea of serious criminal offenses. Under provisions of the statutes which he has violated, he may be subjected to fines totaling $40,000 and may be imprisoned for a period exceeding 30 years.

"To the Court's knowledge," Sirica said, "Mr. Hunt presently has no full-time supervised employment but is self-employed. I believe he is a writer. Mr. Hunt has neither denied nor offered a satisfactory explanation as to why he was in the recent past using names other than his own in traveling. Mr. Hunt has, in the course of prior employment with the Government, lived in foreign countries and has friends and acquaintances therein. After the arrest of the five alleged coconspirators, on June 17, 1972, and after being interviewed by agents of the Federal Bureau of Investigation, Mr. Hunt left the Washington, D.C., metropolitan area, and traveled to California under an assumed name, and did not return to this area until on or about July 3, 1972. During portions of this period of time, the Federal Bureau of Investigation was unable to locate Mr. Hunt.

"In view of all the foregoing, and giving due consideration to Mr. Hunt's length of residence in the metropolitan area," Sirica said, "his family ties, and his appearance before the grand jury and this Court without receiving a formal order of the Court or being taken into custody, the Court finds $100,000 surety bond is necessary to insure the presence of Mr. Hunt at the time he will be sentenced. The only bond he has posted is a $10,000 bond, and he paid in cash $1,000, or ten percent of that bond. He deposited ten percent. So he really had a thousand dollars on deposit. I am going to commit him, and if he gets a reputable surety company, puts up the hundred thousand dollars, I will release him in the custody of the surety company until the day of sentence. All right."

Silbert was familiar with Judge Sirica's habits. So were others in the District of Columbia federal bar. He is a very proud man, and an obstinate one. His verdicts are reversed more regularly than are those of other judges, a circumstance which nettles him enough to impel him to deny repeatedly, in the course of most of his trials, that he is thoughtful in the least of the prospective attitude of the Circuit toward his rulings. He is a man of vast integrity, with concomitant resources of indignation that other men are weaker, and he lacks the subtlety to check his desire to express that indignation. His zeal is didactic, and his position affords him frequent opportunity to compel others to accept his strictures.

"He's a pain in the ass, is what he is," the man said, "a regular pain in the ass if you're trying in front of him, and not just for the defense guys, either. The Assistant's got to keep one eye on Sirica and one eye on the witness when he's trying in front of him, put the evidence in and at the same time do the best he can to stop Sirica from going haywire and setting the thing up to get tipped over on appeal. It's okay for him to run around telling everybody he doesn't care what the Circuit thinks. That's fine for him. He doesn't have to write the brief to save the thing when it gets there, and he doesn't have to try the thing over when it gets reversed and your witnesses've left town or just gotten fed up with the whole thing. Let me tell you something, all right? Earl's a nice guy and he's a damned fine lawyer. He can't see through doors or anything like that, but he's a damned good lawyer. Earl, until Sirica started in on Hunt and put him in the can, when the guy pleaded and was going to come in and see the grand jury and everything, Earl actually thought he was going to try that case himself. He thought he'd done all this work, and he had the evidence, and all right, if they wouldn't plead, he'd convict them, and then he'd get them in before the grand jury and he'd squeeze it out of them, but one way or the other, he was going to get it out of them, if there was anything in them to get out. Those guys didn't know that, at the time, you know. Sy Glanzer, any of them. But they had a way to find out if there was anything, and that was what they were doing. Try a nice lean case, get those guys in the wringer with a verdict that'd stand up, and then go to work on them. And then Sirica put Hunt in the can, and I think that's when Earl started to see it: he was doing all right with the defendants but he was going to have his hands full with the Judge."

Dean had his hands full with the people he'd suborned.

# 10

Magruder was too goddamned ambitious, and Dean knew it. Jeb's whey-faced pseudo-innocence obscured a vaulting and gravely intemperate ego, and no intelligence at all. Magruder was a sort of daredevil among liars; though he was useful, he was dangerous. Dean could coach him, but not control him.

Magruder, before the grand and petit juries, did not take the truth and distort it ever so subtly. Stans had done that, to serve his master, telling the General Accounting Office that cash received after April 7, 1972, was cash received before April 7, 1972. Nor was Magruder content merely to state all facts but time correctly, as Pat Gray did to deceive his champion, Senator Weicker, in the confirmation hearings on his appointment as Director. Magruder did not report the facts, but claim, as Hunt did, that men more powerful than he, had cynically duped him. He was simply not imaginative.

There was in Magruder's perjury no more inventiveness than there is in a child's solemn denial of raiding the cookie jar; he just went down to the grand jury, three times, and before the petit jury, once, and knowingly, maliciously, willfully and with fraudulent intent, denied the truth and swore to the lie. In a matter of such gravity, that took a certain amount of self-confidence, existing in a vacuum where men high in government and politics are supposed to keep their principles. Helpful was the fact that Magruder's wit at best flickered, if it was not uniformly dim.

"He told me," Dean said of a meeting in January, 1973, with Magruder, "that he had talked with Haldeman and Mitchell about running for office in California, and was planning a trip to California to test the water. He said now was the time, because he felt he could get good financial backing. I felt Magruder was in for some serious problems both before the grand jury and the Senate hearings, but without saying this to him, I tried to dissuade him from running for office until this entire matter had been resolved."

Dean and Haldeman prevailed upon Robert Finch and Herbert Kalmbach to discourage Magruder, and he was soon back in Washington with all his teeth exposed, "pushing hard to return to the White House staff, and work on the Bicentennial program," making everybody very nervous and gradually, it seems, tumbling to his actual circumstances: "No one had the heart," Dean said, "to tell Magruder that the President had said that he could not return to the White House staff." Of course not: McCord was badgering Caulfield in the bushes of suburban parkways by then, and had specifically complained about Magruder's existing prosperity: a White House appointment for Jeb would have sent McCord into hysterical orbit.

But you couldn't tell Jeb that. It might piss him off. And Dean had other problems. Smarter than Magruder, and cagier, too, than the President who required his services, Dean by January of 1973 had written off McCord, did not expect much from Hunt (except trouble), and was resigned to the collapse of his second conspiracy. By then he was more savvy; he was preparing for that collapse.

# Part III

*Liddy was joined up; Sirica
knew it, and he hated it.*

# 11

Six months into his felonious mission, Dean, in January of 1973, felt the wall against his back, and reasonably concluded that he and his clients were, at long last, in deep trouble. Part of the reason — a substantial part — was the willingness of Chief Judge John J. Sirica to play prosecutor, and let the judging go.

"Liddy was 'way ahead of Earl," the man said. "If you really looked at that case, at the people that were involved in it, there were only two of them that really started off at the same place, went in there and actually knew what was going on, from the beginning. One of them was Sirica, and the other one was Liddy, and Liddy actually knew more than Sirica did. Sirica got so hot one day he told Maroulis he was glad to see him getting some good advice from his client, and he called Liddy a former attorney, and Maroulis started screeching about the inference that he'd been disbarred, and the Judge sort of apologized and Liddy sat there and grinned.

"Maybe he's stupid," the man said. "In his own sweet way, he's maybe a thoroughly stupid man. Look at what he's doing: Sirica hit him with seven to twenty." Actually, it was a minimum of six years, eight months, to twenty years. "There probably isn't another guy in the United States doing that kind of time for a first offense B and E, unless it's some black guy in Georgia that did it so he could rape a white woman. Now why do you think that is?"

Sirica said it was for the commission of acts which could "only be described as sordid, despicable, and thoroughly reprehensible. The Court has also considered the purposes to be served by imposing sentences in this case. In view of the foregoing, and taking into account the background of the defendants, it seems obvious to the Court that rehabilitation is not the principal purpose to be served. Nor is it appropriate to impose sentence here with the intent of satisfying someone's desire for reprisal. In this matter, the sentences should be imposed with an eye toward a just punishment for the grave offenses committed, and toward the deterrent effect the sentences might have on other potential offenders. I shall not attempt to enumerate every item which the Court has pondered. Numerous other considerations, both favorable and unfavorable to the Defendants, have played a part in the Court's decisions. Suffice it to say that the sentences which the Court will now impose are the result of careful thought extending over a period of several weeks. I think the sentences are appropriate and just. Do you want to say anything? Mr. Maroulis or Mr. Liddy?"

"Nothing at all, your Honor," Liddy said.

"What's he going to say to him?" the man said. " 'Much obliged, your Honor?' People were supposed to think he was getting that kind of time for not talking, that Sirica whacked him because he wanted to scare the other guys. They got conditionals, you notice, but Liddy's was fat and final. Sirica's supposed to've picked Liddy because he knew Liddy'd never scare anyway, if he whacked somebody else, so he whacked Liddy. Take out the guy you're not going to turn over anyway. But five would've done that. The seven to twenty was for getting Sirica pissed off, seven for doing it, fourteen more for doing it on purpose."

Sirica was annoyed by the same circumstances that puzzled Silbert: the appetite of the defendants, and their lawyers, for expensive and time-consuming trial of a hopeless cause before a Judge known to all to be irascible at best, and exasperated, to the great detriment of convicted persons, by useless litigation. Silbert, blessed or afflicted by patience in the abrasion of flinty opposing wills, was willing to wait for things to take their inexorable course: if a case must be needlessly tried to accomplish what ought to have been obtained by plea-bargaining, he would try it without acting upon his speculative views of the defendants' conduct. Either way, he would get the evidence, if there was any.

Sirica was in a better position, at least as Sirica saw it, one that demanded none of the patience which he possessed in such short supply: he did not need evidence, to act, and he was accordingly not constrained by the lack of it to bridle his action upon surmise.

Representing Bernard L. Barker, Virgilio R. Gonzalez, Eugenio R. Martinez and Frank A. Sturgis, Henry B. Rothblatt on the first day of trial "proudly" declared that he spoke for all of them. Rothblatt, lampreylike in his attachments to F. Lee Bailey and other celebrities of the American defense bar, has by unceasing toil established himself as a fairly pedestrian lawyer who toils unceasingly, and thus regularly appears in the wakes of the Baileys of this world, representing the less important defendants in multiple-defendant cases sensational enough to attract a Bailey or two. Rothblatt does the donkey work. He writes books about evidence and procedure, and lets the stars cosign them. And always he labors to outshine them, never succeeding and never subsiding. Rothblatt delivered himself of a great deal of persiflage:

"I am sure that all of you were moved as I was when we heard the story-presentation, the outline of proof presented by the prosecution, by Mr. Silbert." Rothblatt was beginning the argument which importunes the jury to acquit the defendant, who is there — my poor client — because all the majesty and power of the Government were arrayed against him, and that's how come they caught him.

"It was thorough. It was dramatic. And it was moving." Not as moving as Rothblatt intended to be, of course, but moving enough to warrant snide comment. "And it was even difficult for me, speaking as an attorney for four of the accused, to say that I have an open mind, and that a person that has not been acquainted with the evidence in this case and the individuals involved in this case, would say, as His Honor, Judge Sirica has instructed you, and will instruct you again, that these accused as they sit here now are presumed to be innocent under our great system of American justice."

The fellow who talks about the great system of American justice hasn't got anything else to talk about. "And they are presumed to be innocent until good, believable evidence comes from the witness stand which should convince you beyond a reasonable doubt and to a moral certainty otherwise, as to each and every element of the crime charged in this indictment."

You bet it should: Rothblatt's men were charged with burglary and other deeds in the Democratic National Committee headquarters, and that was where they had been caught, with the equipment to do the deeds. "Not only do we labor under the disadvantage of the story, opening address, by Mr. Silbert, of course. He was aided by the most thorough investigation undertaken by the greatest law enforcement agency in the United States, and the evidence will show this was the most thorough investigation undertaken by the Federal Bureau of Investigation, Department of Justice, since the death of President Kennedy."

Rothblatt went on like that, until neither Sirica nor Silbert could stand it any longer. He was at last instructed to save his final argument for the close of the case, and deal with the evidence he intended to introduce during the trial, which is what the lawyer making his opening statement is supposed to do anyway. Rothblatt did the best he could, with nothing. He conceded that his clients were caught in the act. His defense, he said, was motive.

"Mr. Silbert said they can't read the minds of people. I agree. Sometimes we can't." Most of the time, when you come right down to it. "But we can certainly read their character. We can certainly judge their spots, and they don't change after a number of years. A man's character does not change. The evidence will show a man whose character is not to be questioned. Nor is there any slight doubt as to the sterling nature of it." This is the my-client-is-a-good-guy; he-did-it-but-leave-him-go argument.

"Starting with Mr. Barker, a Cuban citizen of mixed heritage. When our country was involved in the Second World War, on Pearl Harbor Day, even though he had Cuban citizenship, the evidence will show that he was the first to go to the American Embassy, to enlist in our Army, to serve our country. He went on to become an officer in our Air Force. He was shot down over Germany, and kept in prison, in a Nazi prison camp, for over a year. And later he was discharged as a Captain, honorably discharged as a Captain in the United States Army, and returned to civilian life."

This was really more than Sy Glanzer could bear. Spliced onto Silbert's case for his tenaciousness, Glanzer had converted to the law from the Juilliard School of Music. He went to NYU, college and law school, and he is one tough son of a bitch. He originated the white-collar crime unit in the U.S. Attorney's Office in Washington in 1967; its conviction rate hovers around ninety-five percent, and most of those convictions are secured by pleas. He rose to protest: what did Barker's record in World War II do to explain what he was doing in the Watergate on June 17, 1972. Sirica admonished Rothblatt.

"The evidence will further show," Rothblatt said, "that Sturgis is of impeccable character and of highest patriotic background. Served our country, the evidence will show, not in one branch of the Service. During World War Two he volunteered and joined the Marines, and after serving through World War Two in the Marines, and was honorably discharged, he immediately enlisted in the United States Navy. Served honorably in the United States Navy and enlisted in the United States Army. Served honorably in the United States Army. Since then, the evidence will show, he has led a life devoted to making himself available to people who want to see democratic systems of justice prevail. Particularly in this part of the hemisphere." Rothblatt intended to prove that Sturgis, also known as Frank Fiorini, had ferried B-26s for the CIA in the Bay of Pigs fiasco. In other words, Sturgis was a mercenary.

"Now," Sirica said, "let's get down to the reason why he went into the Watergate."

"The evidence," Rothblatt said, "will show that all of these four accused were part of our Government and served our Government back in 1951" — if the court reporter was right, Rothblatt had as much trouble with dates as he had with procedure — "that Mr. Silbert referred to as the Bay of Pigs. These were men who took orders in military fashion, and never questioned orders. These were men who were used to serving their Government loyally and following orders."

Rothblatt's best-known previous excursion into a celebrated case was the trial of Lieutenant William Calley. The defense was: following orders. Calley got life, reduced by Nixon to twenty years.

"Let me ask you a question," Sirica said. "Is it your defense that they were taking orders from somebody, were ordered to go into the Watergate? Is this what you are going to show?"

Rothblatt's answer, reduced to terms, was: Yes. Proponent of the view that a jury has the right to nullify a criminal statute by acquitting a man proven, beyond a reasonable doubt, to have violated it, Rothblatt was trying the case for publicity. On January 15, 1973, Alvin Newmyer, appointed by Judge Sirica, entered the case for the Cubans. "They have decided," Glanzer told the Court, "that they wish to enter a plea. Mr. Rothblatt, simply stated, opposes that decision and therefore does not want to be a party to that. However, he has still made himself available to advise them at every juncture."

Their decision was contained in a letter dated January 12, 1973, addressed to Rothblatt and copied to Sirica. "We have been asking you since Sunday, January 7, 1973, to change our plea from not guilty to guilty. You have not complied with our request. We have made it clear from the beginning that the defense" — the Nuremberg defense (it didn't work at Nuremberg, either) — "which you presented in your opening statement and in statements to the press is unacceptable to us. We respectfully inform you that, as of this date, January 12, 1973, you will no longer represent us. We intend to pay any reasonable fees presented by you. Please accept our sincere gratitude for your services." It was signed by the four Cubans.

They went as an entry. The trial transcript of their treatment by Sirica records their answers to his questions: "THE DEFENDANTS: (In chorus.) 'Yes, sir.'"

Sirica went through the indictment. Then he got down to what he thought was hard pan. "Now, I will take Mr. Martinez first, and I will ask you some questions. As I indicated some time ago, I think I indicated this, I posed certain questions to the Government during the pretrial hearing of this case, and I think some of you were present and undoubtedly you heard it. I do not have a jury in the jury box now, and I purposely sequestered them, had them locked up, so they couldn't hear any of the things going on in this courtroom. I indicated more than once, and I am going to say it again, I want you each to listen carefully: This jury is going to want to know, somewhere along the line, what purpose did you four men go into the Democratic headquarters for. You understand that?"

"Yes, sir," Barker said.

"They are going to wonder who, if anyone," Sirica said, "hired you to go in there, if you were hired. I am just assuming they will be asking themselves these questions. They are going to want to know if there are other people, that is, higher up in the Republican Party or the Democratic Party or any Party, who are mentioned or who are involved in this case and should be in this case. Do you understand that?" He continued: "They will want to know where this money came from, who was the money man, who did the paying off, who paid Mr. Barker, how much was paid. They are going to want to know a lot of things before this case is over. We will only have, I think, two Defendants left, which cases will be submitted to the jury."

"That really wasn't much of a trial, you know," the man said. "It was more like an Inquisition. If you gave, say, Daniel Ellsberg that kind of trial, the whole faculty at the Yale Law School'd be down carrying signs in front of the White House. Sirica decided he was going to try that case himself, and I don't mean he just called his own number when the indictment came in."

The fifteen judges of the United States District Court for the District of Columbia ordinarily receive criminal case assignments by rotation. When the indictments come up to the Clerk's office, they are distributed *seriatim* among the judges. But there remains an alternative procedure, for application in unusual cases: the United States Attorney can request that a particular case be specially assigned.

Special assignment, in the District, does not permit the prosecutor to handpick the judge who will sit on the case. But it does assure that the case will be expedited, and it serves to prevent overloading one judge with heavy cases, by accidents of random draw.

Harold Titus requested that the *Liddy* case be specially assigned. He did not request Chief Judge Sirica to handle the case himself, but neither he nor Silbert was distressed when Sirica took that action. Judge Sirica, in the pretrial stages, is unexceptionably the prosecutor's friend: he moves things along, disposes of frivolous motions, and hastens the day of trial. For Silbert's purposes, that was very desirable. He did not foresee what was in store for him when trial began.

Liddy, who recognized no limits during his tenure as a prosecutor, should have sympathized. To the consternation of a presiding judge, Raymond C. Barrata, Liddy had rebutted a defense claim of no danger, in a gun-carrying case, by firing the evidence in the courtroom. In another case he took umbrage at a defense contention that no harm was intended by the defendant in an assault and battery case, and smashed the weapon in question, a length of two-by-four, upon the rail of the jury box with force sufficient to crack the wood. He paid for the damage in each instance, probably considering the expense low for the creation of a reputation as a man subject to some sort of rational fits, best not trifled with by opposing counsel. He had to apologize to the judges, too, but that additional levy was also modest. The judges in Dutchess County came to expect his excesses with the same resignation they manifested in response to his apologies.

"All Sirica was doing," the man said, "was telling Liddy that he agreed with the way that Liddy'd done business. Not that he'd've gone out and hired a bunch of burglars if he was Counsel to the Committee to Re-elect the President. Just that Liddy'd ignored the rules to get the results he wanted, and now there were some results Sirica wanted, and it was in court now, and not a campaign, and Sirica had the power, not Liddy. That probably wasn't what Sirica wanted to tell Liddy, nowhere around that. But that was the way Liddy'd always thought it was, and the way Sirica was acting, you couldn't blame Liddy for not changing his mind. You lose, somebody else gets the power, and they unload on you and if it happens, you take it. Like a man."

Sirica addressed Martinez. "Tell me in your own words, what you did, how did you get mixed up?"

"I believe the facts that you have read in the charges are true," Martinez said, "and are just to the truth."

"That is a blanket answer," Sirica said. "I want to know specifics."

"I am sorry," Martinez said.

"I want specific answers to my questions," Sirica said. "I am not satisfied."

"If your Honor asked me questions," Martinez said.

"I will ask you questions," Sirica said. "When was a suggestion first made to you, if a suggestion was made, that they wanted you, or whoever might have talked to you, Mr. Hunt or Mr. Barker or anybody else, to come up here and go into the Democratic Headquarters or the Mc-Govern Headquarters? When did you first learn about that?"

"I don't recall the exact day," Martinez said, "but it is about the date stated in your charge."

"Those Cubans," the man said. "I don't know who talked to them, but he did a hell of a job." It was Hunt. "Eduardo," as they called him. "Those guys survive on patriotism, and they can handle anything with that. They're like retired drunks, you know? Much worse'n guys that never took a drink in their lives about other people drinking? Converts. All that anti-Castro stuff, they weren't in that for money. They were in that because it was holy."

"What did you go into the premises for?" Sirica said. "What was the purpose?"

"To intercept communications," Martinez said, "and do all the facts the District Attorney has in his charge."

"Here are these guys," the man said, "they live in America and all they can think about is two things: going back to Cuba, and if they can't do that, they'll do anything anybody tells them they got to do to stop this country from going the same way. Anything, because everything these guys do is personal loyalty, and a guy they trust can get them to do anything and they'll never admit it."

"Were you doing this for nothing?" Sirica said. "Or were you getting paid."

"No," Martinez said, mildly startled by such a suggestion, "I did not get paid, your Honor, for my services."

"You didn't get any money," Sirica said. "Did Mr. Barker give you any money at all?"

"Sirica was fascinated by the money," the man said. "Keep in mind that this is the guy who dumped a House Committee Counsel's job when he was in practice, because he thought the way the Committee was acting, somebody might get the idea there was some funny business going on. Not *because* there was funny business going on; there wasn't. Just that somebody might get the idea there was. He's just as buggy about integrity as the Cubans are about Castro. Sirica thinks crookedness explains everything that ever went wrong in this country, and he doesn't like it. His daddy came here in a boat and now here he is, sitting on the bench and giving everybody hell all the time because they're doing things to this place that lets a laborer's kid be a judge."

"For expenses," Martinez said.

"How much did he give you?" Sirica said.

"Maybe four hundred, five hundred dollars," Martinez said. "Something like that, in expenses."

Sirica worried that issue of money until Martinez could stand it no longer. "Your Honor, I don't know if you are familiar, and this is the true facts with our, or my, situation. Money doesn't mean a thing to us, your Honor. I own a hospital in Cuba, one of the best hospitals. I own a factory of furniture in Cuba. I was the owner of a hotel in Cuba. I left everything in the hands of the Communist there. So, money, really, I lose everything, and really, money is not a great deal in my decisions, so I never worry for money."

"Whoever it was," the man said, "I think it was probably Hunt, because he was as much of a nut as these guys were, he thought he was still working for the CIA himself when he talked to them the first time, but whoever it was, he did a hell of a job. First he gets these clowns to break into places, and he tells them it's for democracy and all that kind of thing, and they do it. And they get caught. Now these guys don't know anything, really. All they know is what Hunt or somebody told them. They never had drinks in the Oval Office. They never met Mitchell. They don't know Stans or anybody else everybody knows about now. All they know is what Hunt tells them, if it was Hunt, and when they get to court he's got them convinced that they have to say they're guilty, in an American court, and go to an American jail, for doing what they did for America. And furthermore, they got to keep their mouths shut about it, too. They can't talk."

"Do you know of anybody else that was involved in the breaking and entering of the Democratic Headquarters, either by being personally present or by being somewhere else?" Sirica said. "Do you know of anybody else, no matter who it might be?"

"No, I don't, your Honor," Martinez said.

"And he didn't," the man said. "All he knew was what whoever it was told him, that he was doing secret work and now he got caught and the people he was working for would take care of his family for him if he stood up."

Sirica tackled Gonzalez, the locksmith, next. "Who paid you for doing that, if anybody?"

"Nobody paid me anything, your Honor," Gonzalez said.

"Did you do it for nothing?" Sirica said.

"I do it," Gonzalez said, "because I believe what I did was the right thing to do."

"What did you do it for?" Sirica said.

"Because my idea," Gonzalez said, "I figured that this is the political scene, representing Cuba, and I am an American citizen, and I keep feeling about my country, and the way people suffer over there. That is the only reason I did my cooperation in that situation."

"What did Cuba have to do with breaking in and entering the Democratic Headquarters?" Sirica said.

"I don't know," Gonzalez said. "That is what he told me, and I believed him."

"Who told you that?" Sirica said.

"Mr. Barker," Gonzalez said, "and Mr. Hunt." Hunt, who in his despair would tell the Committee that Liddy conveyed that information to him, and he presumed that Liddy had gotten it from the Bureau, or from Mardian.

"Did you ever work for the CIA?" Sirica said.

"No, your Honor," Gonzalez said.

"Never worked for them?" Sirica said.

Displaying a fine appreciation of the subtleties of clandestine work, Martinez said: "Not that I know, your Honor."

"Who worked for the CIA here among the four of you?" Sirica said, still seeking to know, if it was not money, what motivated these people.

"Not that I know of," Barker said. The transcript records no response from Gonzalez. Richard Helms, Director of the CIA when the Cubans, "amateurish in the extreme," in his view, made the break-in, told the Committee that Gonzalez was on the Agency's payroll at $100 per month when he was arrested.

Sirica went back to money. "Now, does anyone, and when I say anyone, I make no exceptions, is anyone at this time or at any time paying anything to the four of you defendants?"

The defendants answered in chorus: "No one."

"You say: no one?" Sirica said.

"No one," Barker said.

"Has anyone assured you," Sirica said, "if you go to jail, either one of you or the four of you, if you go to jail your families will be taken care of?"

And then they lied some more. "No one," they said, in chorus.

A criminal trial is not, properly, a public investigation. It is a stylized exposition proposed by the prosecutor and opposed by defense counsel. The prosecutor, who starts this mannerly fight by presenting evidence to the grand jury, enjoys the advantage of choosing the terrain. Confronting a general-purpose bad guy, he can reap that advantage by recommending indictment only upon such charges as are supported by the strongest evidence, or dissipate it by shotgunning feeble charges among the strong ones, or opting to allege extremely serious offenses which he cannot prove in preference to lesser offenses which he can prove.

No prosecutor with any brains at all relishes the experience of having his case shot out from under him. If he once indulges his temptation to allege more than he can prove, the humiliation of having those allegations shoved down his own throat shortly educates him to more cautious approaches. The ethics of his office demand that prosecutions, and the anguish which accusation and trial inflict upon the accused, be initiated only when a man of dispassionate good judgment, taking inventory of available evidence, would reasonably conclude that conviction is virtually certain in prospect.

Occasionally, that conclusion is mistaken; exculpatory evidence has eluded the investigators, or inculpatory evidence which seemed solid before indictment turns out to be ephemeral at trial. Witnesses vigorous before the grand jury become tentative before the petit jury, die, forget, leave town or are reached, and the defendant is acquitted. Occasionally, too, the prosecutor may indulge in the exaltation of righteous indignation over rational evaluation of his evidence, a species of behavior which, like the Loch Ness monster, is reported as perceived in cases denominated "political" with frequency sufficient to bar facile deprecation of the possibility. But a careful prosecutor, regardless of what he may suspect, surmise, dislike or loathe about a prospective defendant, will not express his feelings in the form of criminal charges, unless he is damned sure he can prove those charges.

Earl Silbert is very, very careful. Conferring by telephone almost nightly with Henry Petersen, Silbert during three months of grand jury investigation never lost sight of the useful distinction between what the *Washington Post* might rightfully publish as credible speculation from trustworthy sources, and what he would be able to prove by documents and testimony admissible in evidence in a trial in a court of law. Of course, he didn't know that Petersen was innocently hampering his investigation by talking to Dean when Silbert hung up, but that was another matter. Silbert and Glanzer and Campbell, perhaps the only prosecutors in the country during 1972 actually being egged on by the press and the American Civil Liberties Union, confined the Liddy indictment to what they knew they could prove, and eschewed the fool's enterprise of setting out to use the prospective trial as an investigation. If their charges brought convictions, suspects adamantly uncooperative before indictment might prove talkative before sentencing, and then they could investigate some more. But they would not investigate in court.

That was a perfectly legitimate approach. In fact, it was the only legitimate approach. In an ordinary case, it would have brought success; in the *Liddy* case, it brought success. But it was not perceived as having succeeded, because Sirica elbowed the prosecutors aside, took McCord by the arm, and ushered him off to the Ervin Committee: it was perceived as having failed.

Sirica did not share that perception, although he caused it: when Titus resigned, in 1974, Sirica joined the other judges of the United States District Court for the District of Columbia in their unanimous appointment of Earl Silbert as Acting United States Attorney (then Silbert, showing more fortitude than prudence, acceded to the submission of his nomination as U.S. Attorney, to the Senate Judiciary Committee, which was by then disposed to cavil at length about President Nixon's selection of Mr. Silbert, and the reasons therefor).

Dean did not share it either. With increasing pessimism, he had labored from the middle of June, 1972, through the end of January, 1973, to prevent the inevitable by delaying the immediate. Because he was the kind of man he was, extremely realistic, he was not confident about the chances of long-term success for that program. And he was a pretty good judge of character, a much better judge than his principal client was. He got so he knew what to expect, and his expectations were usually justified by what happened.

# Part IV

*The President of the United States, and Dean's other private clients, had not displayed good judgment, and persisted in that deficiency when it was hazardous to do so.*

# 12

Dean didn't fret much about George Gordon Battle Liddy, who rewarded that confidence by adapting moderately well to life in the D.C. jail. Liddy was reliable; he was usefully manic. The former Assistant District Attorney of Dutchess County, New York, and Special Assistant to the Secretary of the United States Treasury Department, for Organized Crime, received a term of up to eighteen months for his contemptuous refusal to tell what he knew to the Watergate grand jury. He spent more than twenty-one months in jail in 1973 and 1974, *got out on appeal* and then returned in 1975, for more jail.

It didn't start out as the Watergate grand jury. It was regularly constituted out of twenty-three District residents drawn by lot to sit for six months or so and listen to evidence presented by Assistant U.S. Attorneys, decide whether the evidence conduced to probable cause to believe that a crime had been committed and that a named person or persons had committed it, and to do this hundreds of times, voting indictments in those cases in which at least thirteen of the grand jurors believed that U.S. Attorney Harold Titus and his Assistants had the bastards cold. There were several other grand juries sitting in the District at the same time, on the same terms and with the same obligations. Earl Silbert chose the one he chose because it was available on the day he needed grand jury time.

The life of the jury, as it is called, was twice extended by Judge Sirica, upon certifications by the prosecutors and the grand jurors themselves that the usual term would not suffice to get to the bottom of Watergate and related matters. Liddy's punishment, for contempt of that grand jury, continued until the grand jury completed its term. He could have gotten out, by talking.

"He was born thirty years too late." The man who said that knew Liddy, and, being able to distinguish between affection and approval, rather likes him. "He was born in the wrong country. He should've been some kind of an assistant to Hitler. They keep pushing him to talk. Liddy's never going to talk. The first thing that anybody has to learn about Liddy is that he's consistent. He never did a one-eighty on anything in his life."

From time to time, while doing time, Liddy drew upon his background as a prosecutor — and, before that, as Special Agent of the FBI — to help an illiterate fellow inmate prepare a petition for a writ of habeas corpus, or a motion to reconsider sentence. Occasionally the Deputy U.S. Marshals picked him up, on a writ of habeas corpus directing them to produce the body of G. Gordon Liddy before a congressional committee, in order that he might give testimony upon matters there pending, or before a court, in order that he might answer to charges returned against him. Before the committees, he refused to testify, and thus subjected himself to further citations of contempt issued by the Congress, and more time to be served. Before the courts, he pleaded not guilty, informed the judges that he could not afford to hire counsel to represent him, and declared his intention to try his own case. He knew that if he lost he would get more time to be served. With the Watergate grand jury finished with its work, he was let out of the jail again by the Marshals, to worry about losing his appeal in the *Liddy* case. He lost, and recommenced serving six years and eight months to twenty years, for managing and supervising the burglary and bugging of the DNC.

Thirty-eight when he went to Treasury in 1969, Liddy was forty-two when Maximum John described his hope that Liddy would do almost seven years, minimum. "All it did," the man said, "was convince him he was right all along."

What made Liddy right, or at least made him think he was right, which got him into his terrible trouble, was the ostensible hospitality of the Nixon Administration to views which had been deemed eccentric at worst and harmlessly aberrant at best to two other bureaucracies. Liddy was encouraged to resign from the FBI; people worried about what he might do in the field. And as a prosecutor he was colorful at least. He got lots of ink, going on raids and generally getting in the way of his investigators, and he ran for the 1968 Republican congressional nomination in Poughkeepsie in the apparent belief that a hysterically conservative approach to law and order was just what the country wanted. He was wrong, but he was close enough to being right to frighten the regular GOP nominee, who got him the job at Treasury to preclude the possibility of a Liddy Independent campaign that would insure the election of a Democrat to the seat.

Liddy used his Treasury job to ramrod Operation Intercept, the disastrous antimarijuana blockade of the Mexican border transparently intended to bludgeon the Mexican government into extirpation of the weed by fouling up tourist and itinerant-labor traffic at Customs gates. Then he went over to the National Rifle Association and made a speech vociferously contradictory of Treasury's position in favor of gun control. By the end of 1971, he was at the Committee to Re-elect the President. There he found Jeb Magruder pliant, and open to intimidation. At the White House, Charles W. Colson, Jr., was hard-nosed in the Special Counsel's office, and nobody at the Finance Committee to Re-elect the President (where Liddy went after he threatened to kill Magruder; annoyed at CREEP, one day, by Jeb's advertisingman tactility, Liddy told him to take his arm off Liddy's shoulder, "or I'll rip it off and beat you to death with it") took very much interest at all in him. The Attorney General of the United States, John N. Mitchell, was the only obstacle between Liddy and the accomplishment of his crackpot plans, in January of 1972; lobbied as he was, and perceiving nothing wrong in what Liddy had in mind, Mitchell also failed to check him.

Sirica was determined to check him. He had a good deal to say about deterrence when he sentenced Liddy. Deterrent effect is what judges and prosecutors talk about when they are made furious or despondent by a crime so heinous or a defendant so pitiably hapless that the meagerness of prison as a palliative for the victim and a corrective for the offender paralyzes the intellectual muscles that apply it, on the accurate reasoning that, meager as it is, imprisonment is all that remains to be done, and maybe if it is done, it will stop somebody else from wrecking his own life, or someone else's. Daniel Ellsberg was prosecuted in such a fury, because his behavior threatened fragile diplomatic transactions and because, if it proved contagious, the ability of the Government to do business would be destroyed; that did not make his prosecution a good idea, but that was the reasoning which impelled it. Sirica laid the lash to Hunt and Liddy because, in part, he abhorred their conduct, and rightly considered that it ought to be discouraged.

In Boston, some years back, there was a loanshark who complained that his trade was widely misunderstood. "You know," he said, "you're in this business because you want to help people. You want them to come to you, to be able to come to you when they're in trouble and they need money. But you have to get the money back, they have to pay you back. You have to understand that. Because if they don't pay you back, then pretty soon you can't help people anymore. And then sometimes there's a fellow"— he was very earnest about this, in his blue suit and his black shoes and his white socks — "that comes to you, and you help him, and then he doesn't pay. So you go up to him and you take his eye and you pluck it out and you put it in a saucer and you show it to him, and then he pays you back, because he understands. Then he understands. You understand, don't you," he said, and it was not a question.

For the others, there were conditional sentences, heavy, maximum terms which Sirica imposed, upon Hunt and McCord and the Cuban Americans, with the promise of review after they had had an opportunity to talk to grand juries and inquisitive legislators. In the autumn of 1973 Sirica was annoyed by criticism that he had distorted the purposes of punishment to his purpose of extracting the truth about Watergate. En route to the cover of *Time*, he divulged his belief that we would all be all right if we got the truth out; cutting back the provisional sentences, he said it should have been apparent that he never intended that Hunt and the Cubans would do twenty or thirty years. But it wasn't apparent; what was apparent was that they would do the full bit if they didn't talk. And Liddy's six-eight to twenty was the eyeball in the saucer for them.

And after the customer looks in the saucer, the shylock was asked, and he pays, what do you do then? "Well," he said, "you give him the thing back."

The Liddys and the loansharks of this world are great problems for the American theory of criminal justice. Its first premise is that it shall be invariably reactive. The notion comes out of the Anglo-American experience which resisted the establishment of professional police. Before Sir Robert Peel invented cops to patrol a nineteenth-century London teeming with anonymous brigands, the laws were enforced by witnesses to crime, who raised the hue and the cry. But society and commerce increased in sophistication, and villains in that new complexity obtained a fair chance to obtain anonymity by traveling, and to escape punishment by the same means. There was a lot of resistance to the idea of a standing constabulary, and the constables themselves raised the devil in Boston and New York when uniforms were proposed for them; we know that there are evil people in the world, but we don't like it, and the dislike we express by restricting the work of the cops to the capture of offenders who are fed into a judicial system that at once reassures them by reminding them that they are innocent until proven guilty, with that to be done only by means of evidence acquired by due process of law, and sufficient to prove their offenses beyond a reasonable doubt.

The rest of the world thinks we're nuts. In Switzerland a young American in court on drug charges asserted his constitutional right to refuse to give evidence against himself; the magistrate, who was a practical man and desired to know the whole story from the person likeliest to know it, advised him that the Bill of Rights does not run in Geneva, and clapped him in irons until he should talk. In London, where we secured the raw materials for our system of justice, Lords of the Bench in Old Bailey chide those who would suppress confessions of defendants, with the firm reminder that they are not in America, where things might be done differently. And here, too, it's often tough to be a cop, and always tough to be a victim; our system of law enforcement is so determinedly idealistic in formal terms that it is gravely inefficient in practice, and that can be frustrating, as it was to John Sirica. A conservative, the sour but realistic definition goes, is a liberal who's been mugged.

John Sirica's daddy was an immigrant. This country, and its system, made John Sirica a judge. Gordon Liddy mugged the system, as far as John Sirica was concerned. That made him angry. The idealism of the system says it's better if ninety-nine escape punishment, though guilty, than that one innocent be punished. The part about the innocent not getting punished goes down easily enough, but Sirica saw at least ninety-nine on the street behind Liddy, and the price was too high for him. Wrathful, he refused to pay it, and for that he was lionized, an experience which he did not find distasteful.

His refusal was not unique. The tension between what we know about viciousness, and what we would prefer to believe about human nature, is constant. It gave us the Smith Act in 1940, congressional action engendered by a fear of Communists titanically greater in degree, but similar in kind, to Silbert's experience of pushers and robbers and rapists incorporated in the D.C. Crime Bill; the national experience of the Alien and

Sedition Acts went unattended. It took *Ex parte Milliken* from the Supreme Court to restore the presumption of innocence to those accused, but denied habeaus corpus, by Abraham Lincoln's stern view that those apprehended in circumstances suggesting participation in Confederate treachery should not be released on bail. Among American law enforcement officers today, there is a persistent belief that the decisions of Earl Warren's term as Chief Justice, deemed unrealistic in the extreme and in several instances (such as, for example, *Mapp* v. *Ohio* and *Escobedo* v. *Illinois*) downright foolish, were nothing more than Warren's efforts to expiate the guilt he felt for his contributions, as Attorney General of California, to the internment of Japanese Americans during World War II, without anything approaching due process of law. The equilibrium of constitutional idealism and practical vengefulness has always been unstable, more perfect by far in the civics textbooks than it has ever been in fact.

John Sirica presided over the trial of *United States of America* v. *George Gordon Liddy, et al.*, Criminal No. 1827–72, in a period of special precariousness of that traditional instability. The national tilt was toward practical vengefulness, a list to starboard which the Nixon Administration, employer of G. Gordon Liddy, had intensified, but certainly did not initiate.

In the Kennedy Administration, RFK, with what seemed to be excellent reason, went after James Riddle Hoffa, the boss of the Teamsters, and Vito Genovese, the boss of all bosses (if he was). In the Kennedy view, they fully deserved the Government's aggressive Strike Force efforts to put them in jail, not because they had, provably, committed acts which would have raised the hue and the cry, but because they were bad bastards generally, the one shafting his union members for his own gain, the other presiding over an economic system masquerading as the Mafia but competing with the orthodox system by offering goods and services either proscribed by law (narcotics and gambling) or detrimental to commerce (labor racketeering, proscribed by statutes enacted commencing in 1961). Having eluded conviction in the *Test Fleet* case, Hoffa was hunted to earth by proof that he had sought to influence one of the *Test Fleet* jurors; he was convicted of mistrust of the criminal justice system, effectuated by bribery. Hoffa's prosecutor was Jim Neal, who led the 1974 prosecution of Haldeman, Ehrlichman, Mitchell and the rest.

Interviewed on television in 1974, Neal conceded new reservations about the Hoffa prosecution: he said he'd begun to wonder if any human being in a high position could withstand such pursuit successfully. The Nixon Administration, by then, had let Hoffa out. Genovese, amenable to the procurement of murders only when all other forms of trade regulation failed, had gone to jail for conspiring to deal in narcotics, and died there, too soon for Nixon's, uh, mercy.

The Chief of the Organized Crime and Racketeering Section of the Criminal Division of the Department of Justice, when those prodigies were accomplished, was Henry Petersen. He had a lot to do with those successes, which accounts, even today, for much of his reputation as a man of utter and incorruptible integrity. But Petersen was Chief, too, when Lyndon Johnson conferred with J. Edgar Hoover in the White House, about some behavior that was against the law, but countenanced by Petersen, others, and LBJ himself. Because it was, well, at least interesting, and potentially useful.

"He'd get very fidgety," a former Johnson aide said. "Hoover never said exactly how he got his information, because he didn't have to. Johnson was very concerned about being bugged himself, because of the way he talked, the words he used."

In 1971, less than elated by the way his successor had conducted the presidency, Johnson visited some editors in Washington, and said that Nixon had done for the country "what panty hose did for finger-fuckin'."

"So, he'd be very impatient, and he'd go this way, and that way, in the chair, cross his legs and uncross his legs, and finally it'd get the better of him. Hoover'd mention the name of one of his worst enemies, somebody'd been mentioned on one of the Las Vegas taps, some skimming connection or something, and he'd stop fidgeting and turn around and look Hoover right in the face and say: 'What'd he say, what'd he say?' He never really wanted it done, and he never really wanted it stopped. He just wanted to know what they got by doing it. He couldn't stand it."

Ramsey Clark became Attorney General of the United States on March 2, 1967, succeeding Nicholas deB. Katzenbach. That occasioned the retirement of Lyndon's friend Tom Clark, from the Supreme Court, to avoid conflict of interest in appeals and petitions for writs of certiorari brought by the Government in the person of the Attorney General's subaltern, the Solicitor General of the United States.

*Buagents,* as FBI Special Agents are called in FBI 302s, say it was 1966 when recruits, in training at Quantico, for some reason ceased to act, individually and spontaneously, upon impulsions of unknown causation, to visit the sixth floor of the FBI's Ident Building down on Second Street in the District at night, there to manufacture lock picks and study the installation of wiretaps and induction coils. This is not to say that there were no FBI bag jobs after 1966, but the manpower trained to perform them dwindled.

Never rash, J. Edgar Hoover as he aged became more cautious still, and more jealous than ever of the seraphic public image he had so painstakingly fashioned for his Bureau and himself in the course of forty years; he had a sure intuition of the public mind, and he shrank from the heat that would follow a bungled burglary. Thus when Hoover made his courtesy call, as one monarch to the other, upon President Nixon in 1969, he carried two pieces of bad news, only one of which he delivered: he told the new President that one of his campaigns had been bugged; he failed to respond to Nixon's instruction to discontinue such practices, when he might have confided that he had done so, and would not, under any circumstances, revive them.

"In 1970," Haldeman told the Senate Select Committee on Presidential Campaign Activities, "the domestic security problem reached critical proportions as a wave of bombings and explosions, rioting and violence, demonstrations, arson, gun battles and other disruptive activities took place across the country — on college campuses, primarily, but also in other areas."

From a legitimately grave concern about the degeneration of dissension into anarchy, the Administration proceeded lamentably into something very like hysteria. Tom Charles Huston, the White House staff assistant who shuttled between Ehrlichman and Haldeman, reporting on such problems, told Haldeman in 1970 that he was "talking about the future of this country, for surely domestic violence and disorder threaten the very fabric of our society." Huston, advocating "surreptitious entry" and bugging because it was cheap (which it is) and efficient (also true), rose above constitutional principle on the wings of the argument from necessity, propelled by the knowledge which he had gained from his service in Army Intelligence that domestic espionage is eminently feasible. Huston thought the way that Liddy was prepared to act, and wrote it down, and only Hoover prevented the immediate implementation of Huston's view that the times and the circumstances demanded an aggressiveness of investigation and prosecution which the system was constructed to preclude. "Mr. Huston," Haldeman said, "was notified by a memorandum from me of the approval of the President."

That was the kind of approval, extended when wrathful denunciations would have comported a good deal better with the words in the presidential oath about upholding the Constitution and the laws of the United States, that unleashed the Liddys, intoxicated the Hunts, attracted the McCords, and created the problems that needed a Dean to repair. Dean, in January of 1973, was engaged in a hopeless enterprise because nobody among his clients had any notion whatsoever of the risk attending a Liddy at large, nor of the even greater risks that went with mistaking a Hunt or a McCord for a Liddy and setting them loose also.

# 13

HUNT WAS MORE worrisome to Dean. Dean, like Magruder, had never dealt with men like Hunt and Liddy before, and they were always surprising him. Hunt practiced the rudiments of extortion during the last half of 1972, and gained both confidence and nerve. By 1973, he was holding the White House indirectly responsible for the airplane crash that had killed his wife in December; his grief made him shrill, and very avaricious indeed. Money, money, money: except for *clemency*, and *pardons*, that was all Dean heard from Hunt, and it disturbed him.

For the wrong reasons, Sirica had focused on money, too. He thought the case was in the bag, and he was pretty close to the truth on that score, but he believed that the Cubans were the ones bagging it, for money, when in fact it was Hunt who was doing that, and bagging the Cubans as part of the quid pro quo. If the Cubans needed bagging, which is doubtful.

Hunt rationalized his behavior by reference to the desperation of his situation. That situation was pretty much his own damned fault. But the opportunity to incur the fault had not been denied him by people who could have denied it, and whose vulnerability to blackmail was the consequence of that failure. There were Dean's clients, who hadn't dealt with Hunts and Liddys either, but assumed themselves, mistakenly, competent to handle them also.

"Now," Sam Dash, Chief Counsel to the Ervin Committee, said to Ehrlichman, "did you know Mr. Hunt or Mr. Liddy?"

"I had met Mr. Liddy once, briefly," Ehrlichman said. "I never met Hunt. I will take that back. He may have been in my office, once."

"Did you ever initiate any instruction to them?" Dash asked, after questioning Ehrlichman about Young and Krogh, the buffers on his staff between him and Hunt and Liddy. *Initiate any instruction to them* meant: Did you ever tell them to do anything?

"I was asked to ratify a number of their decisions from time to time," Ehrlichman said, meaning, one assumes: No. "Their practice would be to send me periodic information reports." They told him what they were doing. "Sometimes these would contain requests"— they asked him something and wanted his opinion —"for either approval of a decision that they had made or proposals that they had or something of that kind," which is close to impermeable by ordinary methods of understanding, but seems to mean: Yes.

"Is this the special investigations unit that later became," Dash said, "began to be known popularly as: 'The Plumbers'?"

Ehrlichman said: "Yes."

"Now," Dash said, *now* being an utterance which is used by trial lawyers and other public interrogators to indicate that a question is being formulated; it has absolutely no reference to any point in time, "did you actually interview Mr. Hunt before he was hired?"

"No," Ehrlichman said. "I had a meeting with Mr. Colson and Mr. Hunt after he was hired. It was in July of 1971 and I believe that is the only time I have seen Mr. Hunt."

"Would it be fair to say," Dash said, "that Mr. Colson very much wanted Mr. Hunt to be hired?"

"That would be fair to say," Ehrlichman said.

Charles W. Colson, Special Counsel to the President for three years until he resigned in 1972, had a bar in his den. He had a Green Beret slogan above the bar: "If you got 'em by the balls, their hearts and minds will follow." In 1970 an Op Art poster seen in San Francisco was described to a Colson friend from Massachusetts; the poster, printed in scriptural style, read: "Yes, though I walk through the valley of the shadow of death, I shall fear no evil, for I am the meanest son of a bitch in the valley." The listener reproved the narrator: "You should have picked one of them up for me; I'd give it to Chuck."

In the first Nixon Administration, Colson was one of the few White

House aides whose mouth was free of meal. Then in his early forties, he was no longer the same son of a bitch that he was when he started out, a Brown graduate and retired Marine captain with fierce partisan instincts, fiercer loyalties and total dedication to his cause; he was older. He was a partisan of stripes different from those of Haldeman, Ehrlichman and Huston; and could bandy ideologies, because he is a brilliant man, but issues for him were primarily personal. It was Colson who fumed at the refusal of Johnnie Walters, Commissioner of Internal Revenue, to start audits on White House enemies. It was Colson who floated the proposal to firebomb the Brookings Institution, in order to grab papers which he suspected might be useful to embarrass the Democrats. It was Colson who called Hunt, when Arthur Bremer shot George Wallace, and vainly attempted to get Hunt to break into Bremer's apartment to see if there might be some papers there that could tie Bremer to the Democrats. It was Colson who said that a "scandal would be most helpful" in subduing Dr. Morton Halperin, a Brookings Institution activist friendly to Ellsberg, and it was Colson who demanded that the Enemies List be kept up to date, in order that opponents of the Administration be denied Government contracts and other goodies: "so we can figure out ways to screw them," he dictated, in his delicate way of hinting his intentions. He had his hounds out moments after Teddy Kennedy's sunken Oldsmobile was found to contain the body of Mary Jo Kopechne at Chappaquiddick, because he thinks that dirt's effective in campaigns and he believed Ted Kennedy had a campaign in mind for 1972. He was a ruthless, energetic adversary who believed that the One Great Scorer will write against your name whether you won or lost, and that's all, and he was as bashful about his views as he was timid in expressing them. Except for Richard G. Kleindienst, and Richard M. Nixon, and maybe Daniel Patrick Moynihan, Ehrlichman's predecessor as Domestic Adviser, Colson was the only man in the first Nixon Administration who could swear proficiently; Nixon wouldn't, at least in public, and he was terribly awkward when he did it in private; Moynihan left, and Kleindienst, able to cuss also in Navajo, adopted a more seemly vocabulary when he reduced his opinions to writing. Colson called things by their right names.

What Colson did not do was act as a tempering influence upon imaginative and irrepressible folk about him, laboring perhaps with some neglect of constitutional and statutory precepts toward a mutual goal. He had not found Jesus, then. He liked having Hunts and Liddys around.

"Now," Dash said, "you said that the major responsibility of this unit developed because of the need for the unit to go ahead on an investigation of the so-called Pentagon leaks. Were there any other responsibilities or assignments given to this unit?"

"Yes," Ehrlichman said.

"Could you state what they are?" Dash said. "Were?"

"Well," Ehrlichman said, "I can state some of them. I cannot state all of them. The strategic arms limitations negotiations were under way in the summer of 1971, and a newspaper obtained the U.S. negotiating position, in effect, the secret U.S. negotiations in that negotiation. That came close on the heels of the *Pentagon Papers* episode and was a major cause of concern for the President and for those dealing in this area of foreign policy. This special unit was asked to see if they could determine the source of that leak."

This was properly the concern of the FBI, if it was properly the concern of any governmental agency. The FBI was strenuously investigating all of the aspects of the *Pentagon Papers* case in the summer of 1971. There were grand juries sitting in the Southern District of California and the District of Massachusetts. Assistant U.S. Attorney Warren Reese, from San Diego, and Justice Department lawyer David Nesson, detailed from Mardian's Internal Security Division to work with Reese, spent more time in Boston than they did in California. Nobody, then, asked what the hell an ad hoc White House squad was doing, meddling in an FBI investigation, because no one knew about it.

"Do you know," Dash said, "what actions the special unit took in seeking to carry out that responsibility?"

"In general terms, I do," Ehrlichman said. "I know that they worked through the security people at the State Department and the Defense Department. They narrowed down the probable source of that leak, and I believe there were some personnel actions taken as a result of that."

They did a few other things, too, such as tapping the phones at the Embassy of Chile, but Ehrlichman couldn't talk about those and Dash didn't want him to talk about them. Reasonably enough. McCord had, but that was different.

"Now," Dash said, "you did become aware at some point in time" — Dash by July 24 had been listening and talking to Administration people for almost three months, and their usage had started to get to him — "of the activities of staff members of the special investigations unit, Mr. Hunt and Mr. Liddy, with regard to the office of Mr. Ellsberg's psychiatrist?"

"Yes," Ehrlichman said. "It was around Labor Day of 1971." It was September 3, 1971, the Friday before Labor Day. And Ehrlichman had "become aware" of the proposed activity by a memorandum from Colson, to which he responded on August 27, 1971: "On the assumption that the proposed undertaking by Hunt and Liddy would be carried out and would be successful, I would appreciate receiving from you by next Wednesday a game plan as to how and when you believe the material should be used."

Hunt and Liddy had cased the joint during the week of August 20. Before the Committee, Hunt called it a "feasibility study." Colson, testifying before a California grand jury inquiring into the burglary at Dr. Lewis Fielding's office, said Ehrlichman called him in August and "asked if I could obtain $5,000 for Mr. Krogh, and he indicated that the money was needed rather quickly. I obtained it from Mr. Joseph Baroody, who was at that time a partner in a public relations firm that was organizing the Committee for the New Prosperity," a Nixon campaign organization. Hunt and Liddy stayed outside during the burglary; it was the Cubans who went inside, and came up empty.

"In late November of 1971," Hunt told the Committee, "Mr. Liddy approached me saying that the Attorney General of the United States, Mr. John Mitchell, required the establishment of a large-scale intelligence and counterintelligence program. That he, Mr. Liddy, was about to become its chief, and Mr. Liddy would like to assure himself of my cooperation."

"Was this the plan," Dash said, "that came later to be known as Gemstone?"

"Yes, sir," Hunt said.

"Did there come a time," Dash said to Jeb Stuart Magruder, former Director of the Office of Policy Development in the Department of Commerce, "when Mr. Liddy did present his plan to the Attorney General, Mr. Mitchell?"

"The first meeting," Magruder said, "was February twenty-seventh. I'm sorry, January twenty-seventh, 1971." Magruder was off by a year. "And we had a meeting in Mr. Mitchell's office." Mitchell was also confident, then, about his mastery of men who did not acknowledge limits.

Mr. Mitchell's office was then in the United States Department of Justice. He was still Attorney General of the United States, a position he utilized to exhort the public about the need for law, or, at least, order. John Dean had attended the meeting.

"Mr. Liddy," Magruder said, "brought in with him a series of charts. They were professionally done charts, and had color, some color, on each of the charts. As I recall there were approximately six charts. Each chart contained a subject matter, and was headed by a code word. I cannot recall many of the code words. The one I do recall is Gemstone. I think one was called Target, but I cannot specifically recall the other code words. Each chart had a listing of certain types of activities, with a budget, and, as I recall, there was one chart that totaled up the activities and the budget totaled to the million figure that he had mentioned previously."

"Mr. Liddy was presenting this in the form of a show-and-tell operation?" Dash said.

"Yes," Magruder said, "that is correct." He went on: "This was, of course, the projects, including wiretapping, electronic surveillance, and photography. There were projects relating to the abduction of individuals, particularly members of radical groups that we were concerned about on the convention at San Diego. Mr. Liddy had a plan where the leaders would be abducted and detained in a place like Mexico, and then they would be returned to this country at the end of the convention. He had another plan which would have used women as agents to work with members of the Democratic National Committee at their convention, and hopefully, through their efforts, they would obtain information from them."

There was some commotion in the gallery. There was, as a matter of fact, a lot of commotion in the gallery. Sam Ervin liked to instigate it, by provision of a lot of Southern molasses, allow it to die down, and then pretend to be offended, whamming his gavel vigorously.

"With regard to the use of these women as agents," Dash said, ever circuitous, "did this involve the use of a yacht at Miami?"

"He envisoned renting a yacht at Miami and having it set up for sound and photographs," Magruder said.

"And what," Dash said, "would the women be doing at that time?"

"I could really only estimate," Magruder said, "but . . ."

"Based on his project," Dash said, "from your recollection, what did he indicate?"

"Well," Magruder said, squirming endearingly, "I think you could consider them call girls."

This was what Liddy had in mind for a million dollars.

"Mr. Magruder," Dash said, "what was Mr. Mitchell's reaction, Mr. Dean's reaction, and your own reaction, when you heard this presentation?"

"I think all three of us were appalled," Magruder said. "The scope and size of the project was something that, at least in my mind, was not envisioned. I do not think it was in Mr. Mitchell's mind, or Mr. Dean's, although I can't comment on their state of mind at the time. Mr. Mitchell, in an understated way, which was his method of dealing with difficult problems like this, indicated that this was not an acceptable project."

Cholerically, Mitchell assured the Committee that he had roundly disapproved Liddy's plan, and told him to burn the charts. He described the first Liddy plan, he said, as "a complete horror story," a "mishmash" of "code names" that went "beyond the pale." Liddy, Mitchell said dispiritedly, "didn't exercise any responsiveness to my desires in this matter."

All of that permitted the inference that Mitchell had rejected the Liddy plan, January 27, 1972, on moral and ethical grounds. But Mitchell never said that, directly, and he said other things which warrant the inference that his disapproval, then, was based only upon financial and strategic considerations. His forehead littered with the residue of burst blood vessels (which lent credibility to reports he had prepared for his Committee appearance by assiduous attention to a gallon of Dewar's White Label set in a wooden pouring cradle in his New York apartment), Mitchell said he would have opposed the offer of Hoover's job to the judge in the Ellsberg case because an "improper approach to a judge is, in my opinion, the surest way to get the opposite result." He retrospectively disapproved another such feeler as "unproductive," and said he never used any influence "because it wouldn't work." He acceded to Ervin's suggestion that he had exalted Nixon's reelection above his obligation to see that the laws be faithfully executed, and when Dash asked him if he would have committed perjury to insure that reelection, the former Attorney General of the United States said: "I think, Mr. Dash, that that subject matter, that I would have to think very long and hard about."

It was only when Mitchell found himself before the Committee — as an anonymous friend told the *Washington Post*: "He's under indictment, he can't practice law, he's a prisoner in his own apartment and he's married to a screwball" — that he professed to think that he should have thrown Liddy out the window when the million-dollar plan was proposed, so it is likely that adversity resulting from what Liddy finally did, and got caught doing, was responsible for Mitchell's hardness of heart in 1973.

Liddy and Magruder appear to have perceived no such repugnance in

1972. Liddy submitted a reduced plan on February 4, again in the office of the Attorney General of the United States. The half-million-dollar proposal "related only to the wiretapping," Magruder told the Committee, "and photography, and not to any of the other projects. They had been basically discarded." But what remained for discussion was piquant enough: "We did discuss potential targets," Magruder said. "We discussed the potential target of the Democratic National Committee headquarters, primarily because of information we had relating to Mr. O'Brien, that we felt would be possibly damaging to the Democratic National Committee." Mr. Mitchell was so horrified by that idea that he told Liddy about some possible dirt on Senator Edmund Muskie — "At that time," Magruder told the Committee, "we did not know who the candidate would be, so it was simply an indication that that would be a target of interest" — in a safe in the Las Vegas office of publisher Hank Greenspun, and directed Liddy to determine the "potential for an entry into Greenspun's office."

"How did that meeting end?" Dash asked Magruder. "What was Mr. Mitchell's reaction to this presentation at the end of the second meeting?"

"It still was disapproval," Magruder said, "or, let's say, I should say we agreed that it would not be approved at that time, but we would take it up later; that he just didn't feel comfortable with it even at that level."

"But again," Dash said, "it would be true to say that at least Mr. Liddy was encouraged to continue in his planning?"

"Yes," Magruder said, "I think that is correct."

"Who finally approved Mr. Liddy's position at the committee?" Dash said.

"Mr. Mitchell," Magruder said.

Magruder admired Mitchell, and professed to the Committee that his respect had not been diminished by postelection developments, although he said that before John Mitchell visited the Committee and called Magruder a liar. Which, of course, he was. "A tremendous liar, tremendous," Silbert said, having damned good reason to know. In March of 1972, Magruder was still depending upon Mitchell's acumen, and gave Liddy the benefit of a doubt that perhaps did not exist. Of Liddy's proposal to kill him he said: "But I want to make it clear that I did not, and I do not now, regard that as a specific threat. It was simply Mr. Liddy's mannerism. I think he was indicating to me that he did not care for his relationship with me. That was all." But it was enough to cause Magruder to see Fred LaRue, right off, because he was scared.

The meeting with LaRue brought only a partial severance of Liddy's connection with CREEP. "What we then agreed to," Magruder said, "was to terminate him from our committee as general counsel, but retain him in the area of intelligence gathering." Liddy was manumitted to the position of general counsel to the parallel Finance Committee to Re-elect the President, under the putative supervision of Maurice Stans, former Secretary of Commerce, but left in place as CREEP's snoop.

"By the way," said Dash, "did you know at that time that Mr. Hunt was working with Mr. Liddy?"

"At that time," Magruder said, "I think by that time, I had been encouraged by certain staff members at the White House to be sure that Mr. Hunt was not employed by us directly, but employed by Mr. Liddy. So I think I was aware at that time that he was." Magruder said that Richard Howard, Colson's assistant, "indicated that Mr. Hunt had completed his assignments at the White House," among them, presumably, the forgery of State Department cables meant to lend specious authenticity to what had been widely rumored: that the Kennedy Administration had acquiesced in the assassination of President Diem of South Vietnam, "and since we were now engaged in intelligence activities, he thought I would find Mr. Hunt very valuable. I only met Mr. Hunt once, so I was not really sure in what terms he would be valuable. So I indicated to Mr. Howard that he should refer Mr. Hunt to Mr. Liddy and that Mr. Liddy would employ him. I did not know at that time that he and Mr. Liddy had worked together before."

Magruder, in his eagerness to please like a huge spaniel in a Hickey-Freeman suit, evidently experienced less than total remission of what he claimed to have been no trepidation at all in the reception of Liddy's threat. Dean had had to soothe him: "I received a call from Mr. Dean encouraging me not to become personally concerned about Mr. Liddy, that I should not let my personal animosity and his get in the way of the projects. And then I went over to the White House and was working with Mr. Strachan" — Gordon Strachan, a younger version of Magruder with more brains, who worked for Haldeman but reported to Colson — "on normal campaign matters, and he brought up the same subject, and, as we walked back to the committee — it was a Friday afternoon, as I recall, and it was raining — he indicated that although he had the same personal difficulties with Mr. Liddy, that probably Mr. Liddy was quite a professional in this intelligence gathering, and we should retain him in this area." Egil Krogh, Jr., who had been Liddy's keeper for Ehrlichman, also talked "to me about Mr. Liddy, and mentioned to me a number of times, we should keep tight control over him, but he was very effective."

It is difficult, now, to select just which of these men in Magruder's estimation, or Krogh's, for that matter, had been charged by that *we* with controlling Liddy. Whoever it was, he didn't do it, and there was very little advance prospect that he'd be able to. Liddy had overthrown Magruder's authority by scaring the living daylights out of him; now he was working for Stans on the Finance Committee, but, apparently, reporting to Mitchell, through Magruder, on intelligence activities for CREEP. Krogh had no actual influence upon Liddy, and neither did Dean; that vanished, if it had ever existed, in fact, when Liddy left the White House for CREEP. In fact, nobody controlled Liddy; he was on his own, a juggernaut looking for a track.

"All right now, Mr. Hunt," Dash said, "after the February fourth meeting that Mr. Liddy had with the former Attorney General, in which there was another turn-down on the so-called Liddy plan, did Mr. Liddy ask you to introduce him to Mr. Colson?"

"He did," Hunt said.

"And what reason did he give you for this?" Dash said.

"He indicated to me," Hunt said, "that, first of all, he admired Chuck Colson as a man who got things done. He expressed his own desire for a substantial position in the forthcoming Administration. He indicated to me that inasmuch as John Mitchell would be leaving the Administration, and he, Liddy, was known and identified as a Mitchell man, that Mr. Liddy would like to touch base with Mr. Colson, who would be staying on in the Administration, at least through the election, and so have another power base, as it were, on which he could depend at such time. . . ."

"Well," Dash said, "did you arrange such a meeting?"

"I did," Hunt said.

"After you did," Dash said, "what did you do?"

"I withdrew to the back of the room," Hunt said, "and sat and smoked my pipe, leafing through a magazine, while Mr. Liddy conversed with Mr. Colson."

"And why did you withdraw to the back of the room?" Dash said.

"Mr. Liddy having given me the preamble," Hunt said, "the reasons for his desire to meet Mr. Colson, I felt that it was a personal matter, and did not want to involve myself with it or interpose myself in any way."

"How long did the meeting take place, Mr. Hunt?" Dash said.

"Approximately ten, twelve minutes," Hunt said.

"Did you observe Mr. Colson use the telephone during that meeting," Dash said.

"On several occasions," Hunt said.

"After the February fourth meeting in Mr. Mitchell's office," Dash asked Magruder, "when the plan was still not approved, did there come a time when anyone else at the White House urged you to get the Liddy plan approved?"

"Yes," Magruder said. "Mr. Charles Colson called me one evening and asked me, in a sense, would we get off the stick and get the budget approved for Mr. Liddy's plans, that we needed information, particularly on Mr. O'Brien. He did not mention, I want to make clear, anything relating to wiretapping or espionage at that time."

"But in the discussion," Dash said, "did you get the impression yourself that he knew what the Liddy plan was?"

Colson swears he didn't, and nobody's ever proven that he did, or lied when he said he didn't.

"Again," Magruder said, "I want to be careful. I knew Mr. Hunt was a close friend of Mr. Colson. He had been referred to me earlier by Mr. Colson. I did make the assumption that he did know, but he did not say that he was aware of the specifics and never did say that to me at any time." LaRue was in Magruder's office when the Colson call came through.

"After the meeting," Dash said to Hunt, "did you have a conversation with Mr. Liddy?"

"I did," Hunt said.

"What did Mr. Liddy tell you?" Dash asked.

"He said," Hunt said, " 'I think I may have done us some good.' " Liddy now had his track.

"Now," said Dash to Magruder, "did there come a time when you had a third and final meeting with Mr. Mitchell on the Liddy plan, on or about March thirtieth, 1972?"

"Yes, we had," Magruder said. "There had been a delay in the decision-making process at the Committee. . . . Mr. Mitchell was on vacation at Key Biscayne. I went down to Key Biscayne. Mr. LaRue was there. And we met and went over approximately thirty-some decision papers, mainly relating to direct mail and advertising, the other parts of the campaign. The last project we discussed was the final proposal of Mr. Liddy's, which was for approximately $250,000. We discussed it, brought up again the pros and cons. I think I can honestly say that no one was particularly overwhelmed with the project. But I think we felt that the information could be useful, and Mr. Mitchell agreed to approve the project and I then notified the parties of Mr. Mitchell's approval."

"Would it be fair to say, Mr. Mitchell," Dash said, "that the so-called quarter-million-dollar Liddy plan for wiretapping and break-in was actually different in degree and kind than any other agenda item that he was presenting to you?"

"Mr. Dash," Mitchell said, "you can rest assured of this: there were no other such plans in the documents that were submitted."

"What would have given Mr. Magruder the idea that you would even consider this proposal again," Dash said, "if you had indeed, as you stated, rejected it so categorically, twice before?"

"Well," Mitchell said, "I would have presumed that you would ask Mr. Magruder that question when he was here, Mr. Dash. But in hindsight, I presume there were other people interested in the implementation of some type of activity in this area. Because I believe that Mr. Magruder was very clearly aware of the position that I had taken in connection with it."

"So that it is at least your present feeling," Dash said, "that he was acting under some pressure for somebody to represent this plan to you?"

"This has continued to be my feeling," Mitchell said, "but I have no basis for knowing that."

"Do you know who might have been involved?" Dash said.

"No," Mitchell said, "I do not."

"Now," Dash said, "what is your recollection of what decision you made in Key Biscayne on the so-called Liddy plan?"

"Well," Mitchell said, "it was very simple. This, again: 'We don't need this. I am tired of hearing it. Out. Let's not discuss it any further.' This sort of concept."

"Then how do you explain, Mr. Mitchell," Dash said, "Mr. Magruder's sworn testimony that you, however reluctantly, approved the quarter-million-dollar Liddy plan at Key Biscayne?"

"Mr. Dash," Mitchell said, wearily, "I can't explain anybody's testimony up here but my own."

"Did you have a conversation," David M. Dorsen, Assistant Chief Counsel to the Committee, asked Richard Helms, "with General Cushman concerning Howard Hunt in the summer of 1971?"

"Yes," Helms said. "I recall that General Cushman informed me that he had authorized giving to Howard Hunt a tape recorder and a camera, and I asked for what purpose and he said he wanted to conduct a one-time interview and that he had been properly authenticated by the White House and that he was working at their behest."

General Robert E. Cushman, Jr., Commandant of the Marines in 1973, was Deputy Diréctor of the Central Intelligence Agency in 1971, when Helms was director.

"Now," Dorsen said, "you have indicated that in your conversation with General Cushman that you indicated to General Cushman" — *indicated* meant *said* in Watergatese — "that John Ehrlichman should be called. Why was it that John Ehrlichman was to be called?" All actions were stated in the passive voice, in that tongue.

"Because it was my distinct impression," Helms said, "that he was the one who had arranged with General Cushman to have Hunt get these pieces of equipment."

"And what can you say," Senator Joseph Montoya inquired, later, "about Mr. Hunt?"

"Yes," Helms said, "I knew him."

"What was his reputation?" Montoya said, in his vocal imitation of Mr. Magoo.

"Well," Helms said, struggling, "ah, Mr. Hunt was . . . had a . . . well, he had a good reputation. There was some question at various times during his employment about how well he carried out certain assignments, but there was nothing malign about this." In other words, Hunt, retired after twenty-one years with the CIA in Paris, Vienna, Mexico City, Madrid and Montevideo, notwithstanding his participation in the successful overthrow of the government of Guatemala in 1954, wasn't very good. That estimate might have proceeded from his work as "Eduardo," when he represented the CIA on the Cuban Revolutionary Council, which took the, uh, credit for the Bay of Pigs invasion in 1962. "It was just a question of his effectiveness," Helms said. "Mr. Hunt was a bit of a romantic. He used to write books in his spare time" — forty-six of them, to be precise, the forty-seventh out in 1974 — "and I think there was a tendency sometimes for him to get a little bit carried away with some of the things he was involved in. But he had never done anything illegal or nefarious that anybody was aware of."

Except, of course, labor successfully to overthrow the government of Guatemala, which was probably at least nefarious in Guatemalan terms, and take an active role in the clumsy effort to topple the Castro government, which Castro took very ill indeed, demanding tractors and potions and poultices before he would let Mr. Hunt's hapless charges out of the Cuban jails. "And when he left the Agency he left a decent record behind," Helms said.

"What would you say," Montoya said, "about his reputation for veracity?" In other words, would a man practiced, if somewhat erratic, in espionage, sabotage and fomenting of rebellion, misrepresent the truth?

Helms got it down. It choked him for a minute, but he got it down. "Well, I have said, sir, that he was a romantic." In other words, he might lie. "I think that I just do not have any way of being able to answer that." My problem is that I think he would lie, if the circumstances were exigent; he didn't exactly go into Guatemala with a statement of his purposes taped to his forehead, you know. "I would have assumed that in matters of importance he would tell the truth." When he was reporting to us, he told the truth, but of course his skin wasn't at stake when he reported to us.

Senator Ervin was curious about CIA hospitality to Hunt. "So, didn't it strike you, when you learned of these things, didn't it strike you as strange that the White House would engage in undercover work on its own initiative rather than resort to the use of the FBI?"

Hoover was still alive in 1971. The White House had resorted to the use of the FBI, and Hoover had repulsed the resort, calculating — with some prescience, as it turned out — that what the White House had in mind was going to get somebody in a whole lot of trouble. And it was not going to be Hoover, or the Bureau.

"Well," Helms said reflectively, "you know, Senator, at that time there was no intimation that this was even undercover work. What I understood Mr. Hunt had told General Cushman was that he wanted to conduct an interview and there was no intimation that this was undercover work."

"Well, now," Ervin said, "here is a wig. That was. . . . You didn't think that the wig was to improve the appearance of the, the pulchritude of Mr. Hunt. Did you?"

"I assume," Helms said painfully, "that in retrospect, because I didn't remember about the wig at the time, Mr. Chairman, as I have testified, but I have assumed in retrospect that Mr. Hunt wanted to conduct this interview disguising himself as someone else, but we didn't know that at the time." Or: Yeah, it was undercover work, but they asked Cushman and we gave them a wig.

"Well," said Ervin, in one of his very occasional efforts to obtain some

*121*

actual facts, "when a man undertakes to disguise himself as someone else, he is engaged in undercover work, isn't he?"

"Well," Helms said, patrician, urbane, privy to unspeakable secrets, former proprietor though not inventor of the Phoenix program, which in a manner consonant with Colson's Green Beret poster accomplished the reformation of Viet Cong by killing those whose intransigence withstood torture, "we run into a definitional problem, sir."

"Well," Ervin said, as tenacious in his interrogation of a spy as he had been, nine years before, in his opposition to civil rights legislation, from darling of the Right to darling of the Left in a decade without any cognizable mutation of *his* ideology, "you didn't think that he applied for this voice alteration device in order to sing a different part in the choir, did you?"

Now Helms bit the bullet. "Mr. Chairman, my problem here is that at the time that this was going on, I do not recall having been told that he had been given a wig and a voice alteration device. I found that out in May of this year [1973]."

Nobody ever leaves the Agency. Or, for that matter, the Bureau. They resign, as Hunt did, because he had family medical bills and he couldn't make enough on the Government's salary to pay them. They resign, as Liddy did from the Bureau after two years or so as a Special Agent. Or as Helms, who acceded to the President's plain desire in 1972 that he step down as CIA Director to accept the sinecure of Ambassador to Iran, not because he had not done a good job — which he had, an excellent job of managing the Republic's dirty work, which someone must manage — but because the President made it perfectly clear that he wanted a new Director. Helms was more compliant than Hoover, who had had the decency to expire; still he had exploded when Hunt, after getting phony identification for himself and Liddy, then demanded that the Agency repatriate his former secretary from Paris, and loan her to him for his White House work. That was when Helms told Cushman to call Ehrlichman and get Hunt off his back, and Cushman, on orders, told Ehrlichman that Hunt had become a pain in the neck. Still the connections remain, and it was those connections which Hunt exploited. Cushman gave him the stuff because Hunt said he was from the White House, and Cushman checked, and he was, and Hunt was an old boy. So the pros, who could have controlled the Hunts and Liddys, deferred to the amateurs, who couldn't.

As a result, Silbert got himself six defendants — McCord's zeal was leavened, at least, by a thoughtful interest in self-preservation — who broke into buildings in the same subjective assurance that inspired Daniel Ellsberg to steal and publish the *Pentagon Papers*; with beautiful malice, the CIA produced an Ellsberg personality profile which denominated his motive as "a higher order of patriotism," content to leave unremarked the fact that this was the justification advanced by Kim Philby for his treasonous defection to the Soviet Union. Such people are zealous instruments, not thoughtful instigators, as ill adapted as Nathan Hale to malleability by pressure.

Silbert did not know this, either. There was no way he could have proven it, if he had. Sirica, if he sensed it, sensed it dimly. In the shadows behind Liddy and Hunt and the Cubans there were men with motives familiar to both judge and prosecutor: greed, fear of disgrace, pride sufficient to precede a great fall, and the arrogance of vicarious power. Magruder was the man who kept them in the shadows.

"They knew we'd have to believe Magruder," Silbert said. "That's why they sent him; because they knew in the end we'd have to believe him." But Dean was the man who had sent Magruder, coached him, prepped him and made sure his ears were clean, and he knew also how Magruder would react to pressure. Dean only used Magruder because he had to. He had to because Hunt had been left to prowl, with Liddy, by his clients.

# 14

John Dean did not have an original mind. He did not, as Liddy did, imagine great enterprises, or propose brilliant strokes. He lacked Liddy's fondness for sneakiness, which McCord and Hunt, from their spy work, not only shared but exacerbated. Dean was only a technician, a situational improviser, of no ethics at all, who excelled chiefly in the taking of inventories and the gimlet-eyed, passionless evaluation of options. He did not get a lot of guidance from his clients, who gave him their problems only because they themselves could think of nothing to solve them, and thus designed to be rid of them. He was delegated the task of solving the insoluble, and they did not give him any help.

He was forced back upon his intuition. It wasn't bad. It was nowhere near good enough, but it wasn't bad. Short of bright ideas himself, he'd been expert in the recognition of bright ideas divulged by others. What he had needed, for the satisfaction of Ehrlichman, Haldeman and the President in the week after the burglars were caught, was something that would divert the FBI. He got it from Pat Gray on June 21 and 22, 1973: the Gray theory of the investigation, which included the materials for the CIA smokescreen. But that was blown away, by people who wanted things in writing; and Dean was reduced to seeking guidance. The people he sought it from, couldn't give it.

On June 23, Dean said, he "reported my conversation with Gray, of the preceding evening, to Haldeman and Ehrlichman. We discussed the

Dahlberg and the Mexican checks, and the fact that the FBI was looking for answers regarding these checks. I had the impression that either Haldeman or Ehrlichman might have had a conversation with someone else about this matter, but this was mere speculation on my part at that time.

"Within the first days of my involvement in the cover-up," Dean said, "a pattern had developed, where I was carrying messages from Mitchell, Stans, and Mardian, to Ehrlichman and Haldeman — and vice versa — about how each quarter was handling the cover-up, and relevant information as to what was occurring. I was also reporting to them all the information I was receiving about the case from the Justice Department and the FBI. I checked with Haldeman and Ehrlichman before I did anything."

President Nixon had three meetings with Haldeman on the twenty-third of June. They included these discussions:

"Now," Haldeman said, "on the investigation. You know, the Democratic break-in thing. We're back in the problem area because the FBI is not under control. Because Gray doesn't exactly know how to control it, and they have, their investigation is now leading into some productive areas. Because they've been able to trace the money. Not through the money itself, but through bank sources, the banker. And, and it goes in some directions we don't want it to go. Ah, also, there have been some things, like an informant came in off the street to the FBI in Miami, who was a photographer, or has a friend who is a photographer, who developed some films for this guy Barker, and the films had pictures of Democratic National Committee letterhead documents and things. So, it's things like that that are filtering in. Mitchell came up yesterday," Haldeman said, "*and John Dean analyzed very carefully, last night, and now concludes, concurs now with Mitchell's recommendation, that the only way to solve this, and we're set up beautifully to do it*, ah, in that, and that, the only network that paid any attention to it last night was NBC. They did a massive story on the Cuban thing."

"That's right," said the President of the United States.

"That's the way to handle this now," Haldeman said, "is for us to have [General Vernon A.] Walters [of the Central Intelligence Agency] call Pat Gray and just say: 'Stay the hell out of this. This is, ah, business, here. We don't want you to go any further on it.' That's not an unusual development, and, ah, that would take care of it."

"What about Pat Gray?" the President said, not realizing that Pat Gray had unwittingly suggested the whole idea to Dean on the twenty-second. "You mean Pat Gray doesn't want to?"

"Pat does want to," Haldeman said, meaning, does want to conduct his usual thorough and complete investigation, but he's so damned stupid he's telling Dean, without meaning to, how we can obstruct that investigation. "He doesn't know how to," Haldeman said, which was perhaps the most mordant comment anyone was to make about Pat Gray's leadership of the FBI that anyone in a position to know ever made. "And he doesn't have, he doesn't have any basis for doing it. Given this, he will then have the basis. He'll call Mark Felt in, and the two of them — Mark Felt wants to cooperate because he's ambitious. . . ." Haldeman didn't know much about Mark Felt, either: Mark Felt knows more reporters than most reporters do, and there are those who think he had a *Washington Post* alias borrowed from a dirty movie.

"Yeah," the President said.

"He'll call him in," Haldeman said, "and say: 'We've got this signal from across the river,' " meaning Langley, Virginia, where the CIA hangs out, " 'to put the hold on this.' *And that will fit rather well, because the FBI agents who are working the case, at this point, feel that's what it is.*"

Haldeman, being the journeyman liar that he was, declared to the Ervin Committee his "full confidence that when the entire truth is known, it will be clear to the American people that President Nixon had no knowledge of or involvement in the Watergate affair itself or the subsequent efforts of a 'cover-up' of the Watergate. It will be equally clear," he continued, "despite all the unfounded allegations to the contrary, that I had no such knowledge or involvement." That left the allegations with foundation, which were many.

"This is CIA?" the President said. "They've traced the money? Who'd they trace it to?"

"Well," Haldeman said, "they've traced it to a name. But they haven't gotten to the guy yet."

"Would it be somebody here?" the President said.

"Ken Dahlberg," Haldeman said.

"Who the hell is Ken Dahlberg?" the President said.

"He gave $25,000 in Minnesota," Haldeman said, thus providing a lesson of potential instructiveness to fat cats dreaming of lasting remembrance from politicians to whom they give $25,000: it was Andreas who was from Minnesota. "And, ah, the check went directly to this guy Barker."

"It wasn't from the Committee, though," the President said, "from Stans?"

"Yeah," Haldeman said, "it is. It's directly traceable, and there's some more, through some Texas people, that went to a Mexican bank, which can also be traced to the Mexican bank. They'll get their names today. And. . . ."

"Well," the President said, "I mean, there's no way. I'm just thinking: if they don't cooperate" — which will sink us pretty good, Harry Bob, if they decide to — "what do they say?" Or: we'd better think of something for them to say. "That they were approached by the Cubans," the President said, having thought of something for the Dahlbergs of this world to say. "That's what Dahlberg has to say. The Texans, too." In other words, they have to lie. "That they. . . ."

"Well," Haldeman said, "if they will. But then we're relying on more and more people all the time." You might find yourself with a weak sister in there. "That's the problem. And they'll [the FBI] stop, if we could take this other route." Much more economical. Instead of dragooning a whole bunch of unskilled fellows to lie to the cops, and thus render the investigation fruitless, get a few spooks to lie to the cops, and thus abort the investigation. Pat Gray really had some great ideas, and since he was Acting top cop, his ideas received a very respectful hearing. Much more respectful than he knew.

"All right," the President said on June 23, 1972. On August 29 he said to the nation: "What really hurts is if you try to cover it up." On October 15, 1972, he had some further pieties for us: "I agreed with the amount of effort that was put into it" — the FBI investigation. "I wanted every lead carried out to the end, because I wanted to be sure that no member of the White House staff, and no man or woman in a position of major responsibility in the Committee for the Re-election had anything to do with this kind of reprehensible activity." What bullshit.

"And you seem to think," Haldeman said, less than a week after the burglars were arrested, "the thing to do is get them [the FBI] to stop?"

"Right," said the President of the United States. "Fine."

Now Haldeman had the tough one. "They say the only way to do that is from White House instructions. And it's got to be to Helms. And to, ah, what's his name?" Beware of Presidents and their assistants bearing requests for favors dangerous to grant: most of the time they can't remember your name. "Walters."

"Walters," the President said.

"And the proposal," Haldeman said, "would be that Ehrlichman and I call them in, and say, ah. . . ."

That proposal had to come from Dean. He reported to Ehrlichman. It was Ehrlichman who got him cracking on the case. It was Ehrlichman who had obtained CIA assistance for Hunt some time back, when what was wanted was merely a red wig and some stuff.

"Remember," Ehrlichman, also a journeyman liar, instructed the Ervin Committee, "Dean testified that keeping Watergate covered up was a tremendous drain of my time and told of all the conferences and meetings I was having with him about it. Let's be clear: I did not cover up anything to do with Watergate. Nor were Mr. Dean and I keeping steady company during all those weeks."

"All right," the President said. "Fine. How do you call him in? I mean, you just. . . . Well, we protected Helms from one hell of a lot of things."

Damned right. Of course he got protected for doing those things for the United States of America, but the USA that he did it for was LBJ, and RMN, and when the Congress started to get curious about it, the Nixon Administration had covered his ass for him. So there's another lesson for people who go to work for governments, and find themselves directed to do things that they don't really think are quite kosher: instead of getting to assert the Nuremberg defense of following orders, which won't work, by the way, you're likely to end up finding yourself obliged to do further dirty tricks, in restitution for being protected from being found out in the commission of previous dirty tricks performed in behalf of your obligees.

"That's what Ehrlichman says," Haldeman said. Ehrlichman would scarcely have said that if he hadn't been keeping some kind of company with Dean; there would have been no reason to.

"Of course," the President said, "this Hunt. That will uncover a lot of things. You open that scab, there's just a hell of a lot of things. 'And we just feel that it would be very detrimental [to us] to have this thing go any further. This involves these Cubans, Hunt, and a lot of hanky-panky that we have nothing to do with ourselves.' Well, what the hell, did Mitchell know about this?"

"The President," Haldeman told the Committee, "and all of us at the White House, were determined that the campaign organization and operation should be set up outside the White House, and this was the reason for the development of the Committee to Re-Elect the President. The Committee operated autonomously under the direction of John

Mitchell and later Clark MacGregor, but, of course, with close liaison and communications with the White House at many levels.

"The President looked to me as *his* basic contact with the campaign organization, and I maintained communication with John Mitchell in this regard until July 1972, and then with Clark MacGregor."

"Now," Dash said to Mitchell. "I think you have indicated that Mr. Haldeman also played a role in both the creation of the Committee to Re-Elect the President and the selection of personnel. What was the relationship between you and Mr. Haldeman in the operation of the committee?"

"Well," Mitchell said, "it was one of liaison, I would think, at the highest level, in which he, of course, would be representing the President and interest of the President in connection with the campaign, and that most major decisions were discussed with Mr. Haldeman and/or the President, and I say: very major decisions." The problem of controlling the Hunts and Liddys was a negative one: it was not done, because no one had perceived it as needful of doing. The cover-up was urgently needed, once Hunt and Liddy spun out of control. That *was* a very major decision.

Dean had reported to Ehrlichman on the afternoon of June 19. "He just gave me a rundown of the identity of the individuals," Ehrlichman told the Committee. "He told me that he had talked to Liddy. That Liddy had told him that it was his operation, in effect, that he, Liddy, was involved, but that nobody at the White House was involved."

"I think so," Haldeman told the President on the twenty-third. "I don't think he [Mitchell] knew the details, but I think he knew."

"He didn't know how it was going to be handled, though?" the President said. "With Dahlberg and the Texans and so forth? Well, who was the asshole that did it? Is it Liddy? Is that the fellow? He must be a little nuts."

"He is," Haldeman said.

And there it was. There was a place where two paths diverged in a wood. Nothing had been done, that could not be undone. There was more than a week before Baldwin would lose his nerve outside Earl Silbert's office, and tip Liddy in. The President, unless he was much more mindful of his taping machines than he appeared to be, plainly had not known in advance of the break-in. Not the one that was causing all the trouble, at least. To that point, he had not done anything that anyone could hang on him, disastrously, like the albatross on the ancient mariner, to deprive him of 895 days of his tenure as President of the United States. There was his opportunity, to rid himself of the onus of "a third-rate burglary." All he had to do was call Ron Ziegler in, and tell him that he wanted a press conference. All he had to tell the reporters was that a nutcake, whose name he was providing to Earl Silbert, had gone off on a frolic of his own, and that some of his people on CREEP had failed to watch the fellow carefully enough. That was all he had to do. And that would have removed the necessity for Dean to take on-the-job training in obstruction of justice.

"I mean," the President said, "he just isn't well screwed on, is he? Is that the problem?"

That was the problem, but it was the problem as it then existed. If you work hard enough, you can transform any problem into a calamity.

"No," Haldeman said. "But he was under pressure, apparently, to get more information. And as he got more pressure, he pushed the people harder, to move harder. . . ."

"Pressure from Mitchell?" the President said.

"Apparently," Haldeman said.

"Oh," the President said, experienced with Mitchell's loyalty, "Mitchell. Mitchell was at the point [unintelligible]. . . ."

"Yeah," Haldeman said. Okay, throw Mitchell in. Right now.

"All right," the President said, "fine. I understand it all. We won't second-guess Mitchell and the rest. Thank God it wasn't Colson." Nothing doing.

"The FBI interviewed Colson yesterday," Haldeman said. "They determined that it would be a good thing to do."

Colson had sedulously cultivated the "bad guy" image for himself in the Administration. He worked hard and he succeeded. That cost him jail: he got one to three and served a lot of it, for having nothing to do with Watergate, the cover-up of Watergate, the Ellsberg burglary, the President's tax returns, the Cambodian bombing orders, the impoundment of congressionally appropriated funds, the approaches the Judge Matt Byrne in the *Ellsberg* case, or anything else. Chuck Colson is a tough son of a bitch, but doing time for talking tough (he said he'd run over his grandmother if Dick Nixon asked) is a pretty heavy remonstrance; Humphrey Bogart would've gone away forever. Judge Gerhard Gesell, sentencing Colson for intending to defame Ellsberg so as to make it more likely that Ellsberg would be convicted — Colson never actually did it; he pleaded to intending to do it — was altogether too responsive to the Sirica sentencing model: he thought the public expected Colson to go to jail, and so he put the man in jail.

"To have him [Colson] take an interrogation," Haldeman said, "which he did. And that, the FBI guys working the case concluded that there were one or two possibilities: one, that this was a White House. . . . They don't think that there is anything at the election committee." Where most of it was, but the President and Haldeman, because they were being remarkably stupid, were importing it to 1600 Pennsylvania Avenue, Northwest, just about as fast as they could. "They think it was either a White House operation, and they had some obscure reasons for it, non-political. Or else it was a, Cuban and the CIA. And after their interrogation of Colson yesterday, they concluded it was not the White House, but are now convinced it is a CIA thing. So the CIA turnoff would. . . ."

There wasn't any need for a turnoff. There was a positive, pressing need, that no turnoff be attempted.

"Well," the President said, "not sure of their analysis, I'm not going to get that involved."

They called it *deniability*.

"No, sir," Haldeman said. "We don't want you to."

"You call them in," the President said.

"Good deal," Haldeman said.

"Play it tough," the President said. "That's the way they play it, and that's the way we are going to play it."

John Dean had a pedestrian mind, but his was better than the minds of those to whom he gave advice. Good enough to come close to saving him, at least, when, in their desperation, they designed to throw him to the wolves; as an hors d'oeuvre, the President would call him, to keep the investigation from the main course.

# 15

TRUSTING DEAN WAS easy, if you needed something done and wanted somebody who was competent, industrious and efficient to do it, without raising a lot of irksome questions about the legality of what you wanted done. But it was also risky, because a man like that can be fairly cold-blooded, likely to reserve some of his identity, and thus to demarcate a point beyond which he will not go. And then keep it to himself. Unlike Magruder, who was thoroughly stupid, or Mitchell, who kept nothing back, or Haldeman or Ehrlichman, who saw no need to keep anything back, Dean had taken lessons from Br'er Fox, and knew how to lie low, and when to do it. McCord worried Dean. That was not an act of circumspection for McCord.

In the summer of 1973, Karla Hennings, Dean's ex-wife, daughter of the late Senator Thomas Hennings of Missouri, professed to the *Washington Star* no particular astonishment that her former husband was acquitting himself so well before the Ervin Committee. Dean had many good qualities, she said, among them his paternal attentiveness to their son: he had visited the kid at Christmas, she said, and called him around Easter. She thought it was Easter anyway.

That aspect of his character eluded the President. The President was used to dealing with Haldeman, who would do anything he said, promptly, and some things he hadn't said because he hadn't thought of them, with equal promptitude. The President subsided gratefully into the cocoon of Haldeman's autocratic, manipulative, servile protectiveness, and he luxuriated also in Ehrlichman's ministrations. They, and Ziegler, absorbed the buffets of an exasperated press, a restive Congress and a potentially mutinous bureaucracy, leaving him at liberty to think about large matters, like the People's Republic of China, and how Kissinger — who insulated him, in similar fashion, from difficult visitors from foreign lands, and the Middle East and Southeast Asian wars — was doing. The President tended to lump Dean in with the rest of them.

That was a mistake. Though Counsel to the President, Dean lacked that daily access to the Oval Office which contented Haldeman and Ehrlichman in their roles, because they saw themselves, in part, correctly, as surrogate Presidents. Dean had a nice title for a lawyer in his early thirties, but he was still an errand boy, drafting estate plans for the President, seeing him very seldom, spending a lot of time on the phone with his broker, disdaining a White House car and driving in to work in his maroon 911 Porsche. The very quality which made him so useful to the cover-up — his technical resourcefulness — in that situation militated against the development of strong personal loyalties, assuming that he had the capacity for them in the first place. So while he resembled, in appearance, those indistinguishable Junior Chamber of Commerce types who infested the Committee to Re-elect, and survived on the fact that they were working for the President (without any urgent need to have direct, personal contact with the true anointed one), he was not like them in fact. He was strictly a mercenary, an apprentice mechanic who would do the best he could to make the system malfunction as desired.

In that respect, he was unique in the Nixon White House. Haldeman and Ehrlichman were ideologues: to them, Mr. Nixon was "the body" that could gain the presidency for their uses in 1968. For Mitchell, Mr. Nixon was a cause. For Dean, he was an employer. Period.

He was just as cold-blooded about the other people that he encountered, whether they were his clients (who had problems) or third parties (who could make problems for his clients). One of the third parties was Jim McCord. By January of 1973, McCord had become a big pain in the ass for Dean, and he commenced cutting the guy loose. He used Caulfield for that, too. Without telling him, of course.

John J. Caulfield, having a good deal in common with Dean, should have known better. He, too, was a man after the main chance. But he lacked Dean's precision of judgment. So Dean got away with using him.

McCord knew, when they did it, that Porter and Magruder had perjured themselves. The college students were phantoms. Liddy, the stand-up guy, was tolerant of any self-protective measures which might appeal to his nervous superiors. But McCord sat there on January 23, 1973, and listened to Magruder and Porter lie, and he was furious.

In a declining mood, by October 1972 — unknown, of course, to Silbert — McCord was thrust by circumstances into a renewal of the relationship that had brought him to his sorry estate. "Conversations with Mr. Hunt began, to the best of my recollection, in late September or early October 1972, when I was seeing him at the courthouse on various pretrial exercises or events, motions, that were transpiring, in which we would talk about various matters, including the situation that we were in, what the trial appeared to be at that point in time, that is: what the future looked like for us, and in telephone conversations, with him to me. In other words, both in person and by telephone, Mr. Hunt stated that the defendants were going to be provided with, given, executive clemency, after a period of time in prison, if interested, if they would plead guilty, and were sentenced, in a plea of not guilty. That they were going to be given financial support while they were in prison, that is: their families would be. And that rehabilitation, not specified, but rehabilitation, perhaps a job, would be provided for the men after the release from prison."

Hunt, in September and October, presumably partook of his lawyer's fair confidence that the evidence against him was going to be suppressed anyway, because tainted by its source in Hunt's notebooks. Before the Committee, at any rate, he told Senator Gurney he was never promised executive clemency by anyone, which would imply that he did not in turn relay such a promise to any of his codefendants.

McCord was not elated by Hunt's assurances. If Hunt, in fact, made them. He commenced a rather pitiable struggle to extricate himself from the bind which had claimed him, despite the best efforts of Alch and Caulfield to the contrary. He made a couple of telephone calls.

"In September of 1972, the indictments came out and no one was being indicted among the higher-ups," McCord told the Committee, "so this looked like a further cover-up to me. Also in September and October of 1972, there began to be a series of telephone anomalies on my phone, that indicated to me that the phone had been tapped. Further, I had read in August, 1972, in *Newsweek* magazine, I believe, that Ellsberg had tried for five months to get the Government to admit to wiretapping of his phone calls, and those of his attorney, and the Government denied such calls until a court order forced a search of 12 separate law enforcement agencies and turned up telephone interception of Leonard Boudin's calls to the Chilean Embassy. I knew that the Government had also lied about wiretapping in the *Coplon* case and in the *Hoffa* case for several weeks until disclosure was forced upon them. In an effort to test the truthfulness of the Government on a forthcoming motion for disclosure of wiretapping of the defendants' phones in the Watergate case, including my own, I made two calls in September and October, 1972, to two local embassies. On October 10, 1972, I asked for the filing of a motion for Government disclosure of any interceptions, and two weeks later the Government came back with a denial of any, saying a search of Government records had been made. I knew two weeks was too short a time to search 12 different Government agencies for such records, and believed the Government was not telling the truth."

McCord probably had some inkling of what Bittman expected to accomplish for Hunt. "Mr. McCord," Alch said, "advised that he had made telephone calls to the Israeli Embassy on September 19, 1972, and to the Chilean Embassy on October 10, 1972. He did not divulge the contents of these telephone conversations. He explained his purpose as follows: He told me he was convinced that the Government had telephone taps on the phones of those embassies, but would not admit to such activity. He was certain that his calls had been intercepted. He instructed that I make a motion in court requiring the Government to disclose any and all intercepted communications in which he was involved. His theory was that the Government, rather than reveal such activity, would dismiss the case against him."

On the evening of January 12, 1972, eleven days before Magruder and Porter took the stand, two days into the trial and Hunt gone from the case on his guilty plea, McCord met Caulfield ("Watson") at the second overlook on the George Washington Parkway. McCord was very edgy, and Caulfield was a little jumpy, too (even though he had arranged the meeting, through Ulasewicz), and with excellent reason.

"Mr. McCord then said words to the effect: 'Jack, I am different from all the others. Anybody who knew me at the CIA knows that I always follow my own independent course,'" Caulfield said. "'I have always followed the rule that if one goes,' I took this to mean: going to jail, 'all who are involved must go. People who I am sure are involved are sitting outside with their families. I saw a picture in the newspaper of some guy who I am sure was involved, sitting with his family.'" That was Magruder. " 'I can take care of my family. I don't need any jobs. I want my freedom.'

"I stated," Caulfield said, "that I was only delivering a message, and had nothing to do with its formulation, or had no control over what was being done. I sympathized with Mr. McCord's situation and made remarks, such as: 'I can't understand how all this happened. I'd give anything if I had not recommended you for your two jobs with the Republican Party.' I did try to impress upon Mr. McCord that I was simply a messenger, and was not too pleased to be even doing that. I did say that the people who had asked me to convey the message had always been honorable toward me, and that I thought it was a sincere offer. He asked me who I was speaking with at the White House" — it was Dean — "and I said I could not reveal any names, but that they were from the 'highest level of the White House.' He continually said that all he was interested in was his freedom, and he was not pleased that others who he felt had been involved were not suffering the consequences that he was. In the context of demanding his immediate freedom, he said that he knew of a way in which his freedom could be obtained, and asked me if I could convey his plan to the people at the White House with whom I was talking.

". . . Mr. McCord and his attorneys would make a motion in court, aimed at dismissing the case against Mr. McCord because of the use of wiretap evidence by the prosecution."

The prosecution wasn't using any wiretap evidence, because Silbert didn't have any, just as he had no access to Hunt's Hermès notebooks. McCord, one of the few tangled up in Watergate who was not a lawyer, was hustling around in the law, and botching it up. The lawyers, to be sure, were not doing noticeably better.

"Mr. McCord's idea," Caulfield said, "was that when the U.S. Attorney was told that at least two of Mr. McCord's conversations had been intercepted over a national security wiretap, he would be forced to dismiss the case rather than reveal that the two embassies in question were the subject of national security wiretaps.

"Mr. McCord," Caulfield told the Committee, "was quite adamant in saying that he was sure the Government could secure his immediate release, if they wanted to help him, and, other than the publicity incumbent upon the Government for being forced to dismiss the case against him, such an approval would save the Administration any real embarrassment. He gave me a note with the dates of the two conversations that he referred to, and told me that he knew this kind of thing had been done before, most recently in the *Ellsberg* case, and that he saw no reason why the Government could not at least accomplish this for him. I told Mr. McCord that I would get back to him on the wiretap situation, and would probably be calling him in a day or two to set this up. I agreed to carry the message to the White House, and the meeting ended."

McCord had seriously miscontrued the import of Watson's surreptitious ministrations. He received them as evidence that the White House was fretful about him, and would be thus submissive to threats. He conveyed his threats, and Caulfield remained solicitous; McCord thereupon concluded that he had extorted a guarantee of salvation. When salvation did not quickly materialize, he reasoned that his hapless allies simply did not know what to do, in order to reach their common objective of saving McCord. Thus he sought to nudge things along with his telephone, patiently contriving the circumstances which would relieve everyone's mind by affording the Administration a way to get him out of things with minimal embarrassment. McCord thought Watson's contact at the White House, and Silbert in the U.S. Attorney's Office, and, for that matter, Lano at the FBI, probably were secretly on his side, and needed only a modest pretext to fulfill his wishes.

"During this meeting with Caulfield," Dean said, "I received a call from either John Mitchell or Paul O'Brien, requesting a report on the meeting. I told the caller that I was getting a report from Caulfield and would call back. Caulfield told me that McCord was very adamant about his plans to gain his freedom through the phone calls that he had made to the foreign embassies. I told Caulfield I really did not understand why McCord thought he could get his case dismissed by reason of the wiretaps, but I would give the matter some thought." He told Caulfield to see McCord again "and keep him happy by telling him we were checking out the matter of his conversations with the embassies. Later that afternoon, Caulfield reported again to me that McCord was only interested in his theory about the calls to the embassies. I told Caulfield to keep in touch with McCord, but I couldn't promise anything about his calling the embassies. I told Caulfield to have McCord give him a memo on why he thought that his calls to the embassies would result in dismissal of his case. I called O'Brien and told him what had transpired. On Monday morning, I reported to Mitchell what Caulfield had reported."

McCord's memo got to Dean about a week later. The trial was still in

137

progress before Sirica, and McCord was desperately pressing Caulfield. Of McCord's memo, Dean said: "I never did anything with these documents, other than inform Mitchell I had received them, and I showed them to Mr. O'Brien in my office. I do not recall ever talking with anyone at the Department of Justice regarding McCord's proposal. At this time I concluded that McCord was going to do what he thought best for himself."

McCord had not quite reached that decision, but he was on his way to it. Each day he had to get out of bed and go down to court and sit there with Liddy and wait for help that never came, and at last he understood that he'd been wrong to think that Watson's people were on his side. They had not been cordial to him because they were intent upon saving his hide; they stroked him only in order to save themselves. They wanted McCord to keep still and go to jail.

He sat there in the courtroom and he watched Silbert methodically nailing the box shut, with him in it, and he raged. Silbert was another guy who wanted McCord in jail. Missing entirely from their acquaintance was the odd camaraderie that commences when the defendant's initial hostility erodes under recognition that the prosecutor is only a professional, doing a job, but acting fairly, with no personal animosity toward the defendant. Nor was there any possibility that such relaxation would occur, thus increasing the likelihood that McCord, coming to trust Silbert, would throw in the towel and see what could be done for him. Silbert and Glanzer had demolished that prospect by offering to put McCord's wife in jail too. McCord, hard up for friends, did not essay to make new ones in the U.S. Attorney's Office.

"On or about October twenty-fifth, 1972," Alch said, "the Government conveyed to local counsel, my local counsel, Bernard Shankman of Washington, and my associate, Mr. Johnson, an offer to accept from Mr. McCord a plea of guilty to one substantive count of the indictment, and in return for his testimony as a Government witness, a recommendation of leniency would be made to the court. The Government indicated, however, that it could not and would not recommend any type of sentence which would allow Mr. McCord to remain at liberty. This offer was transmitted to Mr. McCord," who was troubled by what he found in *Newsweek* about nominees for ringleader, "and was unequivocally rejected.

"In November of 1972," Alch said, "a second plea offer was received from the prosecutors. At this time, the offer was essentially similar to the

138

first offer, except that Mr. McCord would have to plead to three counts of the indictment instead of one. The explanation for this change of position was that the Government's case had grown considerably stronger."

The explanation for that was the Government's suspicion that a Mc-Cord without a prayer might have less motive for silence after his former employers had accomplished the reelection of the President than he had manifested before the election.

"This offer," Alch said, "which also involved Mr. McCord's testifying as a Government witness, was related to, and again rejected by, Mr. McCord."

And the explanation for that lay in the fact that the prosecutors were as little able to calculate accurately McCord's motives and intentions as Caulfield was.

Caulfield's obtuseness baffled McCord as thoroughly as McCord's erratic behavior perplexed Caulfield. He had been promoted in the NYPD in 1955, he said, "for the arrest and conviction of seven people involved in a series of robberies." In 1958, he received the "Meritorious Police Award, owing to the seizure of a store of contraband weapons destined for Ireland." In 1959, the "Excellent Police Award, for arrest and conviction, in cooperation with the FBI, of the prime Castro agent operating in the United States in 1958." In 1964, another "Meritorious Police Award, for the arrest of the perpetrators of the bazooka shelling of the United Nations," and in 1965, Caulfield had received "an award for participating in the arrest and conviction of a group of French Canadians and domestic militants who had plotted to destroy the Washington Monument, the Statue of Liberty, and the Liberty Bell." The *New York Times* could find no official record of these kudos. But Caulfield recognized obstruction of justice when he saw it, and it made him worry when he found himself engaged in it.

"In early January of 1973," Caulfield said, "I was attending a drug conference in San Clemente, California, when I received a telephone call in my hotel room from John Dean. He asked that I go outside the hotel and call him back from a public telephone, which I did. He told me that he had a very important message which he wanted me to deliver to James McCord, that Mr. McCord was expecting to hear from me and McCord would understand what the message referred to. He said the message consisted of three things: One. 'A year is a long time'; Two. 'Your wife and family will be taken care of'; Three. 'You will be rehabilitated with employment when this is over.' I immediately realized that I

*139*

was being asked to do a very dangerous thing, and I said to Mr. Dean that I did not think it was wise to send me on such a mission, since Mr. McCord knew, as many others did, that I worked closely with Mr. Dean and Mr. Ehrlichman at the White House, and therefore it might be quickly guessed that any messages I was conveying were probably from one of the two."

As, in fact, they were.

"The reason I raised this question with him was because, very frankly, I did not wish to convey the message. Mr. Dean asked if I could think of any other way to do it, and I suggested that perhaps I could get Mr. Ulasewicz to convey the message over the telephone anonymously, stating that message had come from me." Which, if the message were intercepted, would require the prosecutor to identify the messenger, and then prove he spoke for Caulfield, before the message could be used against Caulfield. "Mr. Dean felt this would be all right, so I hung up the telephone and called Mr. Ulasewicz in New York." Ulasewicz was a former cop, too. "He did not wish to convey the message at first, but I convinced him to do it merely as a matter of friendship to me.

"Mr. Ulasewicz called Mr. McCord's home," Caulfield said, "and, presumably, delivered the same message which Mr. Dean had given to me. He then called me back in California, and reported that he had delivered the message, and that Mr. McCord's attitude had been one of satisfaction. I was glad to hear this, since I had felt this probably meant that Mr. McCord had been in some stage of negotiation about his status" — or, in other words: I thought he might have been getting ready to make a deal with Silbert — "and that this message had probably relieved his mind." Meaning: it kept the fix in. "I called Mr. Dean and told him that the message had been delivered by Mr. Ulasewicz and that Mr. McCord seemed satisfied."

McCord was not satisfied. During November and December of 1972 he had become very grouchy, and had interpreted various developments as indicators that the White House had it in mind to blame the whole thing on the CIA. McCord did not like that; he was proud of his work with the CIA, and proud of that agency, too, sharing the same affection that Helms demonstrated, paralleling the esprit de corps of the Special Agents who resisted so effectively the efforts made to prostitute the Bureau.

"In two separate meetings in December, 1972," McCord told the Committee, "it was suggested that I use as my defense during the trial the false story that the operation was a CIA operation. I refused to do so."

Alch would angrily deny what came next. "The two December, 1972, meetings with me were on December twenty-first, 1972, and December twenty-sixth, 1972. Present at the first meeting with me at the Monocle Restaurant in Washington, D.C., were Gerald Alch and Bernard Shankman, my attorneys. Present at the second meeting was Gerald Alch, and the meeting was at his office in Boston, Massachusetts. Alch stated that he had just come from a meeting with William O. Bittman."

Bittman was the message center among defense counsel for Parkinson, O'Brien and Dean. He reported wavering defendants to CREEP and to Dean, and they dispatched money and promises, as seemed appropriate, to keep the boys quiet if not happy. It was that unprofessional servility, and not the pro forma presentation of Hunt's guilty plea, which earned, if that is the word, $156,000 for Mr. Bittman's firm.

"In the first meeting," McCord said, "Alch stated that he had just come from a meeting with William O. Bittman, attorney for E. Howard Hunt, and I received the impression in the discussion that followed that Alch was conveying an idea or request from Bittman."

Alch conceded that he talked to Bittman. "In December of 1972, I attended one of several meetings of defense counsel, the purpose of which was to discuss various aspects of trial strategy. I proceeded to explain the defense I was contemplating: duress. A discussion ensued, wherein some of the other defense attorneys reasoned that this 'security motive,' and by that they were referring to my contemplated defense of duress, based on what Mr. McCord had told me, would be applicable only to Mr. McCord, in view of his position as chief of security for the Committee to Re-elect the President. In the general discussion that followed, the question arose as to whether or not the CIA could have been involved."

That, in December, had to be smokescreening. According to Dean, Mardian conjured up the specter of the CIA on June twenty-third or twenty-fourth, Gray, to better effect, on the twenty-first. Ehrlichman anointed the idea on the twenty-sixth, and Generals Vernon A. Walters and Robert E. Cushman, backed by Helms, knocked it down on June twenty-eighth.

"On the morning of June twenty-eighth," Dean said, "I arranged again to meet with General Walters. I was first embarrassed about requesting the meeting, because he had been most explicit and convincing to me at the first meeting."

That was on the afternoon of June 26, when Walters told Dean that

Helms would camouflage Liddy and the rest "only on a direct order from the President." Ehrlichman, Dean said, received this intelligence with the observation: "Very interesting," and told Dean to "push a little harder to see if the CIA couldn't help out." Dean said he didn't push; the Agency's stubbornness, tardy as it was, stuck. But that did not preclude defense counsel, six months later, from toying with the possibility of befuddling the *Liddy* trial jury with dark hints that the CIA had dispatched McCord, Barker, Martinez, Gonzalez and Sturgis to bug Larry O'Brien's phone and take pictures of his files; in trial law the maxim is: when the law's against you, argue the facts; when the facts're against you, argue the law; when the law and the facts're against you, hammer the table.

Alch didn't put the issue of the December meeting quite precisely; it was not "whether or not the CIA could have been involved"; it was whether there was any CIA dust around, that the defendants could tramp up to make it look like the Agency was messing around in domestic politics in the same purposive fashion that it fooled around in foreign politics.

"It was pointed out," Alch said, resorting to the passive voice again, which left unidentified the pointer-outer, and the Committee let him get away with it, again, "by others, and I emphasize *by others* because at this point my defense of Mr. McCord had been formulated based upon what he had told me, and with his concurrence, it was pointed out by others that all of the individuals apprehended in the Watergate complex had some prior connection with the CIA, and that one of the Cuban Americans had been in possession of what appeared to be CIA-forged documents."

Those were the papers that Hunt wheedled out of Walters, some for Liddy ("George Leonard") and some for himself, and some for the other guys.

"Before the meeting went on to other topics," Alch said, "it was agreed that each lawyer would ask his respective client whether or not he had any knowledge of any CIA involvement," which meant: can we fly this thing?

"There followed," McCord said, and by December of 1972 he was very tense, "a suggestion from Alch that I use as my defense during the trial the story that the Watergate operation was a CIA operation. I heard him out on the suggestion, which included questions as to whether I could ostensibly have been recalled from retirement to the CIA to participate in the operation. He said that if so, my personnel records at CIA could be doctored to reflect such a recall. He stated that Schlesinger, the new Director of CIA, whose appointment had just been announced, 'could be subpoenaed, and would go along with it.' I had noted in the newspapers of that day, December 21, 1972, that it had been announced by the White House that Mr. Schlesinger had taken over as Director of CIA, and that it had been decided that Pat Gray would be supported by the White House to be permanent Director of the FBI."

Helms told the Committee he felt the CIA had been used, and explained that he gracefully accepted the appointment as Ambassador to Iran, in November of 1972, because the White House had made it perfectly clear that his services at CIA were no longer required.

A lot happened to McCord between that quick lunch on December 21, 1972, and his public discussions with the Committee, commencing May 18, 1973. Most of those events conduced to the sense of isolation experienced by convicted defendants; McCord felt himself abandoned by men whom he had thought at least obliged by circumstances, if not by morality, to rescue him.

The usual concomitant of that reaction, limited in ordinary cases to the despairing belief that the defense lawyer, before trial, vastly overstated his capabilities, is the compensating effort to preserve one's dignity by constructing a self-image of martyrdom. It is as common among convicted loansharks as it is among convicted embezzlers, and it is expressed in woeful declarations that the true story was never told at trial, that the defendant was misunderstood, and that his character, notwithstanding the stain of conviction, remains pristine.

Dealing with a convicted felon, out to make some repairs to his life by regurgitating in the direction of his former associates, still at liberty, the prosecutor is first constrained to dissipate the messianic fog which the newly talkative convict has conjured up around his wounded pride, lest the jury sitting on the cases of his confreres translate disgust for his posturings (perceived as the results of hypocrisy, and not as reactions to devastating psychological damage) into disbelief of his evidence.

Nobody on the Committee appears to have shouldered that stern duty vis-à-vis McCord; if anyone did, the curative instructions did not take. He wanted only a crown of thorns and a cumbersome crucifix to complete his costume when he testified, and, if Alch was telling the truth (startled as *he* had been, in the midst of a Florida vacation, to switch on the television in the motel room and find his professional reputation under vigorous attack before the whole country), he had developed from

*143*

his broodings the vengeful sentiment requisite to justify in testimony certain adjustments of the facts.

It was the existence of those adjustments, asserted by Alch, which occupied both the Committee and the press, and not the relative significance of the alleged adjustments. Each of the Senators was a lawyer, and the Committee was surrounded by lawyers, and Alch is a lawyer, and all of them, by osmosis if not by actual courtroom experience, tended to indulge themselves in uncritical action upon the law's axiom: *falsus in unum, falsus in omnia*. Lawyers and leakers for the White House seized upon that same principle, which determines many a trial in a court of law, to support the position that McCord was a liar from start to finish.

The trouble is that a demonstration of falsity in the witness's assertion of Fact No. 5 is not, per se, ineluctable proof that he also lied in asserting Facts 1 through 4, and 6 through 10. The suspicion of a propensity to fabricate important stuff is legitimately indulged, perhaps, in a criminal case, where the American criminal justice system demands virtual certainty — proof beyond a reasonable doubt — of every material fact, when the witness is caught in the misrepresentation of a minor matter. Liars, after all, are abroad in the land, and must be treated skeptically when a man's life, liberty, property and reputation hang in the balance.

But there remains the possibility, though hazardous for consideration by a trial judge, that the witness was selective in his improvements of the truth, and that much of what he said was true. And there persist the complementary possibilities that the witness was mistaken when he declared a falsehood, believing it true, or self-deceived when he spoke deceitfully, and himself credited the falsehood that he uttered.

"I did not see or hear from Mr. McCord again," Caulfield said, "until I received an anonymous letter at my home in December of 1972. It was typewritten, a note approximately two paragraphs in length and, to the best of my knowledge, said:

" 'Dear Jack —

" 'I am sorry to have to tell you this, but the White House is bent on having the CIA take the blame for the Watergate.

" 'If they continue to pursue this course, every tree in the forest will fall, and it will be a scorched earth, Jack. Even you will be hurt in the fallout.'

"I examined the letter," Caulfield said, "and found that it was postmarked in Rockville, Maryland, and thereby believed that the letter was from James McCord, because he lived in Rockville. I called Mr. Dean's office and spoke with Mr. Fielding, an assistant to Mr. Dean, and read the letter over the telephone to him. Thereafter I went to Mr. Dean's office and gave him the letter."

"While I was in California," Dean said, "during the late December, early January, I referred to a moment ago, 1973, I received a call from Mr. Fielding, who told me that Jack Caulfield had received a letter from McCord. Fielding was not explicit regarding the contents of the letter, and said that he had taken down the letter and that I could read it when I returned in the next day or so to the office. I have submitted a copy of the letter, transcribed by Fielding, to the Committee."

McCord remembered the contents somewhat differently. He told the Committee, on May 22, that he wanted to add something to his second prepared statement. "A letter was written to John Caulfield during the week of December 25, 1972. Reference to it appeared in the press the last weekend. And geared, speaking of my own feelings, and at the time the letter was written, and geared because of what appeared to me to be a ruthless attempt by the White House to put the blame for the Watergate operation on CIA, where it did not belong, I sought to head it off by sending a letter to Caulfield. This letter was couched in strong language because it seemed to me at the time that this was the only language that the White House understood. The letter read in substance, to the best of my memory:

" 'Dear Jack: I am sorry to have to write you this letter. If Helms goes, and the Watergate operation is laid at CIA's feet, where it does not belong, every tree in the forest will fall. It will be a scorched desert. The whole matter is at the precipice right now. Pass the message, that if they want it to blow, they are on exactly the right course. I am sorry that you will get hurt in the fallout.'

"The letter was unsigned," McCord said, "and did not contain any message requesting any contact with Caulfield, nor any request for the White House to get me off in the case. I, in fact, sought no such contact at any time. If I had wanted to talk with Caulfield, it would not have been necessary to go through any complicated arrangements, and a trip to William Bittman's office as occurred on January 8, 1973. I need only have made a phone call to Caulfield's office or home. At no time did I ever initiate any such call to Caulfield."

To the Committee, McCord professed an integrity of purpose which to him plainly demanded corroboration by demonstrable consistency of action. McCord, in May, was a stool pigeon. It was not a comfortable role for him. He sought to stop the chafing by convincing himself, as much as anyone else, that he acted out of disinterested concern for a greater good. That was the unbesmirched reputation of the CIA, which he venerated for the same sort of reasons which prompted Helms, however tardily, and Hoover, however abrasively, to recoil from proposals which to them threatened the Agency and the Bureau. Pat Gray, as rueful as Dean on the bench outside Harbour Square Apartments about the loquacity of Special Agents, never comprehended that kind of reasoning. McCord, of course, did not act entirely out of chivalrous protectiveness of the Agency; he acted mostly to save Jim McCord. But he *was* protective of the Agency, and he warded off the subjective conception of himself as informer by attributing his actions to the existing motive of protectiveness.

"Now," McCord said, "the above letter to Caulfield brings to mind another set of communications of mine on December 6, 1972. On December 4, 1972, Judge Sirica had stated in open court that the jury, in January 1973, would want to know who had hired the men for the Watergate operation, and why. On December 6, 1972, the *Washington Star* carried an article which appeared to me to be an Administration-planted story, answering Judge Sirica's query, stating that 'Reliable sources state that McCord recruited the four Cubans and that they believed that they were working for the President on an extremely sensitive mission.' This was untrue. This appeared to me to be laying the groundwork for a false claim at the trial that I was the ringleader of the Watergate plot. This would draw attention away from Hunt and Liddy, and, I believe, possibly away from the White House, since both of them had formerly worked at the White House and I had not.

"That some evening," McCord said, "December 6, 1972, I sent telegrams to William O. Bittman, attorney for Hunt, and Bernard Barker's residence in Miami, Florida, stating that the story was untrue, as they both knew, and I asked for comments by return mail from Barker. I also wrote Hunt a letter on the matter, stating that, as he also knew, the story was untrue, and he could either correct it or I would do so."

Hunt was not about to do any such thing. His wife was four days away from death when McCord sent the letter, and Hunt was still of a mind to fight the case, an enterprise which would have been seriously compromised by a public disquisition by Hunt on the recruitment of Cubans for burglaries.

"With the letter to Caulfield in late December 1972," McCord said, "I was trying to head off an effort to falsely lay the Watergate operation off on CIA. In the telegrams and letter to Hunt and others in December 1972 that I have just referred to, I was trying to head off an effort to falsely lay the recruitment of the Cubans off on the writer, which would, in turn, shift the focus of the trial off of those formerly connected with the White House, namely: Liddy and Hunt, than from those who in effect actually recruited them, namely: Mr. Hunt."

Hunt's taciturnity, in December, apparently caught McCord by surprise. "In July 1972," McCord told the Committee, "Mrs. Hunt had told me that Paul O'Brien, attorney for CRP [CREEP], had told her husband that when the Watergate case broke in June, the Committee for the Re-election of the President told O'Brien that the Watergate operation was a CIA operation."

This was probably a ripple from the Dean-Walters meetings on June 26 and 28: Dean had reported the CIA's intransigence to Haldeman and Ehrlichman, and Dean was talking frequently with Parkinson and O'Brien. Dean had left the remnants of that plot in place, six months before, to precisely such purposes.

"She said," McCord said, "that Howard Hunt had exploded at this, and told O'Brien that this was not true. That it was not a CIA operation."

There was nothing in Hunt's testimony, before the Committee, to gainsay McCord, but neither was there anything to support it: Hunt said he had acted on the authority of the Attorney General of the United States, John N. Mitchell, or thought he had, anyway.

Inexperienced as they presumably were in the frustration of investigations, and the obstruction of justice, McCord's contacts might nevertheless have been understandably puzzled by his conduct. He accepted "salary," and he accepted attorneys' fees, under the table. He proposed shams to divert the orderly processes of justice, at least insofar as justice was processing him. He sneaked around, meeting Watson in wooded areas and speaking obliquely about bagging his case. He looked like the standard-issue, frightened felon. Yet he professed a great patriotism, which seriously cluttered the discussions, and while he wanted the case fixed, he wanted the truth told. In the Mob there is a variation, probably unwitting, of Napoleon's estimate of politicians who like omelets, but disapprove of the means of producing them: of spineless men, the gangsters say: "He couldn't break an egg." McCord is a complicated man, far more complex than Liddy, Hunt and the rest.

Of McCord's scorched-desert letter to Caulfield, Dean said: "I know that O'Brien and I discussed the matter, because he told me that McCord was not cooperating with his lawyer, Mr. Alch. O'Brien also told me that Bittman had planned a CIA defense to the case, but McCord, who had initially been willing to go along, later refused."

Dean said that on June 25, 1973, more than a month after McCord and Alch had protested, about each other, to the Committee. Dean was attentive to the newspapers; he said he had verified his chronologies by reference to newspaper articles. McCord and Alch did not escape media attention. Given McCord's frantic activity, between indictment and conviction, it is hard to fault a man who concluded that McCord might have indicated in 1972 a transient willingness to escape punishment by blaming the CIA. That would not have pretermitted McCord's valorous defense of the CIA in May of the following year.

"It was on January tenth," Dean said, "that I received calls from both O'Brien and Mitchell, indicating that since Hunt had been given assurances of clemency, and that those assurances were being passed by Hunt to the others, that Caulfield should give the same assurances to McCord, who was becoming an increasing problem, and again I was told that McCord's lawyer was having problems with him. Both O'Brien and Mitchell felt that McCord might be responsive to an assurance from Caulfield, because Hunt, Bittman, and his lawyer, Mr. Alch, had lost rapport with him. I told Mitchell I would do so."

That was the reason for Caulfield's meeting on January eleventh, at the second overlook. McCord, having watched Hunt cop out on the tenth, importuned Caulfield to see to his redemption by means of the calls to the Israeli and Chilean embassies.

"I called Mr. Dean on Friday night," Caulfield said, "January twelfth, and reported that Mr. McCord did not seem interested in accepting the offer made in Mr. Dean's original message to him: that Mr. McCord wanted his immediate freedom and that he, Mr. McCord, felt that he had a way to obtain that freedom. I then mentioned, over the telephone, McCord's idea for securing his freedom, because of the use of national security wiretaps, and said that I wished to discuss this matter with Dean.

"The following day," Caulfield said, "I saw Mr. Dean in his office at the White House" — that would have been Saturday — "and explained to him Mr. McCord's suggestion for obtaining his freedom, as Mr. McCord had explained it to me. Mr. Dean said: 'Well, I'll check on that.' He then turned the conversation back to the offer of executive clemency.

To the best of my knowledge, he said: 'Jack, I want you to go back to him, [McCord] and tell him that we are checking on the wiretaps. But this time impress upon him as fully as you can that this offer of executive clemency is a sincere offer which comes from the very highest levels of the White House.'

"I said," Caulfield said, " 'I have not used anybody's name with him. Do you want me to?' "

Not hardly. Dean had been a lawyer in the Department of Justice.

"He said," Caulfield said, " 'No, I don't want you to do that. But tell him that this comes from the very highest levels.'

"I said," Caulfield said, " 'Do you want me to tell him it comes from the President?' "

Caulfield, trapped by ambition into behavior which he preferred to think uncharacteristic of himself, was playing dumb, and very craftily, too. Dean was just as crafty.

"He said," Caulfield said, "words to the effect, 'No, don't do that. Say that it comes from way up at the top.' " Or: Are you out of your goddamned *mind*?

"I told Mr. Dean," Caulfield said, "I would get back to Mr. McCord. And that, indeed, I had told Mr. McCord that I would.

"At the meeting," Caulfield said, "with Mr. Dean, he also impressed upon me that this was a very grave situation which might someday threaten the President, that it had the potential of becoming a national scandal, and that many people in the White House were quite concerned over it. Mr. Dean said that none of the other then-defendants in the Watergate burglary 'were any problem,' and that Mr. McCord 'was not cooperating with his attorney.' " Which was right on both counts.

"I then called Mr. McCord," Caulfield said, "and arranged a meeting with him, again at the second overlook of the George Washington Parkway, early in the morning on Sunday, January fourteenth. On this occasion we both got out of our cars and walked down a path from the overlook toward the Potomac River.

"This meeting lasted only ten to fifteen minutes. I did most of the talking. I told Mr. McCord that the White House was checking into the wiretapping situation" — which, as Dean later testified, it was not — "and that I had been asked to impress upon him once again that the offer of executive clemency was a sincere and believable offer, coming from the very highest levels of the White House. I explained to him," Caulfield said, "that among the reasons why I believed that such a commitment would be kept were that the White House officials with whom I was in contact were extremely concerned about the Watergate burglary developing into a major scandal affecting the President, and that therefore such a promise would not be given lightly. I told him that the White House officials with whom I was talking were complaining, because they felt that Mr. McCord was the only one of the Watergate burglary defendants who was refusing to cooperate."

That was not strictly true; he was the only one who looked like he might cooperate, with the Government, but in this case, relationships were inverted.

Easy as he was to trust, Dean trusted no one else readily. By then he had calculated at zero the probable benefits of further negotiations with McCord. He did not delude himself about the risks attending such negotiations, and the dangers of proffering additional incentives to McCord for silence. He determined to relay no further demands from McCord, and he decided not to seek authority to respond to those demands. He turned to preparation of contingency plans, intended not to prevent the calamity of McCord upon the witness stand, but to mitigate the effect of his testimony upon the Administration. He undertook that task without much spirit, having calculated also that disaster could be averted only by means of a presidential bullet-biting as unlikely to occur as McCord's silence was to endure.

That did not mean that he intended actively to court the disaster. It was one thing to write McCord off; it would be quite another thing to dare McCord to talk. There remained, even after Magruder and Porter, with Sloan's reluctant support, had infuriated McCord, the remote possibility that McCord might for some eccentric motive — and McCord, in his declining state, had behaved somewhat oddly, in Dean's opinion — decide to persist in silence. Dean therefore omitted to inform Caulfield that McCord had been relegated to the Administration's trash. Caulfield, frantically juggling the sharp objects of his cop's ethics with the even sharper objects of his loyalties and ambitions, would have given anything to stop.

Dean danced him along to dodge immediate catastrophe: at worst, an angry Caulfield would advise his friend McCord that the Administration had abandoned him; at best, Caulfield with obvious relief would quit meeting McCord in wooded areas, or else conduct such meetings so desultorily that McCord would divine the fact of his loneliness. Dean had his faults, but he was not a poor tactician, and he knew when time could be bought. He had some reservations about the transactions, but he made them.

Caulfield thus continued on his fool's errands. Sirica, on Wednesday, January 24, recessed the trial until Friday, the twenty-sixth, in deference to the national day of mourning decreed for Lyndon B. Johnson. The Government's case was nearly complete; Silbert was piling up documentary evidence of Liddy's use of the Leonard alias, and with the agreement of Alch and Maroulis, reading, to the jury, gouts of stipulated facts: to save time in a protracted trial, the parties, heartily sick of the whole tiresome process, usually discover by the middle of the second week that they can join in a statement of what a cadre of minor witnesses would say, and set out to shorten things by reading the reports of that testimony instead of educing it on the stand.

McCord had been simmering since the night of the fifteenth, when from the phone booth on Route 355 he had told Caulfield that he had "no desire to talk further, that if the White House had any intention of playing the game straight, and giving us the semblance of a fair trial, they would check into the perjury charge of Magruder, and into the existence of the two intercepted calls previously referred to, and hung up." On the night of the sixteenth, McCord said, "Caulfield called and asked me again to meet him, and I responded: 'Not until they had something to talk about on the perjured testimony and the intercepted calls.' He said words to the effect: 'Give us a week,' and a meeting was subsequently arranged on January twenty-fifth, 1973, when he said he would have something to talk about."

Instructed by Dean to commiserate with McCord, Caulfield to the Committee exerted himself to present, in the best possible light, a clandestine meeting of a high Government official with a defendant reprieved for twenty-four hours from felony conviction on Government evidence. He commenced this effort by disremembering the date of the meeting, it being "unsure in my mind." This, he apparently hoped, would divert the Committee from pointed questions about the use of trial recesses to hush up defendants, and he was right: it did.

"We again met at the overlook on the George Washington Parkway," Caulfield said. "He got into my car and we drove out on the parkway, pursuing a course in the general direction of Warrenton, Virginia. I have no specific recollection as to how long we drove, but I would say it was an hour or two."

Each of them had done that sort of thing before, in the combined

*151*

course of more than forty years with the New York Police Department, the FBI and the CIA; the man working the case takes his own car to the rendezvous, and, because a long discussion of very sensitive matters is planned, gets the contact into that car and starts driving into remote areas. The man on the case knows his car is clear of bugs (unless he has bugged it himself), and the contact prefers the rolling interview because the risk of being spotted is reduced considerably.

That was the sort of expertise, perverted, which balked Silbert — spending the twenty-fifth in his office, taking inventory of the evidence, making sure he had left nothing out — in his efforts to crack the Watergate case by conventional methods of investigation: his ostensible allies were engaged in the employment of the same methods to shore it up.

"I would characterize this conversation as a very friendly one," Caulfield said, "in which a large portion of the time was spent discussing our respective families, how my job at the Treasury Department was going, and various other purely personal matters."

McCord's memory was not congruent to that. "About ten A.M. on Thursday, January twenty-fifth, 1973," he told the Committee, "in a meeting lasting until about twelve-thirty A.M., correction, twelve-thirty P.M., we drove in his car toward Warrenton, Virginia, and returned. That is, we drove there, and returned. And a conversation ensued, which repeated the offers of executive clemency, and financial support while in prison. And rehabilitation later. I refused to discuss it."

"I gave him my private telephone number at the Treasury Department," Caulfield said, "and told him that if he or his wife ever wanted me to do anything for them, they should feel free to call me."

McCord said he got that number back in July, when the feasibility of getting things done for him was considerably greater than it was on January 25.

"I told McCord," Caulfield said, "that if he or his wife should decide to call me, to simply use the name 'Watson.' And I would know who it was. Frankly, this was merely a device to save me from any possible embarrassment."

In Caulfield's version, then, he completed the arrangement of clandestine communication procedures with McCord at their very last clandestine meeting. McCord said he got the Watson password in their first conversation; it seems probable that Caulfield was at least as apprehensive of potential embarrassment when he set Ulasewicz to scurrying around Maryland, as he was when he went for a drive with McCord, and in fact he and McCord had managed to converse face to face, and by phone, for six months, without suffering the ignominy that might have resulted from careless meetings.

"I do not have a specific recollection as to how it arose," Caulfield told the Committee, "but I believe he asked me if he was still the only one of the Watergate defendants that the White House was concerned about."

Hunt had pleaded. The Cubans had pleaded. Liddy, stoic in the face of certain conviction, was the only other survivor. The Acting Director for Enforcement, AT&F, was setting up meetings with McCord, in the midst of his trial, completely innocent of the purpose of those meetings.

"I said," Caulfield said, "that I thought he was, but that I had no knowledge of what relationship existed between the White House and the other Watergate defendants. He said that the Cuban defendants were quite nervous and, in his opinion, might make a statement at any time, and that I 'could pass that along for whatever it was worth.' "

The Cubans had pleaded on January 11, fourteen days before, and Sirica had jugged them in high bail. Nowhere does anyone report that McCord was taking them cakes and ale in the slammer, or carrying on an affectionate correspondence elusive of the jailkeepers who read their mail for censoring.

"I told him," Caulfield said, "there was absolutely no hope, in my opinion, of the White House ever doing anything about the wiretap situation, and asked him when he thought he might make a statement. He said that he had not decided that yet, but that he had spoken to his wife and family, and that he felt free to make a statement whenever he thought the time was right.

"I again asked if there was anything I could do for him," Caulfield said, having painstakingly cultivated McCord's belief, for six months, that he *could* do something for him, without ever managing to do it, and: "He said one thing that I could do was to see whether bail money could be raised for him, pending an appeal in his case."

Alch told the Committee that McCord came up with Bernard Fensterwald, attorney and conspiracy buff, to hustle the bail money for McCord, and Fensterwald did it.

"I said I would check into this," Caulfield said, "toward the end of our conversation, realizing that he definitely was going to make a statement on the Watergate burglary at a time of his own choosing, and that such a statement would in all probability involve allegations against people in the White House and other high Administration officials" — to wit: the

Acting Director for Criminal Enforcement of AT&F, John J. Caulfield, who had spent the summer and the fall in the bushes with McCord, trying to keep the bastard quiet so he wouldn't blow the goddamned election, for Christ's sake.

"I gave him what I considered to be a small piece of friendly advice." You remember the gangster movies, Jim, old buddy. You know what happens to guys that rat.

"I said words to the effect that: 'Jim, I have worked with these people, and I know them to be as tough-minded as you and I. When you make your statement, don't underestimate them.' " Then Watson added a little something to veer the Committee away from grabbing him by the throat, " 'If I were in your shoes, I would probably do the same thing.' "

There were two people in that car, and they didn't go out to look at the bare trees of winter in eastern Virginia. They went out to talk, in private, and they drove, at a minimum, for one hour. That's if Caulfield is to be believed; two and one-half hours if McCord gets the nod. Each of them deemed the meeting of some urgency; McCord had a day off from watching Silbert approach the end of a trial that would sink McCord, and Caulfield was away from his desk at Treasury on a meeting that he had worked very hard to set up, hoping McCord would not talk. Human speech, among reasonably articulate people, varies from, say, one hundred words per minute to over four hundred. Caulfield's sanitary summary reflects his problem: he had to account for, say, two hours of talk, without putting himself in the soup.

"I later called Mr. Dean," Caulfield said, "and advised him of Mr. McCord's request for bail funding, and he said words to the effect that: 'Maybe we can handle that through Alch.' Some time later, Mr. Dean called me and asked me to tell McCord that the bail money presented too many problems, and that maybe consideration could be given to paying premiums. I later called McCord, and reported this. His reaction was: 'I am negotiating with a new attorney, and maybe he can get it handled.' This was the last conversation I had to date with James McCord." That new attorney was Fensterwald, and he did get it handled.

McCord's account of that conversation, on the face of it, does a great deal more to account for that extended drive and the time it required for conversation.

"He stated," McCord said, speaking of Watson, "that I was 'fouling up the game plan.' "

Ehrlichman's principal chore, he would say, was "downfield blocking."

"I made," McCord said, "a few comments about the 'game plan.' He said that 'they' had found no record of the interception of the two calls I referred to, and said that perhaps it could wait until the appeals."

Appeals follow criminal trials only when the defendant is convicted. That must have soothed McCord.

"He asked what my plans were, regarding talking publicly, and I said that I planned to do so when I was ready. That I had discussed it with my wife and she said that I should do what I felt I must, and not to worry about the family. I advised Jack" — *advised* is pure Bureauspeak; the interviewee always "advises," he never "says," and the use of it suggests that McCord's perception of his adverse relationship to the Administration was a fact on the twenty-fifth — "that my children were now grown, and could understand what I had to do, when the disclosures came out.

"He responded," McCord said, "by saying that: 'You know that if the Administration gets its back to the wall, it will have to defend itself.'

"I took that," McCord said, "as a personal threat" — which was reasonable enough, under the circumstances — "and I told him in response that I had had a good life, that my will was made out, and that I had thought through the risks and would take them when I was ready. He said that if I had to go off to jail" — and it was precisely McCord's disinclination to go off to jail that had kept the two of them whispering for six months — "that the Administration would help with the bail premiums. I advised him that it was not a bail premium, but $100,000 straight cash" — which was what Sirica had demanded to know from Hunt and the Cubans, to no effect — "and that that was a problem I would have to worry about, through family and friends." Better them than Dean.

# 16

OUR NATIONAL MYTHOLOGY commences with mean-tempered colonists so insolent of mitered bishops that they damned near died to get away from them; rustic merchants, lawyers and farmers who got so mad that they risked their lives in order to tell the King of England to go shit in his hat, and sailors like Stephen Decatur and John Paul Jones, whose effrontery was equaled — and perhaps excelled — only by the extravagance of the admiration which we have since conventionally accorded it. Wild Indians, savage outlaws, natural conditions of extreme danger and privation: they may have killed some of us, but enough survived to overcome them.

Turned in upon itself, that willingness to fight, when trespassed upon, inspired the South to battle the North, and the North with commensurate vigor to take up arms against the South. The popular notion is that we went into World War I because the Kaiser at long last went too far. And we congratulate ourselves for the forebearance we displayed until intolerably affronted by Hitler, and Tojo, whereupon we rolled up our sleeves and thrashed them. It was not until Korea, really, that any cognizable number of influential Americans commenced to wonder if perhaps we might not have gone a little overboard in our indulgence of the view that we are mighty and righteous enough to do as we damned right well please, in the event that we are not damned well pleased by what some-one else has done or is doing.

It was not until Vietnam that such speculation became widespread. And through it all, we have clamored, individually, for handguns, and then gone and used them at a horrifying rate, to settle personal scores regardless of the laws proscribing homicide. We see ourselves as placid, reasonable, decent and God-fearing folk, desirous of no trouble, but per-fect terrors when our self-restraint, like Shane's, is pushed, at last, too far. Because we think we are that way, we think we ought to act that way; because we think we ought to do, we do.

Of all people, Richard M. Nixon should have known that. Old Law and Order, Old Middle America, partisan of the Washington Redskins, Foe of International Communism, unofficial President of the John Wayne Fan Club (maybe vice-president, if Spiro Agnew's unseemly adoration is con-sidered to displace Mr. Nixon's comparatively temperate affection), re-peatedly engrossed in *Patton*, boastful time and again of irresistible com-bative urges when aroused by wicked opposition, he had managed his political career by reference to the premise that a latent national grouch-iness perdures through our most peaceful days. So it was more than *should have known*: he did know, and so did Haldeman and Ehrlichman, who in 1968 had recreated him in his own image and likeness. He em-bodied that consensus. He was President, because of it. But he didn't think it applied to him.

It did. But (perhaps because he had seen the liberals exhorting paci-fism toward the Viet Cong, and had assumed from that that only those against him were pacific; or wishy-washy about Alger Hiss, and Major Peress, and killing the Rosenbergs; and that they, in addition to advocat-ing pacifism, either could not or would not fight) he behaved, solipsisti-cally, in conformity with his mistaken judgment.

It was probably all three of those premises, each wrong, synergistically reacting in his head, contributing to miscalculations and misjudgments which fed upon each other, and led to chaotic disruptions of his Adminis-tration. He could, and did, become choleric when pacifism was aggres-sively propounded.

("After the inauguration there was a church service meeting, as I recall," Dean said, "where I had a brief encounter with the President, where he actually stopped me in the reception line as a result of an incident that had occurred during the inauguration.

("Apparently there was a demonstrator who ran through the police line and toward the President's car. That night the head of the Secret Service protective detail, protecting the President, called me and told me the President was quite angry and anxious to do something about this man charging at the President's car. The man had made it about five feet from the curb before he had been knocked down by Secret Service Agents. I do not think anybody in the whole world who was watching the inauguration on television saw it. I certainly did not. Mr. Taylor, when he called me, said 'What can I do? The President wants something done.'

(" 'Well, you just tell the President you reported it to me and I will check into it,' " Dean said, "which I did."

("The next Sunday morning, when I was going through the reception line, the President pulled me aside and said to me, 'I want something done about that man, that fellow that charged the car.'

("I had looked into the case. The best this man could be charged with was a collateral offense for breaking police lines. There was no assassination attempt, there was no evidence of anything like that. He was merely trying to make a point, as many demonstrators do, by being arrested in a public forum to make his protest. I had occasion to request the Secret Service to make a full investigation of the matter. They said they, after examining the man, had released him. I also talked to Mr. Petersen at the Justice Department, and Mr. Silbert at the Justice Department, and they said they had no case there. They had talked to the Secret Service. Meanwhile I was receiving further reports from Mr. Haldeman, saying 'What are you going to do with this man? We want a case made against him.' That is one where I just quietly let it go away because there was no case.") But he could not see that he was treading upon a steadily increasing minority of Americans who liked being underfoot no better than any other Americans did, and had not been conditioned any differently, to like it. And who would fight him, if they were obliged to, to make him stop.

Neither did he see that his opposition had some power, which they could use if they deemed themselves driven to fight. Thus neither he, nor Haldeman nor Ehrlichman, bestirred themselves to remember that while they did in fact control a lot of the prizes which the Magruders coveted, there was another parcel of behavioral conditioners which they did not necessarily control: the punishments. With the Department of Justice putatively in their hands, they blissfully arrogated to themselves a monopoly of the punishments, and prodded the Internal Revenue Service of the Treasury Department into application of those penalties to their enemies. They did not allow for the possibility that punishments would be visited upon the Magruders, and therefore they were caught by surprise when it happened. Jeb, the President said ruefully, was weak. When you took his presents away, and prosecutors replaced his presents with goads, and judges with jail, why, the first thing you know, he collapsed.

Which brings up a contingency which they neglected: the survival, both within and without the Administration (more of them without than within) of unreconstructed Americans. Dean apprehended their survival, if not their numbers or individual identities. That was why he shifted from activist obstruction (soliciting hush money, monitoring investigation conferences, soothing jangled conspirators' nerves) in 1972 to passivist obstruction of justice in early 1973 (stringing McCord along; tantalizing Caulfield but not going beyond that, because there might be somebody out there who could hammer Caulfield, and Dean didn't care to go to jail himself): because he had a fine nose for danger. That was why he put an increasingly pessimistic tone on the briefings he gave to Haldeman and Ehrlichman in the early months of 1973: he was a realist. He could see what was coming.

They, it seems, could not. The Nixon White House was a colony of enclaves (Colson, who brought Hunt into it, didn't know — and didn't wish to know — what Hunt had done, or was doing, for Ehrlichman; Haldeman said he didn't know what Ehrlichman was up to; the President, unless he was much more thoughtful of his taping machines than he appears to have been, didn't know what Colson was doing, and he respected his Attorney General's principal legal adviser — as he publicly claimed when naming William Rehnquist to the Supreme Court of the United States — so passionately that he called him, privately, "Renchberg"). Before the Committee, Haldeman and Ehrlichman bragged of the compartmentalization they had contrived for their pet President.

So while it is feasible, now, to examine what the accessible few in the Nixon Administration had to say about what was going on in those embattled years between June 17, 1972, and August 9, 1974, and to draw inferences from what they had to say, it is difficult to be confident that what was backgrounded and deep-backgrounded, and said not for attribution, faithfully reflected what was actually thought, reasoned and believed by those who were not accessible. Herb Klein, for example, would tell a television audience what he thought. But now the transcripts have come out, and they show that the President, deep in skulduggery, had nothing but contempt for his long-time associate. Didn't have his head on straight, the President thought. Something of a marshmallow. Skunk that he was, Mr. Nixon would get all the mileage that he could from a Klein, use him to float trial balloons, reap any advantages he could from Klein's credibility with the press, and then orally despise him in closet conferences with his actual confidants. He did the same thing to Liddy, of course, but Liddy took it philosophically, while others (Hunt, for example) took it very ill indeed, when the tapes came out. Either Mr. Nixon and his henchmen allowed the Administration's candid members glimpses which, though few, were accurate depictions of inner circle thinking (so that those glimpses would be relayed to the press; the inner circle people were as aware of the press as they were hateful of it, and they were very hateful indeed), or else they staged things *for their own people*, in the expectation that what was staged would be reported in good faith, and published in good faith, to influence a public expectant of good faith, in order to mislead the whole bunch of them. Us.

Mr. Nixon lied to his lawyers. Mr. Haldeman and Mr. Ehrlichman lied to the Senate, lied to the grand jury, and lied when deposed under oath in the Democratic National Committee and Common Cause lawsuits. Mr. Nixon lied to the country, to two Attorneys General of the United States, to any number of United States Senators, to his own Vice-President, and, apparently, to his family. Rage did not wither, nor custom stale, his infinite variety as liar. It seems likely that he and his principal varlets lied to those wide-eyed types who had found their way into his White House and yet remained on speaking terms with the press, and thus, by extension, with the country.

And yet, and yet. The President was expert at wishful thinking. And he believed that his wishes were superior to those of beggars, so that he could ride them: self-fulfilling wishes, as it were, which if propounded with adequate gravity to the country, perhaps by a presidential press conference which televised what Special Prosecutor Leon Jaworski was to call his "affidavit face," would render so what was not so, and fool us all. Deceit, in the Nixon view, was not just corrosive of the truth, which would have been entirely bad enough: it was eradicative of the truth, and affirmatively supplantive of it. What was true disappeared, and what had been false, by the erasure of the truth, became the truth. Teddy

Roosevelt, in their view, had barely touched upon the reality when he called the presidency a bully pulpit: it was, in their estimation, Mount Sinai, and what came down from it was true, because it had come down from there.

Accordingly it may well be that what now seems to have been the most egregiously cynical employment of press-credited White House people as unwitting middlemen in the public distribution of falsehoods, was, subjectively speaking, a naïve exercise, by a bunch of lying bastards, to manufacture from thin air a series of truths which would assist them. They thought, after all, that the press had manufactured from similarly vaporous substances the truths (which they knew, subjectively, to be lies) which plagued them. They had a nice, though fatal, sense of symmetry. It seems probable, therefore, that they fed their lies to the press because they genuinely believed that the press would accept them, at face value, and thus make them into the truth.

On that assumption, what the accessible White House people purveyed was but a slightly warped version of what the White House inner circle at least hoped, and may very well have believed. As such, now, it does not have to be comportable with the facts, in order to be significant of the way in which the inner circle saw the facts. As late as the end of July 1974, with the Supreme Court ruminating about a judicial emetic to force up the tapes that Jaworski wanted, what was coming out of the approachable White House people was that the President was secure, innocent, embattled but undaunted, and certain to prevail. In May of 1974 he was said to be proof against so much as a vote, in the House Judiciary Committee, recommending articles of impeachment. In June, well, the Committee might recommend, but the House would reject, and there would be no trial in the Senate. In early July: the full House might, *just* might, excitedly vote, say, one article of impeachment, but it would last about as long as the proverbial snowball in the upper chamber.

It was that kind of fantasizing which made John Dean's loyalist career so difficult. Steadfast as long as it seemed opportune to be steadfast, he shifted to caution, admonition and outright bleak prognostication of doleful prospects, as the *Liddy* trial went forward and McCord diminished like a sugar cube in hot coffee. But no one listened to him. The Ervin Committee annoyed the inner circle: their response was to get Kleindienst on a silver leash, subvert Senator Howard Baker (he was hospitable, but also personally ambitious), and make a greater fool out of Senator Edward

Gurney, thus improving on nature. McCord, the inner circle agreed, was a credible threat: they would seek, in vain, to discredit him. Hunt was a fool: no one would listen to him; and thus did they position themselves for the country to draw inferences from his reticence. They were safe. They were in the White House. Draw up a report. Stand fast. Form a hollow square.

Dean despaired.

Sirica (Don't Tread on Me) had found something to try: the patience and aspirations to martyrdom of those who, caught, designed nevertheless to protect the Nixon Administration. They were found wanting. Dean prepared to jump ship. He had run out of ideas.

# Part V

*Dean's private clients were incompetent, by choice or deficiency of ability, to assist in their illegal defense, and the ranks of volunteers became depleted.*

# 17

Dean ran out of ideas because he ran out of people who supplied ideas. Between June 19, 1972, and January 31, 1973, he exhausted the volunteers, and what they volunteered. Gray's contribution inspired the first Dean conspiracy (lay it off on the CIA, and buncombe the FBI: Walters, Cushman and Helms declined to go along, and the FBI proceeded). Magruder's management of Sloan and Porter, helped along by Mitchell's reticence and falsehoods, abetted the second Dean conspiracy (heap it all on Liddy, Hunt and McCord). But after them, he was fresh out, just when he most needed reinforcements. Dean's modus operandi was reactive: he did not dream up obstructions, but improvised them from ideas derived from others. When they were neutralized, he was paralyzed.

It was less of a loss than it seemed, but more of a loss than he could afford. Less of a loss, because the ad hoc stimuli that galvanized him were, by any objective standard, of poor quality. The CIA gambit, after all, was not a very good one. The Magruder ploy was transiently serviceable, but, Jeb being weak, was vulnerable to any attack that would middle old Jeb, and put him in fear of his skin. Mitchell was of little help: he was good at denying things that were true, but scant when it came to thinking things up, and besides, he was in New York. Kalmbach would do anything you asked, but he didn't propose anything. Haldeman was aloof, Ehrlichman was abrupt, and Nixon, perforce, didn't know anything and would insist, at the drop of a hat, that he didn't want to know anything, that everything was going to be all right.

But that vacancy was also much more of a burden than Dean could bear, and thus more than the rest of them could shoulder. They weren't doing anything, when he was, but if what he did, didn't work, it wouldn't matter whether they did anything. Not in the long run, at least, and (except for the President) the long run was what interested them. The statute of limitations, after all, precludes no prosecution until five years have passed, and the time doesn't start running, in a conspiracy case, until the conspiracy is over.

What Dean did, didn't work. And as early as December of 1972, he knew it wasn't going to.

Being shrewd, though previously inexperienced in the management of illegal schemes, Dean deduced from his own dealings with McCord several of the central principles of treachery. Paramount among them is the understanding that while the conspirators may hope, desperately, for the permanent success of their undertaking, they may not achieve it. Thus adjustments may be necessary, and when, in the course of criminal events, it becomes needful to leave one of the plotters holding the bag, one leaves him, without piercing remorse, holding the bag. The necessity is regrettable, of course, and it would be nice, from the point of view of those still in the clear, if the sacrifice were not demanded, but there it is. It is permissible to sigh when the decision is made.

Because he had direct empirical knowledge that time and external events can bring about attrition in the ranks of conspirators, Dean, by the end of February 1973, had started to get nervous. Nearly six months before, he had counseled his client not to expect perpetual care of his political well-being from the cover-up. Then, and thereafter, Dean's recommendations for permanent repairs (full disclosure, or something) were rather airily disregarded, and he had been obliged, with increasing foreboding, to apply temporary patches instead. So, if his lawful business with the President had not convinced him of the Nixon-Haldeman-Ehrlichman view of time and its uses, he had ample direct experience of it just in the administration of the cover-up.

The President, conformably to his credo that his problems at home were mere malicious fabrications of his enemies, always began by assuming that they were consequently ephemeral. If he waited long enough, they would go away, because no matter how lathered Dan Schorr and the *Washington Post* became, Out There were the People, who would accord the liberal ravings no credence. Mr. Nixon's faith in the efficacy of stalling was equaled only by its inadequacy, repeatedly demonstrated, as a corrective for his difficulties.

Dean was thus relegated to a position which frightened him severely. At the direction of the President of the United States, he had long since begun to play a very dangerous game. In its course, he had identified a major hazard: the longer a conspiracy goes on, the greater the likelihood that it will give way. But when he tried to tell the President that time was the probable demolition agent of the plot, the President blandly told him to play for time. Obedience to that had required Dean to deal the Old Maid to McCord, without telling McCord; to get what the President seemed to want — time — he had to set McCord up. The cost of that purchase — at the most, Dean got in exchange for McCord only October, November, December and January — was the special menace McCord presented in February as he practiced his scales for his upcoming appearance before the Ervin Committee.

At first Dean cast wildly about the Executive Office Building, looking for some ally who could accomplish what had proven impossible for him: persuade the President and the inner circle that the extremity was at hand. All he found was Richard Moore, who professed concern but was as malleable as all the others under the President's pressure to play for more time, and who persisted in the micawberish notion that something external would turn up to save them from what was an essentially cosmetic problem anyway. Senator Howard Baker was waiting upon the President, to receive his marching orders for the hearings. Attorney General Richard G. Kleindienst was a faithful retainer. Everything would be all right.

By the middle of March 1973, Dean was scared, no longer because he thought the President merely unrealistic, but because he could predict the certain cost of that persistence in unrealism: he thought it was going to take another body to buy time when Sam Ervin warmed up the Mighty Wurlitzer, and he divined that the next body was going to be John Wesley Dean III. By the third week in March he was meeting almost every day with the client he had seen so little until then. The play for time was ostensibly geared to saving Dean, and thus his client, by putting the umbrella of attorney-client privilege over their presidentially incriminating discussions. But Dean, who had done it to McCord without much compunction, had no eagerness to have it done to him.

He was still willing to concede that there might be a doubt of which the President ought to have the benefit. Perhaps Mr. Nixon's conduct, endangering Dean as it did, was not meant to do so. "As I have indicated," Dean told the Committee, talking about March 21, 1973, "my purpose in requesting this meeting particularly with the President was that I felt it necessary that I give him a full report of all the facts that I knew, and explain to him what I believed to be the implication of those facts. It was my particular concern with the fact that the President did not seem to understand the implications of what was going on. For example, when I had earlier told him that I thought I was involved in an obstruction of justice situation, he argued with me to the contrary after I had explained it to him. Also, when the matter of money demands had come up previously, he had very nonchalantly told me that *there was no problem,* and I did not know if he realized that he himself could be getting involved in an obstruction of justice by having promised clemency to Hunt. What I had hoped to do in this conversation was to have the President tell me that we had to end the matter — now."

The President's response was disappointing to Dean. "I began by telling the President that there was a cancer growing on the presidency, and that if the cancer was not removed, that the President himself would be killed by it. I also told him that it was important that this cancer be removed immediately, because it was growing more deadly every day." Dean reminded the President of what he had done, what Kalmbach had done, what Magruder had done, what Haldeman had done, what Ehrlichman had done, and what the *Liddy* defendants were likely to do: "I told the President that I did not believe that all of the seven defendants would maintain their silence forever. In fact, I thought that one or more would very likely break rank."

The President, having asked a few questions, "suggested that it would be an excellent idea if I gave some sort of briefing to the Cabinet, and that he was very impressed with my knowledge of the circumstances. But he did not seem particularly concerned with their implications." Filled with consternation, Dean left the President and conferred with Haldeman. In the afternoon, he met Mr. Nixon again, this time with the German Shepherds present, and it became "quite clear that the cover-up, as far as the White House was concerned, was going to continue." Where-

THE FRIENDS OF RICHARD NIXON

upon Dean said that they were going to get themselves indicted, an observation which made Haldeman and Ehrlichman "very unhappy." The next day they tried to get Mitchell to take the rap. Mitchell was not cooperative. On the twenty-third, McCord's declaration of war was released to the press by Sirica. The President called Dean at home, where he was barricaded by reporters intrigued by Gray's Senate hearing allegation that Dean was probably a liar. "Referring to our meeting on March twenty-first, and McCord's letter," Dean said, quoting the President: " 'Well, John, you were right in your prediction.' He then suggested I go up to Camp David and analyze the situation. He did not instruct me to write a report. Rather, he said to go to Camp David. 'Take your wife and get some relaxation.' " Also, get the hell away from where the press can watch you.

Now the flags were starting to go up. "He then alluded to the fact that I have been under some rather intense pressure lately, but he said he had been through this all his life, and 'You cannot let it get to you.' He said that he was able to do his best thinking at Camp David, and I should get some rest and assess where we are, and where we go from here, and report back to him. I told him I would go.

"My wife and I arrived at Camp David in the midafternoon," Dean said. "As we entered the cabin in which we were staying, the phone was ringing. The operator said it was the President, but Haldeman came on the phone. Haldeman said that while I was there, I should spend some time writing a report on everything I knew about the Watergate. I said I would do so. I asked him if it was for internal or public use. He said that would be decided later."

They *would* keep on underestimating Dean, thinking that because he'd been willing to do everything they'd asked, he'd be willing to do anything they asked. "I spent the rest of the day," Dean said, "and the next day, thinking about this entire matter."

It would have taken a great deal of recklessness to do what they requested of Dean, the sort of recklessness that allows a man to give a statement and sign a paper after some marble-eyed cop has advised him that he has a right to remain silent, and a right to an attorney, and a right to have an attorney appointed to represent him if he cannot afford an attorney, and that if he makes any statement, it will be taken down, and used against him at a trial in a court of law.

Dean was not a reckless man. "I reached the conclusion," he said, being by then about as naïve as a used-car salesman, "based on earlier conversations I had had with Ehrlichman, that he would never admit to his involvement in the cover-up." Canny lad, John Dean, in March of 1973: put to trial on that very charge in September of 1974, Ehrlichman had his lawyer tell the jury that President Nixon had misled the poor fellow, deceived him, lied to him and used him. And that was probably true, too.

"I did not know about Haldeman," Dean said, but this time gave himself the benefit of the doubt: "but I assumed that he would not because he would believe it a higher duty to protect the President.

"The more I thought about it," Dean said, and here he was a bit too crafty in his profession of ingenuousness, "the more I realized that I should step forward" — because they were after my ass and that was the only way I could see, to cover it — "because there was no way the situation was going to get better. Rather, it could only get worse" — by leaving me out there, all alone, to take the rap, without a prayer of getting off because my buddies have got this signed confession that I wrote.

"My most difficult problem," Dean said, "was how I could end this mess without mortally wounding the President."

When they had Adam Clayton Powell on the congressional griddle, several years ago, and he was off in Bimini with a then-current version of an Argentine Firecracker, the Congressman's wife was invited to testify before the roasting committee, and she did it with relish and duende, leaving the philanderer for dead. Then, outside the Capitol, reporters inquired of her motives for testifying, and, demurely, she said: "He's my husband, and I love him." That, as Jimmy Breslin observed at the time, is letting the guy know where it came from.

"I had no answer," Dean said, about how to gore Nixon without spilling any blood, "because I felt, once I came forward, the matter would be for the American people to decide, and not for me to decide."

The popular reaction to what Dean would have to say was then, to be sure, speculative. But it was not *that* speculative. The opposition was out there, with its newspapers and its commentators and its columnists; Dean knew that because he'd seen the fellows swooping around his house on the twenty-third. And he'd heard the President talking like a man under siege, about having no friends, and about the war he was fighting. Dean knew exactly what he was doing, and he had a pretty good idea of the probable results. But he also had that self-preserving instinct which says that when it's him or me, it's him.

"I finally concluded," he said, "that I would have to think of some way for the President to get out in front of the matter" — i.e., take the ground-zero, firestorm heat, because, goddamnit, he's the son of a bitch that made the heat and I'll be damned if I'm going to take it for him — "despite what happened to everybody else." Or, more accurately: so that it wouldn't happen to me.

Dean, to his astonishment, had heard the President tell the country, back in August, that Dean had investigated the whole thing and found no malefactors in the White House. Not even, presumably, Haldeman, who was running the cover-up, or Ehrlichman, who may have imagined that he was. It was one thing, as far as Dean was concerned, to have your name blatted out all over the country as the author of a direct falsehood; it was quite another to prepare your own signed confession as the evil genius who coordinated the falsehoods, or, in the alternative, to draft a detailed denial that falsehoods had been coordinated, only to be burned at the stake when Magruder and McCord and the other shaky types finished yammering to the Senate.

Dean started laying backfires. "I called Mr. Moore and talked to him about it. We talked about a presidential speech, where the President would really lay the facts out. We talked about immunity for everyone involved." They should've copied Gerry Ford in on that part of the conversation. "We talked about a special Warren-type commission, that would put the facts out." And, incidentally, take the play away from the Ervin Committee. "We talked about some half-measures, that might satisfy the public interest. But we both realized that nothing less than the truth would sell."

Moore's tongue was hinged in two places; Dean, by then at least an advanced amateur if not a junior professional in the art of transmitting threats, was using Moore the same way that CBS uses Telstar: he was bouncing messages off the man, for reception by the President and the inner circle. Dean was trying to use Moore the same way that McCord had tried to use Caulfield, but there was an important difference: Dean's strategy was succeeding.

Dean spent March 24 working on his statement. On Sunday, the twenty-fifth, he heard that the *Los Angeles Times* and the *Washington Post* were going with a story "that Magruder and I had prior knowledge of the June seventeenth bugging of the Democratic National Committee. I considered the story libelous" — and, more than that, an instructive hint that somebody was setting him up.

First he called a libel lawyer. Then, after the papers had been put on notice that he'd sue if they printed what they had, he conferred further with that lawyer:

"I also told Mr. [Tom] Hogan that when I returned from Camp David that I wanted to talk to him about this entire matter, and asked him to think about someone who was a good criminal lawyer, because I was planning to take certain steps in the near future." Then, for the Committee, a bit of piety: it was fraternal concern for all which impelled him to seek counsel. "I might add that it was my thinking at that time that I would explain all the facts to a knowledgeable criminal lawyer, to determine the potential criminal problems of everyone involved, from the President on down, to get independent advice on what I should do." To get them hanged instead of me, if possible, but at least to get them hanged along with me.

There Dean possessed an advantage, of then-incalculable significance: on this whole planet there were but four men who could make the President fine, fat and final on the cover-up. The other three were Haldeman, Ehrlichman and Mitchell, and in 1973, they didn't want to. None of the investigators knew this, but Dean did, Mitchell did, Haldeman did, and so did Ehrlichman. Where McCord got form letters when he hectored the White House for succor, and Hunt got only money, Dean got a very respectful hearing. Several of them, in fact.

So many that he was confirmed in his judgment that the next patsy in line to walk the plank was John Dean. Pausing only to record a self-serving conversation with Magruder, Dean on Monday, the twenty-sixth, gave Moore another light jab, quoting to him a memorandum about creating an independent panel to punish Watergaters. Moore, who hadn't had much to do with things until very recently, suggested that Dean "call Haldeman, which I did. He was intrigued, but not overwhelmed. It was becoming increasingly clear that no one involved was willing to stand up and account for themselves." It was becoming increasingly clear that everyone involved was greasing for Dean the same skids that Dean had greased for McCord.

"After I had read in the newspaper on Tuesday, March twenty-seventh, that the President had called me on Monday morning, March twenty-sixth — which he had not," Dean said, with some malevolence, "and expressed great confidence in me, and the fact that I had not had any prior knowledge of the break-in at the Democratic National Committee, I decided to attempt to contact Mr. Liddy, who was the one man who could document the fact that we never had talked about his plans following the February fourth meeting in Mitchell's office."

Dean knew what was going on. The President and the inner circle knew very damned right well that he'd had no knowledge of plans to bug Larry O'Brien. The next public utterance, or the one after that, would reassert that he knew nothing of the cover-up. Then from some mysterious source would float the rumor that Dean had run the cover-up, which in fact he had, and then there would be some startled-fawn official reactions, and perhaps an investigation by Ehrlichman, and then, by God, a shamefaced admission: old Dean fooled us. String him up, the bastard. That, as a matter of fact, was the Haldeman-Ehrlichman-Mitchell defense strategy at trial before Judge Sirica. Dean didn't go for it, and neither, as it turned out, did the trial jury.

But Liddy wouldn't talk to Dean. Liddy was the kind of man that the President expected to have performing dirty tricks at his indirect behest, the kind of clown who'd go to jail for him. And before that prop was cut out from under Dean, Haldeman called again, on March 28, to summon Dean back to the White House for a little chat with Mitchell and Magruder.

Mitchell was just about everybody's first choice for whipping boy, and it is easy to see why: he had all the necessary qualifications. To Nixon, Haldeman and Ehrlichman, he was the man who had made the mistake of loosing Liddy in the first place; by overlooking the presidential impetus to get what was wanted, by whatever means, it was conceptually possible to isolate Mitchell as the first cause of all the trouble, and thus, the appropriate selection as kamikaze pilot to get them out of it. Further, Mitchell had been Attorney General of the United States, and chairman of the Committee to Re-elect: opponents of the White House were baying for large game, and might be satisfied with Mitchell. Finally, Mitchell was regarded as both a villain and a Nixon intimate by the press, which, in the White House view, might content itself therefore with worrying his remains and quit plaguing the President.

The shortcoming in this plan was its condition precedent: Mitchell had to subscribe to the propriety of his own destruction. He did not.

The existence of that condition, and the way it was observed, are matters of some interest. Haldeman and Ehrlichman, on March 28 and 29, set out to talk him into it, but went about their tasks with uncharacteristic timidity, and never really put it to him. John Mitchell knew how not to volunteer for hazardous assignments; he had, after all, spent the previous summer "not volunteering anything" to people who interrogated him, under oath, in civil depositions and grand jury proceedings, and he knew how to suck on his pipe and look thoughtful. Clearly, Haldeman and Ehrlichman (and thus, by extension, the President) were not in a position, vis-à-vis Mitchell, which they thought safe enough to permit them to tip him in without first getting his consent. Given their barbaric unconcern for the feelings, fates and futures of his predecessors in a sacrificial line, their solicitude for Mitchell's continuing amity fairly shrieks for the inference that they feared his rage because they thought it would be fatal to incite.

That is a very pregnant inference. The tapes and Dean's extraordinary memory do not disclose facts sufficient to explain that fear. Reduced to essentials, the public facts establish that Mitchell unleashed Liddy, apologized to Nixon when Liddy was caught, perjured himself as circumstances thereafter required, and stayed out of sight as much as his wife and the press would permit.

He had little to do with management of the cover-up. He did not raise money to buy silence; although he was asked to do so, and made some tentative moves to do so, he finally refused. There was evidently no one in the Administration who could compel him to perform even that menial assistance to the program of covering up what he, after all, had instigated.

It therefore follows that Mr. Nixon, Mr. Haldeman and Mr. Ehrlichman feared Mitchell not just because he might help some prosecutor to fray the cover-up, but because the reason for their fear was so great that it was never confided to Dean, or discussed during the recorded conversations that have been released. Hunt had to issue specific reminders that he might, if crossed, make public recollection of some seamy jobs he had done for the White House. Mitchell's threat was so great he didn't have to mention it. They talked tough about him when he wasn't there, snarling that he had gotten them into it, and that it was only fair that he jolly well get them out of it. But when he came in, and did not come around, the President scurried back to a pep-talk position, and instead of upbraiding Mitchell, told him to stonewall it, take the Fifth, and save the plan. Precisely what Mitchell had intended to do in the first place, and had been doing since Liddy was caught.

Dean was ignorant of Mitchell's bludgeon. But Dean's ignorance was the ignorance of an intelligent man: when he did not know, he was aware of his deficiency, and either set out to remove it (as he had done by asking Gray and Petersen questions when he needed information and ideas to thwart their investigations) or took it into careful account when removal was impossible. He did not, as far as we know, devote much time to speculation about the source of Mitchell's power, but he saw that power for what it was, and for what it meant to him.

"I told Haldeman," Dean said of the twenty-eighth, "that I really did not wish to meet with Mitchell and Magruder, but he was insistent that I return and meet with them. I returned from Camp David about 3:30 and went directly to Haldeman's office. He told me that Mitchell and Magruder were waiting in another office for me. I asked him why they wanted to talk to me, and he said they wanted to ask me about my knowledge of the meetings in Mitchell's office" with Liddy. "I told Haldeman that they were both aware of the situation and I was not going to lie if asked about those meetings."

Haldeman, appraising Gray's confidant (by then a public suspect because a branded liar) as a potential substitute for the obdurate Mitchell, gave Dean more hints of his intentions than he meant to. "Knowing how freely and openly he had discussed matters in the past, I could tell that he was back-pedaling fast. That he was now in the process of uninvolving himself" — a semantic coinage suggestive of the inner circle solipsism which made real what the sovereign declared real — "but keeping others involved. This was a clear sign to me that Mr. Haldeman was not going to come forward and help end this problem. Rather, he was beginning to protect his flanks."

Dean knew what procedures were customary for that business, because he had employed them on McCord. "It was my reaction to this meeting with Mr. Haldeman, and his evident changed attitude, and my earlier dealings with Ehrlichman where he had told me how I should handle various areas of my testimony, should I be called before the grand jury, that made me decide not to turn over to them the report I had written at Camp David."

Mitchell did not choose to take the rap, and in March, at least, there wasn't anyone around who was brave enough to order him to do it. As he would not be cajoled into doing it, so Dean was scrambling to avoid being dragooned into it. On March 30, 1973, four days of clandestine conversations between Dean and Tom Hogan led to five hours of discussions between them and Charles Shaffer. On April 2, 1973, Shaffer and Hogan went to see Silbert and Glanzer and Campbell, "and told them that I was willing to come forward with everything I knew about the case."

# 18

EVEN NOW, WITH proof beyond a peradventure of a doubt in hand, it is difficult to comprehend what a scoundrel we selected, twice, to be President of the United States.

It was not that he was arrogant, not merely that, at least: to get to be President of the United States, you probably have to be arrogant (Lyndon Johnson's Lincoln Continental sorties through the ranch on the Pedernales necessitated disposal not only of the beer cans, but also of the contents processed through the presidential kidneys. Procedure called for a Secret Service agent — one was named Henderson — to stand at the Connie door and shield the presidential anatomy from vulgar view. One day Henderson, disbelievingly, felt at his station something warm and wet on his trousers. "Mr. President," he said, when continued sensations precluded further disbelief, "you're pissing on my leg." "Hinderson," the President said, "Ah *know* Ah am. That's mah prerogative"). But Johnson, thus regally relieved, was scarcely the inventor of presidential highhandedness: Thomas Jefferson found his own strict construction of the Constitution no bar to the Louisiana Purchase. "I took the Canal Zone and let Congress debate," said Theodore Roosevelt, "and while the debate goes on, the Canal does also." Woodrow Wilson thought a lot of his idea for a League of Nations, but not enough to treat with the Senate over it, and thus himself assisted in the ruination of his hopes. At the zenith of his popularity, Franklin D. Roosevelt thought it his prerogative to pack the United States Supreme Court; the Congress, unlike Henderson, did not agree.

A Richard G. Kleindienst or an Elliot L. Richardson, long since graduated from his political novitiate, anticipated a certain vaulting pride in a President of the United States, and allowed for solipsism in his practice of the office.

It was not that he was ruthless. Most successful politicians have a capacity for ruthlessness entirely adequate even by measurement to the high standards of private industry. Elliot Richardson had survived in Massachusetts with his political throat uncut, and acknowledged the necessity for occasional political sacrifices. Kleindienst, Nixon's 1968 campaign director of field services, was remembered in action by a friend: "He'd go into a state and analyze what had to be done — one, two, three. If some important local guy was standing in his way, zip," and he drew a finger across his throat. In 1971, as Deputy Attorney General, he instituted the mass arrest policy used to discourage May Day antiwar protestors bent on exercise of their civil rights; to the suggestion that there might be some constitutional difficulty inherent in such action, the man responsible for management of the United States Department of Justice replied: "Fuck the Constitution, we can worry about that later."

It was not that Richard Nixon was petty, ungenerous, somewhat bigoted, and monumentally cynical. Richardson and Kleindienst had been playing with real money for a long time, and knew what beats two pair. Kleindienst, in fact, harbored some attitudes of his own which squared neatly with the President's nasty little streak of anti-Semitism (to reporters in January of 1973, Attorney General Kleindienst gave a glimpse of his thinking in that line as he protested that he could not have bagged the Watergate investigation if he had wanted to: "You take this fellow Silbert. I don't know his political affiliation, but I'd guess he's a Democrat, considering his age and the fact that he's Jewish . . ."). It was simply that he did not keep his word.

It is impossible, now, to ascertain with any assurance when it was that Richard Nixon first began to practice to deceive, although for those of us with a decade or two of tardiness beginning to wonder if Alger Hiss really was a spy, it would be nicer if it were possible. But it is clear that Mr. Nixon, over the years, perfected his art at least to the point at which he trusted his monstrous craftsmanship completely, and believed it sufficient unto the most anxious of days. He became a virtuoso of deception, a wizard doing things with reality and facts, and the nation's trust, that

Harry Houdini would have been hard-pressed to imitate with a few paltry swords. Remembering now how the Kennedy Administration writhed when impaled upon the allegation that Arthur Sylvester, an Assistant Secretary of Defense for Public Affairs, had posited a limited right in the Government to tell a useful falsehood now and then, if necessary to the national defense, it is difficult to stand less than awestruck before the feat which President Nixon set for himself, and very nearly brought off: he was out to deceive the whole country, the courts and the Congress, any time he wanted, on any subject that he chose, and he damned near got away with it.

He guarded his ambition closely. A few intimates — such as Bob Haldeman, for example, who knew for more than two years what whoppers the President was piously reciting to the country on the subject of the cover-up — may have guessed at his prodigious skill in mendacity, but he was enough of an artist, with others, never to confide in them the truth about his fondness for lies, the final conceit of his mastery. It was that which led to Elliot Richardson's stunned fury, and to Richard Kleindienst's disgrace, and to the helpless rage and sorrow of Jim St. Clair, and Leonard Garment, and William Ruckelshaus, Charles Wiggins, Hugh Scott, Robert Dole, and everyone else who placed himself in hazard in order to assist the President in his travail. "First," Lyndon Johnson said, to a Texas politician who had promised one thing and done the other, "Ah'm gonna give you a two-minute lecture on integrity, and then ah'm gonna *ruin* you."

As requested, Secretary Richardson, of Health, Education and Welfare, late in 1972 supplied to the reelected President a letter of resignation from the Cabinet, along with all the other Secretaries. "Before my pilgrimage to the mountain, as we called it," Richardson said of the Camp David conferences scheduled by the President, he had no idea of what Nixon had in mind for him. He thought he might be asked to stay on at HEW, and he preferred that above all other possibilities because he thought he was making progress there. He allowed for what he thought was the relatively unlikely possibility that his resignation might be one of those taken up, and prepared himself to behave gracefully if it was. Less probable, he thought, were invitations to return to State as Secretary, or to move to Justice as Attorney General, or to run the Department of Defense.

"State? I decided I would take it, and be glad to get it. Defense? I would take it, with somewhat less enthusiasm. The things I was doing were too interesting. Justice? I would decline it. It was important, but it did not compare with what I considered the importance of what I was doing."

Richardson's view — and it was shared by Henry Petersen, and cited by him to account for the fact that a demoralized Department, its top prosecutors castigated and former administrators under criminal charges, did not lose personnel, but gained applicants under Watergate siege (Petersen perhaps discounted the possibility that the economic climate, no-fault insurance laws, and the sheer proliferation of lawyers, militated against maintenance of previous attrition rates at Justice) — was that the Department was not a fertile field for innovation.

RFK, galvanic as he desired to be, and was, as Attorney General, permanently affected Department policy in only two areas: Organized Crime and Civil Rights, and there his hortatory influence went more to accelerate and intensify efforts than to initiate them. Justice is a housekeeping agency, charged with enforcing the laws that the Congress and the President agree to insert in the pocket parts of the United States Code Annotated, together with the laws which previous Presidents and Congresses have provided for the main volumes. An Attorney General can improve upon the performance of his predecessor only if his predecessor somehow put the place, or parts of it, to sleep, or was corrupt, or a hydrophobic ideologue (such as Mitchell Palmer was in the Red-baiting days after World War I), or an utter fool (which Richardson, rightly, did not think Kleindienst had been). And if he inherits such an opportunity, the new Attorney General cannot realistically credit himself with more than a restoration of function. Which, at worst, is always partially discharged by the obstinate bureaucracy which chiefly ignores the political winds that blow at the top of the agency, and goes about its business. There are now more than 49,000 employees in Justice. Only a few of them come and go with new Administrations. The rest, like the ravens of the Tower of London, remain, and do their jobs, and disregard the rhetoric. The lawyers stay for three years, or five, if jobs in private firms are hard to find after three, or twenty-five or thirty, if they really like it there, or if they haven't gotten new jobs by the time they're halfway to pensions, and the clerks and other personnel stay forever, expert, steady, doing the best they can. Richardson was aware of that.

The President struck a nice balance between what Richardson really wanted (State) and what he really didn't want to do (exchange a policy-making position for a primarily administrative one). The President asked Richardson to take over at Defense, dangling a new opportunity to influence from the Pentagon the same emerging national consensus he had endeavored to germinate from his desk at Foggy Bottom. "The President said Laird had been very valuable at Defense, but that changing circumstances required a Secretary with more background in conceptual issues, one better able to moderate a dialogue among foreign specialists."

Richardson fell for it, persisting in his belief, then innocuous enough because fortuitously correct, that when the President said "national interest," he meant, at a minimum, that he expected national along with personal benefits to flow from the proposed action.

Richard G. Kleindienst had been somewhat chagrined, at the end of the reelection year. Acting Attorney General for more than three months after Mitchell's resignation took effect March 1, 1972, Kleindienst's customary ebullience had suffered a hard thrashing in twenty-one days of hearings by the Senate Judiciary Committee. In December his resignation as Attorney General was declined, but lest he become overweening, his selections for executive assistants in the Department were disapproved. He began the new year with a plug for Pat Gray, who, all unbeknownst to Kleindienst, had been obediently destroying evidence while serving as Acting Director of the FBI: Kleindienst said he thought Gray had been doing "a great job," which was true, but later embarrassing. He credited Gray as being "a patriot of America, not just a flag-waver," and a man who believed that "the Constitution is worth preserving and defending." And also, presumably, a man who would not dismiss it, to worry about it later. He professed inability to understand why Gray had not been nominated for Senate approval as permanent Director of the FBI. But in March, spurred on by Ehrlichman, he unhesitatingly relayed to Gray the White House directive that no more be said to the Senate about Watergate.

April 2, 1973, was the beginning of an extremely busy fortnight for Dean, who discovered, as he went along, that the cover-up had succeeded as well as it had because the prosecutors had not dreamed that it was under way.

By April 8, Haldeman and Ehrlichman had begun to fret about the change in Dean's degree of commitment to White House interests. "They asked me if I had met yet with the prosecutors, or knew when I would be called before the grand jury. I avoided a direct answer to the question by saying that my lawyers were still having discussions with the prosecutors about my appearance before the grand jury. I was then asked some questions about testimonial areas, but I gave them evasive answers."

Those gentlemen had their faults, but stupidity was not among them. "Even those evasive answers," Dean said, "which raised matters which related to them, brought forth responses that they did not remember it quite as I did.

"During the week of April ninth to April fourteenth," Dean said, "I had several conversations with Ehrlichman and Haldeman, but I tried to avoid them as much as possible. I recall some discussions, however, regarding getting Mitchell to step forward. The theory that had been discussed before they went to California was becoming the policy: 'If Mitchell takes the rap, the public will have a high-level person, and be satisfied, and the matter will finally end.' I felt, during each encounter that I had with them, that I was very much a problem for them, but they did not want me to know that they felt so."

Mitchell called on the ninth and asked Dean for a meeting. "I informed Ehrlichman and Haldeman," Dean said. Then he talked with Mitchell, and told his mentor "that if and when I were called to testify, I would testify fully and honestly. Mitchell said that he understood, and did not suggest that I do otherwise. He did, however, believe that my testimony would be very harmful to the President, and said that he felt that I should not testify if at all possible. I reported my meeting with Mitchell to Haldeman and Ehrlichman later."

That was among several discussions with the President's chief minions that week, and the talks seemed to make the two of them very edgy. They were talking about "pinning this whole matter on Mitchell. I listened with some interest," Dean said, "because I did not feel that they would succeed at this." He'd seen too much of Mitchell's implacable strength. "And I felt also they would have to be thinking about how to handle the cover-up activities, and felt that I would undoubtedly be the target for them to pin everything with regard to the cover-up on. As Haldeman and Ehrlichman began to discuss more, about getting Mitchell to take the blame for authorizing this plan in the first instance, I began to increase my conversations with the prosecutors about the cover-up." John Dean was not the most charming fellow in the Administration, and he lacked scruples, and he was loyal only to a point, and those qualities served him very well in his milieu. "The more I told the prosecutors about the cover-up, the more interested they became in it. At this time,

Haldeman and Ehrlichman were unaware of my direct dealings with the prosecutors."

By April 13, a Friday as it happened, the fat was well into the fire. "I went to Ehrlichman's office," Dean said, where Ehrlichman and Haldeman were present and discussing a meeting that they had just had with Colson and his attorney, Mr. Shapiro.

"They informed me," Dean said, finding this all very instructive, but not very deceptive, "that Colson had developed a plan to deal with the matter, and that was that Mitchell should be smoked out." He said he might "add that Ehrlichman and Haldeman were most cynical about Colson's suggestions, and said to me that he was really scrambling to protect himself." As they were, Dean most cynically thought, really scrambling to protect themselves.

"After discussing the Colson plan," Dean said, "they told me Mitchell would be coming down to talk about this entire matter. There was some discussion as to how to smoke Mitchell out. By the week's end, it had been decided that the President would meet with Mitchell and ask him about his knowledge, and hopefully the President would be able to get Mitchell to come forward."

That was waltz music, played for Dean's benefit and intended to program him to deliver misleading testimony if he were called. The President knew damned well what Mitchell knew; he had a working grasp of it six days after the break-in, when he told Haldeman to divert the FBI by shouting "CIA" in a loud voice. He probably got it on June 20, when Mitchell called him to apologize for not keeping closer track of what Liddy was doing. Haldeman and Ehrlichman surely knew it. If they said what Dean says they said, they were adding a fillip to the cover-up, preserving the fiction that the President didn't know, had no idea, what Mitchell knew.

"I told them," Dean said, "I doubted very seriously if Mitchell would say anything to anyone about this matter. While these discussions were going on, the President called Ehrlichman, and they had a brief discussion about the matter. I also recall that, at one point in the conversation, Ehrlichman said that 'He's right here,' referring to me."

That was enough for Dean. "On Saturday, April fourteenth, I requested my attorney, Mr. Shaffer, to come to my office. I told him that Mitchell was coming down to meet with the President, and that there was going to be an effort to smoke him out. I asked him if he had any ideas, as Ehrlichman and Haldeman had asked me if I had any ideas. Mr.

Shaffer gave me a former prosecutor's answer, that what Mitchell needs is a good cross-examination."

Mitchell did not need any such thing, but Dean didn't know that. "I told him," Dean said, meaning Mr. Shaffer, "I did not think that was possible by the President, because the President was not the cross-examining type." Then Dean and Shaffer collaborated in listing those likely to be indicted.

After lunch on the fourteenth, Dean showed the list to Richard Moore, who became "quite upset." Along with Dean's own name, it carried those of Haldeman and Ehrlichman. Later in the afternoon, "I went to Ehrlichman's office," Dean said, "where Ehrlichman and Haldeman were discussing Mitchell's visit. I learned that Mitchell had met briefly with Ehrlichman, but not with the President. Ehrlichman said that Mitchell was not talking, which certainly did not surprise me. And I was certainly not surprised that he would not talk with Ehrlichman, either.

"I then pulled the list I had prepared, out of my pocket," Dean said, "and told them that I had discussed everyone's problems with my lawyers, and my lawyers had had conversations with the prosecutors as well, and I thought that the following persons would be indicted. I told them that my attorney had learned from his discussions with the prosecutors" — which must have jarred the composure of the German Shepherds a little — "that not only was Dean the target of the grand jury, but that Ehrlichman and Haldeman were also very much targets of the grand jury.

"Ehrlichman," Dean said, "said that he had just talked with Kleindienst a few days earlier, and that he had no such report from Kleindienst.

"I said," Dean said, "that my lawyer appears to know more than the Attorney General does, because he is probably more informed in that he had had direct conversations with the prosecutors. I did not tell them at that point that I had had private meetings with the prosecutors, or that I had told the prosecutors of the extent of involvement of Haldeman and Ehrlichman." But he was nevertheless "confident that I had gotten the message through to Ehrlichman and Haldeman that they had a serious problem themselves, and I had put them on final notice that I was not playing the cover-up game any longer."

The President and Haldeman had talked earlier that Saturday afternoon about the probable effects of Jeb Magruder's appearances before the grand jury. And the President, reflecting on Mitchell's upcoming appearance, concluded: "John Dean will have to testify. . . ."

"Well," Haldeman said, "John Dean, that doesn't trouble me." But it would.

Between 2:24 and 3:55 P.M., Ehrlichman briefed the President and Haldeman about Mitchell's visit. "He is," Ehrlichman said, "an innocent man in his heart and in his mind, and he does not intend to move off that position." After some express disapproval of Mitchell's attitudes and plans, Ehrlichman said to Mitchell: " 'Dean has not been subpoenaed. He has not testified, and as a matter of fact, the way they are proceeding down there, it looks like they are losing interest in him.' "

What Ehrlichman said to Mitchell was not what the President, Haldeman or even Ehrlichman actually thought. "I think we owe it to ourselves," the President said, "to find out about John Dean, for example . . ."

"All right," Haldeman said.

"I think that's right," Ehrlichman said. "This is probably a golden opportunity, in a way."

"Right," the President said. "To find out, let me put it this way: you've got to find out what the hell he is going to say. [Unintelligible] which is frightening to me. . . ."

It should have been, given Dean's grocery list. "Dean thinks everybody in the place is going to get indicted," Ehrlichman said. Haldeman morosely recited the names.

The question was: how to find out? Ehrlichman had an idea: "Now," he said, "the question is whether I ought to get hold of Kleindienst for, say, five o'clock, and get this thing all wrapped up."

"Have you determined that it should be Kleindienst rather than Silbert?" the President said.

"Yeah," Ehrlichman said. "Dean's right about that, I am sure."

"How do you know?" the President asked.

"I asked him for his advice on this. He said," Ehrlichman said, "Silbert would ask you to wait a minute, and he would step out of the room, and he would come back to get you, and walk you right into the grand jury."

"Oh," the President said.

By 5:15 on that Saturday afternoon, they had found out all about John Dean. "Well," Ehrlichman said, "he and his two lawyers, who are very bright young guys, came in. So I said: 'Evidently, judging by your phone call earlier, this is moot.' He said: 'Yes, we have just come from our informal conference with the United States Attorney.' He then proceeded to voluntarily give me his whole testimony."

The President's reply was unintelligible.

Ehrlichman went on, summarizing Dean's summary of his testimony before the grand jury.

"Now," Ehrlichman said, "I have the Attorney General of the United States sitting at home, waiting to go to this dinner party," the annual White House Correspondents' dinner, and it would have caused comment if Kleindienst had not appeared as scheduled. Ehrlichman proposed calling Kleindienst and telling him nothing about Dean, confining himself to the statement "that Magruder had just disclosed to me what he has shown to the U.S. Attorney, and I really don't have anything to add . . ." thus perpetuating the myth that Ehrlichman was investigating the matter for the White House.

Then he did it, lying to exclude Dean when Kleindienst asked him who he'd seen. Kleindienst said he would call Petersen. Along with feeding Kleindienst the facts about Magruder, Ehrlichman reported Dean's defection, but none of his proposed testimony. Then he sent Kleindienst off to the dinner, and hung up. The President, Haldeman and Ehrlichman were going also, to dine with the hated press.

To the President, Ehrlichman said: "He wants me to meet with Henry Petersen tomorrow. I'm possessed of information establishing the commission of a crime. And I've got to be darn careful about who I talk to."

Kleindienst did call Petersen. He also went to the dinner and had sufficient refreshments. Dean's lawyers reached Dean around 1 A.M. on Sunday, the fifteenth: Shaffer told him "that the prosecutors had called him and that they were going to have to breach the agreement they had made, regarding keeping all of my conversations with them private. The prosecutors had reported to Mr. Shaffer that the Attorney General had called Mr. Petersen, and them, and wanted a full report on everything that was going on before the grand jury, and where the grand jury was headed. The meeting with the Attorney General was to occur about 2 A.M., at the Attorney General's home."

Accompanied by Harold Titus, U.S. Attorney for the District, and Earl Silbert, Petersen kept Kleindienst up all the night, describing the remarkable story that John Dean had told. Kleindienst had not expected that, and he wept. The next day, April 16, 1973, the Attorney General went to the White House, waited for the President to finish a prayer breakfast, and reported what he had learned.

Now presumably Kleindienst thought he was delivering news. He had been very upset when Petersen talked to him, and destroyed the last vestiges of his confidence in the character of John Mitchell; no evident public relations gambit was performed with the visit to the President — indeed, it was kept very confidential. It seems therefore more likely than not that Kleindienst genuinely believed that he was bearing new information to the President.

He was at least the third one. Pat Gray had told the President that some of his people were inflicting mortal wounds, and Mr. Nixon had taken the news with perfect equanimity, instructing Gray to persist in a thorough investigation, the same one that he and Haldeman, back on June 23, 1972, if not before, had conspired to obstruct. Dean, on March 21, 1973, had admonished the President that the cover-up was about to explode, and the President took that pretty well also, brilliantly contriving later to persuade much of the nation, for a while, that the report of trouble in the obstruction plot in fact constituted his first notice that the plot existed. Kleindienst, on that Sunday afternoon, quite plainly thought that he was sounding an alarm that Gordon Strachan would be compromised by the testimony of Dean and Magruder, and might thus do something that would implicate Ehrlichman and Haldeman. And he personally suspected them.

The President professed inability to understand how that could possibly happen, since Haldeman and Ehrlichman were not, he said, involved:

"I have asked both Haldeman and Ehrlichman," the President said.

"I know you have," Kleindienst said.

"And they have given me absolute . . . you know what I mean," the President said, cleverly allowing the Attorney General of the United States, moved by loyalty, to infer whatever falsehood might suit him best. "You can only . . . it's like . . . you'd believe John Mitchell, I suppose, wouldn't you?" he said, thus invoking the virtue which he sought to pervert. "I don't believe Haldeman or Ehrlichman could ever, you know [unintelligible] hurt . . . to be so close to people, and yet I think of . . ."

"John Mitchell and I were a little off more by ourself," Kleindienst said, thinking about what it meant to have friends but not quite buttoned up on the idea that the President wanted him to get. It took a little more conversation, and another nudge or two from the President.

"Oh, in other words," the President said, "the obstruction they are talking about is what happened after the conviction?"

"Yes, sir," Kleindienst said, one of the few who demonstrated any conversational respect for the President. Dean was another, along with Petersen.

"Rather than before the conviction?" the President said, getting his hopes up a bit that perhaps not so big a lie was needed.

"Yes, sir," Kleindienst said.

"Well," the President said, "who the hell would . . . you mean . . ." — thinking that perhaps the whole secret would yet survive even Dean and Magruder's defections — "I can't see Haldeman or Ehrlichman or anybody in that. . . ." Because, of course, it was Dean he had directed to pay off Hunt after Hunt's plea of guilty, and not Haldeman at all. But he had misunderstood. Kleindienst stuck to his prediction that Haldeman and Ehrlichman were in danger of indictment also for preconviction obstructions.

"Let's get back to this concept of the presidency, sir," Kleindienst said, which concept of his was the cornerstone of the President's ability to fool him.

"Right," the President said, having remarkable grasp of just how such concepts could be used; Henry Petersen, Earl Silbert, most of the country — including, as he would demonstrate two weeks later, Elliot L. Richardson — simply did not believe that the President would obstruct justice and then lie to them about doing it.

"What you do is the right thing," Kleindienst said, exposing his lack of sophistication, "and then, when having done it, it would be recognized as the right thing." Mr. Kleindienst appears to have had here either a failure of memory, or else a very vivid recollection, of the President's respect for the right thing, as he demonstrated it in his directive a year before to drop the ITT appeal.

"Right," the President said, having counseled, commanded, procured and induced the wrong thing about ten months before.

"And I know," Kleindienst faltered, "I don't know, but I *believe, feel,* that we should have . . . I think the options that you have to consider there are two.

"One: do you, the President, what I have told you today, that might be forthcoming. And before that comes out, would you ask 'em to step aside until this whole thing blows over? It all blows over, maybe you're not indicted, or culpable, finally you come back. And they do wind up having been indicted, you at least have off your personal staff, these people who are going to be involved in the criminal justice system. If you don't take that step, and I, I really don't pretend to advise you on it, sir, and then if it comes out, it's leaked out, and then you've got to do it after the disclosure is made publicly. You know, I think, it . . ."

The President was masterfully misleading. "Let me ask you this: let us suppose, let's suppose the worst." Okay: supposing the worst, it was that Silbert and Titus and Petersen and the grand jury and Judge Sirica, and ultimately the press and the country, would find out that the President who had told them that March 21, 1973, was his first information of the cover-up, had in fact demanded that Haldeman get the cover-up going at least as early as June 23, 1972. That was the worst, and the President, in conversation with his Attorney General, knew it.

But he also knew that Kleindienst didn't know it, and he was pretty sure that he would never find out. He knew what concept Kleindienst had of the presidency, after all, and he knew that Kleindienst would never surmise that a presidential supposition of "the worst" was in fact a presidential falsehood intended to conceal "the worst." Thus he implied his own innocence, which Kleindienst assumed anyway, while minimizing what had been done, and thus in turn, surely mindful of Kleindienst's truculent attitude toward the ITT order, precluded a somewhat nettlesome Attorney General (who could, nevertheless, be duped) from inconvenient discoveries that might have provoked another threat to resign in protest. Or, in fewer words, the President added another filigree to the body of falsehoods he had created to obstruct justice. "The worst," he invited Kleindienst to believe, and Kleindienst, of course, did, was "that it does . . . that it does come out, on Haldeman and Strachan, with his testimony that he had papers, et cetera."

Now that was neat. Mr. Nixon was maneuvering Kleindienst into the belief that Haldeman, painted to ultimate blackness, at most had received a few reports and might have casually learned that $350,000 that had left a safe in the White House had turned up in the paws of the Watergate Seven. Instead of what was true: that Haldeman was clerk of the works for the cover-up, at the express direction of the President, who was still touching it up as circumstances required.

"The question," the President said, "really is basically whether an individual, you know, can be totally, totally . . . I mean, the point is, if a guy isn't guilty, you shouldn't let him go."

Again, the quick fake, executed expertly. The fellow had more moves than Bobby Orr. The question in the President's mind was not about Haldeman's guilt: he knew Haldeman was as guilty as hell, and he knew it because he was as guilty as hell himself. And because he was, and preferred, reasonably, not to be caught, he was covering up some more. What the President wanted was to instill in Kleindienst's mind the lie that Haldeman was not guilty, and could not be guilty, because then, given what he knew, he would run less risk of being found out himself. "That's right," Kleindienst said, "you shouldn't."

Before the Ervin Committee, Haldeman and Ehrlichman recalled the President's fondness for playing (as they put it more felicitously than they intended) the Devil's Advocate (presumably not purposefully suggesting a full attorney-client relationship). That was how they explained those conversations which Dean had testified about: the President's words, at face value so replete with the willfulness and malice of a man bent on obstruction, had actually been uttered to the Socratic purpose of drawing Dean out. But they were not spoken to draw him out. They were spoken to suck him in. And they succeeded, and it's too bad Socrates is not in a position to comment on the suggestion that his method for pursuit of the truth may be appropriately cited as a serviceable false label for the practice of inculcating falsehoods. The *fleurs de mal* beauty of the Nixon approach to lying was in the delicacy and subtlety of its practice: inhabiting the veracious atmosphere of the presidency, he murmured sounds which allowed his auditors (eager, all of them, to believe him blameless; certain, each of them, that his reputation as a man of no scruples was a wicked voodoo cult meeting evilly in Eastern liberal dells and ruled by dark satanic superstitions) to fashion for themselves whatever false impressions would best serve his purpose.

Your run-of-the-mill liar, your apprentice perjuror, comes a-cropper because he tries too hard to please, and thus, like John Mitchell denying political activity as head of the Committee to Re-elect the President, or Richard Kleindienst, flatly declaring that nobody in the White House was more than completely bored with the handling of the ITT case, finally delivers himself of a fib so incredible that it reduces the listener to helpless laughter. But the Nixon School of Lying was erected on the premise that people will hear what they want to hear, and all you have to do is give them something, some minimally committing placebo which will seem to deny what they shrink from asserting, some palliating remark which will seem to declare what they find repugnant to deny, and then, like the Congressmen lauded for their religious and civic commitments at White House prayer breakfasts, but denominated "assholes" soon thereafter, the poor silly bastards will tailor your grunts into affirmations, and fit those affirmations beautifully to the contradiction of what you know to be the truth.

The President had Kleindienst well in hand now. "It's like me," he said, reflectively. " 'Wait, now. Let's stand up for people, if they're, even though they're under attack.' " Eisenhower, when I was under fire, didn't stand up for me, the President did not say. Eisenhower, when Adams was under attack, didn't stand up for him, the President seemed to say. But when Goldwater was under attack, and you, Clean Dish, were running his national campaign and getting your own ass clobbered at the same time, running for Governor of Arizona, I stood up for Goldwater. I stumped for him. Did Nelson Rockefeller do that? Did anybody ever do what I've done? I go through, Kleindienst, I'm a stand-up guy."

"I know," Kleindienst said. In 1964 he explained to a reporter on the floor of the GOP convention at the San Francisco Cow Palace that Goldwater's preference for old loyalists was nothing more than rational. "You're a damned fool if you don't have around you, the people you know and trust," he said. "If you have big names working for you, you wake up in the morning, and you don't know what deals they may have done in your name."

"In Haldeman's case, though," the President said, "I want to ask you, if you think . . . I just want to ask your opinion. And the same on Ehrlichman, based on this. Do you think that, where he had no knowledge of Watergate. . . ?"

It was perfect. It was as well machined as a Porsche, as well proportioned as a beautiful woman, as fragile and as strong as Charlotte's Web. Some pig. Kleindienst, radiant, jumped into it, accepting the bait — whether Ehrlichman had any knowledge of the burglary was scarcely germane to what the prosecutors were pursuing, under the guidance of the Attorney General of the United States, on the question of covering up the Watergate — and gushing: "I think neither one of them knew about it before." If they got in trouble, he said, it would be because they'd made inconsequential remarks around John Dean, who was, Dean said, involved in the cover-up, and those remarks might now seem to incriminate them.

The President now wanted to know if letting them go would increase their chances of indictment. When you get the pigeon interested, take him for everything he's got. "You find them guilty before they have a chance to prove their innocence, don't you?" Of course they aren't innocent, but never mind that.

"Which is not very good," Kleindienst said, "precise."

"That's the point that I am making," the President said. "Can, on the basis of this kind of information . . ."

"I don't suggest anything, now," Kleindienst said, backtracking quickly into the trap that had been set for him. "I'm just . . ."

"No, no," the President said, graciously absolving Kleindienst of even the slightest, inadvertent trespass upon the truth, "I know. No, I'm just trying, understand, I want to know what is the right thing to do. And, understand, we are going to come out of this thing. The Justice Department and the presidency are going to come out clean, because I don't tolerate this kind of stuff. But the point is, Dick, I also, I can't, I *can't* let an innocent man down. That's my point."

There wasn't a dry eye in the house. By rebutting a suggestion that Kleindienst had never made — that the President ought to commence a program of abandoning innocent men to their undeserved disgrace — the President had thrown the Attorney General off balance, causing him to be anxious to make amends for proposing so unprincipled a course of conduct. Then the President generously afforded him a penitential opportunity: by agreeing that Haldeman and Ehrlichman should not be abandoned to disgrace, Kleindienst could expiate the sin which he had not committed, and in the fullness of his contrition would find it not only easy, but downright cleansing, to endorse the position that, because they ought not to be sacrificed by the President, Haldeman and Ehrlichman were therefore innocent. Which premise, of course, Kleindienst desperately wanted to believe anyway, because Haldeman and Ehrlichman did only what the President wanted them to do, and to suspect them was to suspect him. It was easy. Weaving their names through the rest of the conversation, the President soon had Kleindienst practically babbling his certitude of their blamelessness.

"You see," the President said, "I realize that the fellows, like up at the Ervin Committee, and now the grand jury, they're going to smash the likes of Haldeman all the time. But you can't let a guy go without a [unintelligible] if he's guilty, if you know he's innocent."

"Right," Kleindienst said.

A bit later: "The obstruction of justice is what's bad," the President said.

"And the perjury," Kleindienst said. "The suborning of witnesses, the perjury, and perjuring yourself."

"You don't have Ehrlichman involved in that," the President said. "You don't have Haldeman involved in any of that?"

"No, no," Kleindienst said.

Kleindienst had gone into that seventy-minute meeting at 1:12 P.M.

192

with two strategies in mind: he thought he ought to disqualify himself from any action in the investigation and prosecution of John Mitchell, and he thought his replacement as supervising prosecutor should be someone from outside the Administration. Barnabas Sears, the Chicago lawyer who gets to handle especially dirty cases there, was his primary selection, but he thought Henry Petersen might be an acceptable alternative.

The tape of the discussion ran out before the conversation did. The transcript is fifty pages long. Each page carries about 250 words; while there are wide variances in the rapidity of speech among individuals, it is unusual to find an articulate conversationalist talking at less than 100 words per minute, and the upper limit of intelligible discussion is probably somewhere around 400. No pauses are noted in the transcripts of the tape, although some probably occurred without notation. What the White House reproduced of that conversation, then, probably represents about forty-five to fifty-five minutes of the seventy passed between Kleindienst and the President, omitting the portion where they reached some sort of understanding, and Kleindienst went out on the understanding that he would be back later in the day (that understanding appears from the transcript of a telephone conversation between the President and Kleindienst, recorded at 3:48 on the same afternoon; Mr. Nixon, placing the call, had evidently expected Kleindienst to return more quickly than he did, and was somewhat impatient. It also suggests that the end of the seventy-minute conversation found them in tentative agreement that Petersen should take over ultimate supervision of the Watergate prosecutions. "May I bring Henry Petersen with me?" Kleindienst said. "Yeah," the President said, "I want to ask him to do something"). What Mr. Nixon had in mind was to blow as much smoke at Petersen as he had managed to get past Kleindienst; the President was of a mood to make converts that day.

What the President wanted Petersen to do was more faithfully, though not completely, reflected by what Nixon said on the telephone to Haldeman right after Kleindienst left the White House to talk to Petersen. Haldeman was mildly surprised that the President was favorably considering appointment of a Special Prosecutor; the suggestion might have made him a little nervous. But the President was reassuring: "For a reason. This is not to prosecute the case. A Special Prosecutor, to look at the indictments, to see that the indictments run to everybody they need to run to. So that it isn't just the President's men, you see."

Haldeman did not fully understand. "In other words, he is above Silbert rather than replacing Silbert?" It was not the best idea he had heard all day.

"Oh, no," the President said. "Silbert runs the case, and that's all. But he is just in there for the purpose of examining all this, to see that the indictments cover everybody."

Now Haldeman was having less trouble with it. He understood that what the President had in mind was only another improvement to the cover-up, not something that would torpedo it. "Uh huh," he said, "well, that does protect you a lot, because if they don't indict some of us, then you have a cover-up problem. If you have that guy, then you have a basis. . . ."

"Then he goes out and says," the President said, quite certain of the behavior which this still-unselected fellow would commit, " 'I have examined all of this. These men are not guilty, and these men are not indictable, and these are.' " In other words: we'll just call him a Special Prosecutor; his real function will be to apply a coat of whitewash to keep the surface of the cover-up opaque.

"Yeah," Haldeman said. That was much, much better.

The President mentioned Charles Alan Wright of the Texas Law School as one prospective choice. There was further conversation. Then the President found another reason to appoint another public relations man, and call him Special Prosecutor: because it "helps in another way. It gets one person between me and the whole thing."

What he was doing was reinventing the Mafia. The Mob's rulers are hard to catch because there are so many layers of underbosses and lieutenants and buffers and *consiglieri* between the man who lets the contract for the hit, and the man who pulls the trigger. It's virtually impossible to break all the people in the chain. The President of the United States was adding another layer of insulation. "Yep," Haldeman said, "that's right, and I think that is a darn good route for it, especially if it can be done. I hadn't thought about it, or understood it at the level you are now talking about, and that would seem to me exactly what you are after."

It was that flexibility which made the cover-up so successful for so long, notwithstanding the fact that it was so badly managed. Whenever something happened to threaten disaster, Nixon stuck the lever of the presidency in place to shift things back in his favor. Magruder was talking, Dean was talking, Strachan was talking, but justice had been obstructed for ten months with responsive modifications to the plot, and a Special Prosecutor would be just one more.

Right after the President talked to Haldeman (who promised to brief Ehrlichman), Haldeman talked to his assistant, Lawrence Higby. Higby was relaying information from John Dean, who had called to declare that his dealings with Silbert, Titus and Petersen were motivated solely by loyalty. Haldeman, for a man in his position, demonstrated remarkable self-control in receipt of this information. That brought him the second part of Dean's message: quoting Dean, Higby said: "I think you, meaning the President, should take your counsel from Henry Petersen, who, I assure you, does not want the presidency hurt."

"Hmph," said Haldeman, momentarily disregarding the fact that Dean, genuinely torn by his decision to talk, and deeming himself forced to it, had empirically developed excellent reason to know whereof he spoke, having mulcted Petersen of information vital to the cover-up for the previous ten months. But it evidently registered on Haldeman, later.

At 8:14 that night, the President called Petersen at home. "Anything further you want to report tonight before our meeting tomorrow at 12:30?" the President said, which indicates that he had seen Petersen sometime that day, and that Petersen had spilled his guts, and that the discussion, if recorded at all, was not disgorged by the Nixon White House.

"Not anything, specially," Petersen said, "that I didn't give you today."

The President's interest stemmed from the fact that Dean had been chatting with Titus and Silbert that afternoon, while the President was snuggling up to Petersen.

Petersen was unfortunately vulnerable to presidential manipulation, though it is hard to say that he was more vulnerable than any other lawyer, in his position, would have been. Fiercely proud of his ironclad reputation for integrity (which was, as he well knew, deserved), he considered that reputation to have brought about his ascendancy in the Department, by an Administration suddenly needful of men of such reputation. Named Assistant Attorney General, because he was indisputably honest, he erred by assuming that the Administration would invariably call upon him, if it called at all, because desirous of irreproachable service, not merely its appearance. In twenty-two years of public service, he had previously visited the White House before only to form part of the background for the signature of new criminal legislation. Until 1973, he had no direct, personal contact with Presidents. Eisenhower, Kennedy,

Johnson, and until then, Nixon, had not sought his firsthand views on matters of national importance; when those views were heard at all, it was by presentation through intermediary Attorneys General. To be called, directly, by the President, did not floor him, but it certainly flattered him.

It flattered him, notwithstanding his visceral fear that the President might be personally involved in the mess that had been dumped on his doorstep, because he shared with the President a powerful confidence in the oughtness of things. Nixon unwisely took on Pat Brown because he thought he ought to be Governor of California, and therefore would be Governor, which fantasy damned near ruined him. Petersen struggled upward in the Department like a salmon bent on spawning, persuaded that decades of fealty to the rule of law, in the realm of oughtness, really should bring the reward of being the boss, and by dint of extraordinarily felicitous (from his point of view) random events, was confirmed and irretrievably committed to the rightness of his expectations. He thought that when the President summoned him, it was because the President needed, *and desired,* the copper-bottomed kind of resolute probity that he so unfailingly brought to whatever he was asked to do. He thought he was a man of principle. It did not occur to him that the President of the United States would wish, viciously, to use him.

"Nothing that adds to what we had earlier, eh?" the President said, using Petersen.

"That's right," Petersen said. "They concluded the meeting with Dean. His counsel says he will not permit him to plead, that a . . ."

The President, trifling most obscenely with Title 18 of the United States Code, had almost no acquaintance with the criminal law. This, paradoxically, inured to his benefit: people like Petersen were always explaining things to him, and thus assisting him, unwittingly, in his purposes. "Permit him to plead?" the President said. "What do you mean by that?"

"To plead guilty," Petersen said. "In other words, he will go to trial."

The President didn't know what the hell that meant, but he was afraid he didn't like it. "He is going to plead not guilty, eh?"

"That's right," Petersen said, "unless we come to some agreement with him. His counsel's position is that it would be a travesty to try Dean and not try Ehrlichman and Haldeman."

"Uh huh," the President said, scared shitless and trying to think of the next thing to do.

"That is the basic information. To the extent that it developed in these preliminary negotiations," Petersen said, "isn't much more than I gave you."

That wasn't good enough. The President waffled. "Well, let me ask you this," he said, perceiving that the issue was whether Dean would make a deal, which meant talk or not-talk. "Based on this, though, you mean this inhibits you from using the information, then?" He wouldn't've minded that. "Or do you use it? Or how do you do it? Or do you use it for leads? But you can't use it unless he pleads, right?"

"We cannot use it for any purpose unless he pleads," Petersen said, which was correct if the prosecutors adhered to the President's dictum that nobody in the White House was to get immunity from prosecution, but wrong if somebody with the bit in his teeth took it in mind to get some immunity for Dean, and thus did it imply Henry Petersen's respect for White House policy.

The President wished to be sure. "For no purpose?" he said.

"That's right," Petersen said. "That's incorrect," he said, meaning *not done*, "unless we strike some agreement with him."

The President knew what he thought of that idea. "Hmph," he said.

Petersen rushed on, heedless of the possibility (well, not heedless, exactly: to him it was unthinkable) that the President of the United States was hustling around obstructing justice, and thus that it might be imprudent to furnish information to him. "He had a call from Ehrlichman," Petersen said of Dean. "Ehrlichman wanted to meet with him tonight."

"I see," the President said, cagily.

"About eight o'clock," Petersen said, ingenuously. "We advised him he would have to make his own determination" — which is disingenuous standing operating procedure for prosecutors: they always tell pro-prosecution witnesses that they don't have to talk to anybody, making it very clear that it would be much better if they didn't, but that they have a right to talk to anybody — "but suggested that he not."

"I see," said the President, with less enthusiasm.

"He then," Petersen said, "through his counsel, informed us that he was writing a note to you, in which he would say:

"One, that what he was doing was in your best interests, and that that would all become apparent as this situation unfolded."

Perfectly gorgeous, as far as the President was concerned, just what he had in mind, ranking right up there with a fall down a flight of stairs.

"Right," the President said. "Let me ask you this: why don't I get him in now, if I can find him, and have a talk with him?"

Henry Petersen for more than twenty years had been a dutiful member of the Executive Department. His job existed in order to enable the President to exercise care that the laws should be faithfully enforced. "I don't see any objection to that, Mr. President," Petersen said, and he didn't.

"Is that all right with you?" the President asked.

"Yes, sir," Petersen said.

"All right," the President said, "I am going to get him over because I am not going to screw around with this thing, as I told you."

"All right," Petersen said, thus ratified in his primary assumption, if he needed to be, and thus in turn reassuring the President in his deliberate hope of successfully perverting that assumption.

"But I want to be sure you understand," the President said, meaning that he wanted to be damned sure that Petersen never even came close to understanding, "that you know, that we are going to get to the bottom of this thing." Meaning, of course, that he was going to do everything in his enormous power to make sure that nobody ever got to the bottom of it, because that's where he was, and part of the means to that end were to convince Henry Petersen to the contrary. The King of the Mountain, as he called himself, to Haldeman.

"I think the thing that . . ." Petersen began.

"What do you want me to say to him?" the President cut in, planning to dazzle Dean to a fare-thee-well to avert the dangers that lay ahead when he started to talk. "Ask him to tell me the whole truth?" The more devious the crook, the more sanctimonious the patter.

"Yes, sir," Petersen said. He also wanted the President to signal Liddy to come clean, which the President, knowing that Liddy had nothing on anybody beyond Mitchell — who was already in trouble, and could take care of himself anyway — swiftly agreed to do, but only (the condition was added by the President in a second conversation the same night) by transmitting a message through Petersen. That assured that Liddy would remain steadfast in his silence; he was, after all, the stand-up guy. It also took care of the small risk that he might in fact know something that would cause further damage. There was no way that Liddy would take the prosecutor's word for something the President was supposed to have said, and the President knew it. No point in taking chances.

Later that evening (at 9:39 P.M.), the President used Petersen again, evidently to program John Dean in his testimony. "I discussed with him," Dean said of the 9 P.M. meeting with the President, "the fact that maybe if Liddy's lawyer met with him, that Liddy would begin to open up, because, I said, that I thought it would be very helpful if Liddy did talk. It was during this part of the conversation that the President picked up the telephone and called Henry Petersen and pretended with Petersen that I was not in the room, but that the matter of Liddy's coming forward and talking had arisen during our conversation. The President relayed to Petersen that if Liddy's lawyer wanted to see him, to get a signal, that the President was willing to do this."

By the time the President made that call, he and Dean had been talking for thirty-nine minutes. It was exactly seventy-three minutes after his second call to Petersen, when the whole Liddy thing had presumably been settled. Petersen must have been absolutely mystified.

"Henry," the President said, "I talked to John Dean, and haven't quite finished, but he stepped out for a minute." Dean was sitting right there, and the President hoped he'd be favorably impressed by the President's prompt action on Dean's suggestion, and reason from it to the inference that the President yearned for complete demolition of the cover-up. And thus to the further inference that he had had no part in arranging it in the first place.

"I wanted to ask you this," the President said. "He," meaning Dean, "says he thinks it is important that I tell Liddy's attorney — I don't know who he is — by the name of Maroulis, do you know him? That, what I told you, a few minutes ago." Remembering, of course, just in time, that Dean and Petersen had talked a lot since the previous June, and guarding against the possibility that they might get together for note comparison again, when Dean started testifying before the grand jury.

Petersen said he had been trying to reach Peter Maroulis.

"Let me say this," the President said. "You tell him, if necessary, you haul him in here and I will tell him. Okay?" Precisely what he had earlier retreated from doing.

"All right," Petersen said. "Indeed so."

"You know what I mean," the President said. "You tell him I have called you directly tonight, and that you have it direct from the President: if he needs it from me, I will tell him."

"Very good," Petersen said.

"Because you see," the President said, ostentatiously relying on Dean's recommendation of Petersen, in Dean's presence, to promote an inference of his own good faith (Dean, after all, seemed rather to admire Petersen, and thought no special evil of the man he had so used, and would therefore assume from the President's call to Petersen that the President had seen the monstrous error of his ways, and was determined to get to the bottom of things), "John felt that maybe he wouldn't take it from you. But I think he would. Or, what do you think? What is your judgment?" Thus demonstrating to Dean that he intended to rely upon Petersen's advice, when in fact he intended to subvert the man's loyalty. Dean, cold and shrewd enough to have acted as cover-up foreman as long as he had, was cold and shrewd enough not to be convinced. Two hours later, the President was back on the phone to Petersen for the fourth time that day, chatting about how Dean would have to resign.

Henry Petersen was fully up to dealing with such duplicity; he had, after all, been supervising the hot pursuit of gangsters for twenty years. But he was only up to it when he began with the expectation that it would occur. He did not have that expectation when he dealt with the President, of whom, as he said, he was in awe.

"One of the most difficult things I have had to do, since I have been in the Justice Department," Petersen said, reflecting upon occupants of offices of far lower stature, "are the decisions with respect to public officials.

"You err seriously if you don't conduct an investigation where it should be conducted, and if you do conduct an investigation where it should not be, you do a terrible disservice to the public official involved."

The conundrum, of course, is in deciding whether to conduct an investigation — which promptly gets out to the papers as soon as somebody prominent is involved — when you need the facts which would be turned up by an investigation to decide whether to proceed. Petersen is quite right, but he is right in a limited way: "It is no help to say: 'Well, Mr. Public Official, we want you to know you have been cleared, and we are sorry about all the publicity.' "

Still, the fact is that public officials, just like gangsters and the rest of us, are obliged to do the best they can with the risk that they will be damaged in property, reputation and career by broadcast notice that they are under investigation, or by indictment procured by some irresponsible jerk with a tractable grand jury under his dominion. One of the constitutional and statutory realities which has consistently eluded the press and the public is the comparative insignificance of indictment, *in a case involving a public figure, or in one involving your next-door neighbor*, who works down at the foundry and finds himself accused of slighting the Department of the Treasury in calculation of his income-tax liability. Indictment wrecks a man's life, at least for the time being; acquittal seldom catches up to correct the harm to reputation, and legal fees requiring a second mortgage on the family homestead are not defrayed by the taxpayers when the defendant is found not guilty. A thoughtful prosecutor has that on his mind every time he strides into the grand jury room with a long white paper beginning: "The Grand Jury charges:

"*Count I*

"That on or about . . . in the District of . . . John Doe, did knowingly and willfully . . ." and then you fill in the offense, and issue a three-paragraph press release conforming to court rules balancing the public's right to know against the right to a trial unprejudiced by publicity, and, to his dismay, assuring that the defendant will have a very public trial indeed, as guaranteed him by the Constitution of the United States, and put it out. At the same time you mail him a letter, which reaches him three days after the papers have published the charges, and enclose a copy of the indictment, together with the suggestion that he get in touch with his lawyer, and await notice of the court of when he should appear to enter his plea ("Congratulations. You have just been indicted by the federal grand jury. After a long life of undetected crimes and misdemeanors, the Government has caught up with you." The letter does not say that. Perhaps it should, if not for accuracy, then at least for candor).

The limitation on Petersen's vision was peculiarly severe when the public official in question was the President of the United States. He was the victim of his own integrity: he thought everybody else, including the President of the United States, was presumptively, at least, as pure, and in the case of the President, the presumption was irrebuttable. The trouble was that Petersen was wrong.

# Part VI

*Disappointed as he was with Dean, and in immediate need of further assistance, the President chose a new lawyer, and called him Attorney General of the United States, and lied to him. That was a bad idea.*

# 19

On Saturday, April 28, 1973, Secretary of Defense Elliot L. Richardson took a day off to visit his daughter's school — the Madeira School — in Virginia. There he was given an urgent message to call William Rogers. Kleindienst, appalled by the prospect of prosecuting John Mitchell, was resigning. Rogers told Richardson "he had been talking to the President about the best possible person" to succeed Kleindienst. Richardson was their choice.

He was not certain he agreed. Conceding that "the President needed somebody promptly," Richardson in conversations with his wife, and a few friends, reached the conclusion which he reported back to Rogers: "I told him I thought it would be a mistake, if I were to take responsibility for the Watergate, because I had been so closely identified with the Administration." At, he might have added, some fairly serious damage to his political reputation in Massachusetts, where editorial eyebrows were raised very high in response to his support, as Secretary of HEW, for the Administration's health, education and busing views. "I said I thought the President needed an independent outsider."

Melvin Laird, participating informally but influentially in the Administration after Richardson succeeded him at Defense, thought so too. Both of them were laboring, independently of each other, on what had been traditionally sound expectations among White House advisers, that the President, whoever he was, would act in good faith.

"Rogers called back an hour later," Richardson said. "He had talked with the President," whose aloofness from direct contact with the course of human events was so complete that he employed an intermediary to conduct conversations with his Secretary of Defense about becoming his Attorney General. It gave Rogers something to do as Secretary of State, while Henry Kissinger conducted the nation's foreign policy. "He said," Richardson said, quoting Rogers, "that it would take too long, to find an independent outsider. The President did not want a pig in a poke," as he had independently demonstrated in his recruitment of Henry Petersen, "and was willing to consider an independent Special Prosecutor."

That handsomeness was the beginning of the fissure between President Nixon and Mr. Richardson. At State and at HEW, and also at Defense, Elliot Richardson acted like a lawyer for the President, according to him the same courtesy which he unfailingly expected as service from his Assistant United States Attorneys, his Assistant Attorneys General, his deputies at State and his assistants at HEW, and the Generals subordinate to his discretion at the Pentagon. He supplied his views to the President, on matters within his jurisdiction. He presented them as forcefully as he thought appropriate. When his counsel was accepted, he declared the decision as the position of the Administration, without claiming authorship of it. When his counsel was rejected, he declared the resulting position without disclaiming the personal endorsement which seemed, incorrectly, to be implied by his making of the declaration. One of the lawyer's functions is to lay out alternatives for his client, recommending that course which seems best to him, but genuinely ready to advocate the other if the client so chooses, so long as there is nothing improper about the client's choice.

Leonard Garment, James St. Clair, J. Fred Buzhardt and Charles Alan Wright governed their relationship to President Nixon by the same rule, unflinchingly supporting the President's right to take actions which they, individually, thought unwise for other reasons, but nevertheless within the purview of permitted conduct. Each endured the wrenching anxiety of a thoughtful man whose judgment has been rejected, and whose franchise to make judgments and proffer them for acceptance (against the hazard of rejection) is conditioned upon his ethical undertaking to give no public hint of his reservations about the selected course.

What was familiar to them, and to Richardson, from long experience with the law, was the principle of fallibility, and the clear-eyed recognition that they, themselves, might be mistaken. Each of them, and many others, repeatedly weighed the disadvantages of continued representation of the President — among them the frustration of frequent disappointments incurred in efforts to persuade the President of what they thought the most judicious course — against the disadvantages of quitting: chief among them, the loss of all opportunity to influence even occasionally the decisions which the President made. None was a liberal in bright flames of zeal, and none thought the President to be a dreadful man, who would obstruct justice and then use one of them to obstruct the investigation of the obstruction. Elliot Richardson did not think the President of the United States would lie to his Secretary of Defense, not even to persuade him to become his Attorney General.

Richardson went back to Camp David on April 29, 1973. "The President told me he needed somebody of established integrity, to create confidence that things would be done right." Two weeks before, the President had talked with Haldeman and defined what he meant by that: essentially, somebody who would create the confidence that things *had* been done right, and thus assure nondiscovery of the fact that things had been done wrong. "I was to have full discretion to determine who the Special Prosecutor should be." But not full knowledge — the President was too cagey to confide that to Richardson — of *what* he would be. "The President mentioned Will Hastings," Richardson's brilliant aide, lured from the Boston law firm of Bingham, Dana & Gould to help him as Attorney General of Massachusetts, as Undersecretary of State, and as Secretary of HEW, "and J. Edward Lumbard," of the Court of Appeals for the Second Circuit of the United States, "as possible men."

Considering what the President had in mind, his choice of auditor, and his selections of names to propound as Special Prosecutor, were very remarkable. Neither of them would have gone into the tank for him, any more than Richardson himself would.

"Those were good suggestions," Richardson said, assuming the intention to enforce the fact of integrity, and consequently stressing the secondary obligation to insure also its appearance, "but Hastings was too close to me. The President suggested John J. McCloy."

Critics of the Establishment have said a lot of mean things about John J. McCloy, but nobody in his right mind has ever said that John J. McCloy will take a dive. By adding McCloy's name to the list of prospective candidates for the job of Special Prosecutor, the President thus reinforced Richardson's basic assumption that the President was sincere in his quest for total disclosure of Watergate and related matters.

The President, of course, was not sincere. If he was rational, he was proceeding with great confidence upon at least one, and probably three, gravely mistaken judgments.

— He unquestionably believed, on April 29, 1973, that the problems of Watergate were still entirely cosmetic, like the unfortunate jowls and the five-o'clock shadow that should have been prettied up before his first television debate with John Kennedy. Nixon accorded the press the sort of hostility which hateful men reserve for their most threatening enemies; he believed that newsmen fabricated the stuff that made voters and other politicians dislike and oppose him. There was that, too: in his mind, opposition was proof of dislike, which he at once requited, with interest; Morton Halperin was transmuted from ally (on Henry Kissinger's staff) to traitorous villain (on the staff of the Brookings Institution) in an instant. When President Nixon fulminated about wallowing in Watergate, during the summer of the Ervin Committee hearings, he was articulating the same basic premise that informed his approach to Elliot Richardson in April: he acknowledged no substantive issue in Watergate, seeing only the fantastic vapors of foul malicious opposition. He was not a hypocrite at all, although he surely looked like one; he was a man of utter consistency, who obtained his power by outpretending those who, in his estimation, had perfidiously mounted spiteful pretenses to resist him, but had luckily, at long last, fallen short.

— He thought Elliot Richardson was of the same mind. The President did not admonish Richardson to take the job at Justice as a living, breathing placebo to dupe the nation into thinking that a disease was being cured when it was not, because the President thought, genuinely and sincerely and devotedly, that the national malaise was psychosomatic, and assumed that Richardson agreed. Recalling that conversation at Camp David, Richardson said: "The President referred to discussions with Haldeman, about the Ellsberg break-in. He said Haldeman and Ehrlichman would have to resign. He mentioned the Kleindienst resignation. *He wanted to make a simultaneous announcement of someone in whom the public could have confidence.*"

But, most emphatically, he did not want that public confidence to be fully rewarded. First at State, then at HEW, then at Defense, Elliot Richardson had served him dutifully, and with high marks from all except a few carpers among the Eastern liberal press, and those high marks had eased, smoothed and graced the Nixon Administration. Richardson had made him look good before, and he rather assumed that Richardson would make him look good again, a treatment which he seriously needed. That much, at least, he knew: he needed somebody to make up those Herblock jowls that Watergate was drawing upon his whole presidency.

Richardson, of course, did not agree. He was more than willing to make the President look good, because the substantive accomplishments which reflected pleasurably upon the President were, to his mind, primarily significant in and of themselves. It was appropriate that the President be credited with the causation of those substantive achievements. But the credit was only a side effect, to Richardson, and he believed, just as mistakenly as the President, that Richard M. Nixon agreed with him. He therefore did not seek presidential assurance that his function would be substantive, and only incidentally cosmetic, because when the President had asked him to do things before, his mandate had been substantive. What he did not know was that the Nixon interest and the national interest veered apart where Watergate was concerned: like Henry Petersen, Elliot Richardson was inexpert in thinking about the unthinkable.

— The President thought we were stupid. He had a mean contempt for the voters so readily duped by the evil forces which arrayed themselves against him. He ordered Haldeman to run the cover-up, June 23, 1972, because he saw the burglars' connection to the White House as a goddamned embarrassment which his enemies would use as vampire makeup, but as makeup nonetheless, to cosmeticize his defeat for reelection. Accordingly, he would apply a little obstruction to prevent that, and then a little more, and some more after that, and that was what he was doing when he massaged Elliot Richardson at Camp David on that April Sunday. Bearing his fardels as best he could, which was not very well, he fell back upon his inveterate practice of being a tactician when he should have been a philosopher, concerned, to the exclusion of what was right, solely with what would work.

For Nixon's ploy to succeed, Richardson had to remain ignorant of the divergence of Nixon and national interests. For a while he did. He talked to his wife again, after the calls to Rogers, and "we agreed, 'Oh, expletive deleted,'" he said, "'it would probably be better that I do it.' I would just as soon have been left alone. But I was the only United States Attorney General in the history of the country who had ever been United States

Attorney and a State Attorney General. The reason why I did it? The integrity of the system."

What he had sought to show unimpaired, by becoming Attorney General, Richardson, a quick study, promptly found to be in direct and immediate hazard. At Camp David he told the President he might be "a useful adviser" as Attorney General. Then, after the President had discussed the Ellsberg break-in without any justification on the basis of national security — "The President mentioned the Ellsberg break-in in connection with Ehrlichman's resignation. Ehrlichman, the President said, had turned it down" — Richardson was startled to hear the White House publicly declare that the burglary had been committed for reasons of national security. The President had said nothing about the authority he had issued to pay off Hunt on March 21: "If I had known about Hunt," Richardson said, "I could not have taken the job. The President would have had to agree that I was taking the job as opposing counsel, heading the investigative, prosecutive drive. The hearings" — by the Senate Judiciary Committee, on Richardson's nomination — "made it clear that we were involved in an adversary situation." After Cox was approved as Special Prosecutor, Richardson had no further personal dealings with the President until the Saturday Night Massacre in October.

"It was hard to take," Richardson said of his knowledge of the President whom it was perilous to trust, and perfect folly to protect, "the same as combat in the war. Unassimilable. My disposition was to believe that he was not involved. He told me so, convincingly. It was implausible to me. He said in effect that 'I've had no part in these things. It's been extremely painful. The hardest thing I've ever had to do. I can only say to you that I have had no part in this, and no knowledge of it. And if you don't believe this, you shouldn't take the job.'"

He was lying. And the best he would manage, even under the guns of virtually certain indictment by the Special Prosecutor, secluded in disgrace and bailed out, intemperately soon, by President Ford, was this: "I can see clearly now . . . that I was wrong in not acting more decisively and more forthrightly in dealing with Watergate. . . . I know that many fair-minded people believe that my motivation and actions in the Watergate affair were intentionally self-serving and illegal." Felonious, as a matter of fact, vicious, unprincipled, deceitful, corrupt, malicious, spiteful, vengeful and dead wrong. "I now understand how my own mistakes and misjudgments" — surely the most delicate phraseology ever employed by a President of the United States to describe a conspiracy to obstruct justice — "have contributed to that belief and seemed to support it." *Seemed*, my lord? If this is seeming, what the hell is fact? "That the way I tried to deal with Watergate" — by paying hush money, and sacrificing friends, and lying to loyalists, and watching subalterns go off to jail while lying some more — "was the wrong way is a burden I shall bear for every day of the life that is left to me." My God, he wanted sympathy.

# 20

RICHARDSON DID BELIEVE it, though he shouldn't have, and he did take the job. But unlike Petersen, who also believed it (and persisted in the belief when he should not have), Richardson credited the testimony of his senses, saw that he'd been wrong in the extension of his trust, perceived that he'd been conned, got mad, fast, and stayed mad, too. It's not wise to fool Elliot Richardson; months after he'd quit, in refusal, as Attorney General, to fire Special Prosecutor Archie Cox, the muscles in that Yankee jaw still bulged when he recalled the sleazy trick that had been tried on him.

Richardson, though, had an advantage which Petersen lacked. It was timing. When Richardson went to Camp David, the Senate had already approved Sam J. Ervin's February 5, 1973, resolution; on February 7, 1973, the Select Committee on Presidential Campaign Activities was created by the Sixtieth Resolution of the Ninety-third Congress of the United States, "to conduct an investigation and study of the extent, if any, to which illegal, improper, or unethical activities were engaged in by any persons, acting individually or in combination with others, in the presidential election of 1972, or in any related campaign or canvass conducted by or in behalf of any person seeking nomination or election as the candidate of any political party for the office of President of the United States in such election, and to determine whether in its judgment any occurrences which may be revealed by the investigation and study indicate the necessity or desirability of the enactment of new congressional legislation to safeguard the electoral process by which the President of the United States is chosen."

Hunt was woebegone in the slammer. McCord was spraying his throat and nursing his grudges. Dean was having heart-to-heart talks with the prosecutors. Magruder was having his ethical compass calibrated. Liddy was stolid in the D.C. Jail, bearing no malice toward John J. Sirica, a man who did what he thought was necessary, but Strachan was edgy, and Alexander Butterfield, who knew about the tape system, was indisposed to lie about it, if somebody asked. The press was in full cry. Hank Ruth was recruiting prosecutors.

Those circumstances conduced to Richardson's benefit. He had the wit and resolution to take their best advantage. What he got was not the best imaginable advantage, but it served, it served.

The Committee was specifically instructed to determine whether new legislation was needed to deal with sixteen kinds of conduct: burglary at the Watergate, bugging the DNC, filching and photographing of DNC papers, the transmission of stolen information, who thought it up, who did it, who paid for it; whether there was hush money in the *Liddy* case; campaign sabotage, payments for acts of sabotage, incitement to sabotage; extortionate fund-raising, deceptive reporting of funds raised, concealment of funds raised, destruction of fund records; the commission of crimes and suchlike in the campaign; and whether new laws were needed to forestall such goings-on in the future.

Laws do not forestall anything or anyone, except those men of riotous imagination combined with timid will and feeble mind, who dream up nefarious outings and then consult the statute books, only to learn that what they have in mind is, well, against the law, and then they don't do it. Name two. Not even the Berrigans were feckless enough to deserve that classification.

The concept of laws as self-executing is a shibboleth of the very school which holds that criminal justice shall be enforced idealistically (and thus inefficiently). The correlative of the theory about the ninety-nine is that appropriate judgments, legislatively expressed, defining the constitutive elements of socially intolerable conduct, will immediately conduce to the universal cessation of such behavior.

Legislators, including those on the Ervin Committee, unaverse to the attention of the media and thoughtful of their own reelections, publicly by implication subscribe to the attitude of self-execution, and propose on a regular basis for enactment laws guaranteed to end all torments of the human condition. Cops and lawyers tend to snicker.

Every item on the Senate's shopping list for the Ervin Committee was illegal under federal law in 1970, when Tom Charles Huston thought it might be a good idea to infiltrate student organizations, bug and bag-job the opposition. It was all illegal in 1971, when John Caulfield's Sand-wedge plan was disdained (this was before Caulfield got to Treasury, as Acting Director for the Alcohol, Tobacco & Firearms Division, which enforces the gun control laws of this country; he was there when he took to meeting McCord in the underbrush), and the way for Liddy's Gem-stone plan was prepared. Each of those species of behavior was punishable by law before Hunt and Liddy ever met. If the Committee had followed Resolution 60 by its terms, and if it found (perhaps by consulting the *Liddy* transcript, where most of the conduct in question had been proved beyond a reasonable doubt) that the posited behavior had in fact occurred, it was unarguably empowered to propose new laws that would have precisely the same effect of prevention as the ones which *Liddy, et al.*, had ignored. And it did, too, when the squabbling between the Republicans and the Democrats was at last resolved to a point of accommodation which permitted the drafting and issuance of a report which nobody read. If Resolution 60 meant anything about what the Senate had in mind for the Committee to do, the Committee had nothing to do.

There is no such thing as a committee with nothing to do. A committee with nothing to do was not what the Senate had in mind, and the Committee knew it. The Senate can investigate whatever it damned well pleases. The Senate was pleased to investigate.

What the Senate had in mind, wanted to know, what Sirica wanted to know, and, for that matter, what the people wanted to know, was, as Senator Howard Baker was inclined to ask with tedious regularity, at whatever cost to a line of questioning that was developing circumstantial evidence to precisely his point, was: "What did the President know, and when did he know it?" The Committee found something to do, just as Judge Sirica found something to occupy his mind while Silbert prosecuted a case that should have been pleaded. Just as the people who employed Liddy and Hunt had found something for them to do when Hoover recoiled in repugnance from what *they* had in mind, and said that what they wanted the FBI to do was illegal, dangerous and likely to be mortally embarrassing. Huston had scornfully summarized Hoover's objections to his intelligence plan: "If we do these things, the 'jackels

214

(*sic*) of the press' and the ACLU will find out . . . " and they did, too. And Hoover was right. By the expedient of ignoring what the language of the law said they were to do, they carved out a territory for operations. Just as, come to think of it, Liddy had done.

The Senate Judiciary Committee, in May of 1973, thus functioned to advance Sirica's cause. It was not that the Committee, including Mr. Kennedy, of Massachusetts, distrusted Elliot Richardson. But there was a profound sense among the Democrats of the Committee, charged with vetting Mr. Richardson as Attorney General, that President Nixon was not entirely candid, and not totally disinclined to keep his paws off the Department of Justice. Of Mr. Richardson, therefore — and, by extension, of President Nixon, who needed Richardson desperately in that new slot because he is a man of probity — the Committee required a hostage. They wanted an independent prosecutor.

Earl Silbert was pissed off. "It's bad enough," he told a friend, "you expect it, a big case comes along, and they take it away from you when it's ready. Or it's tough, and they let you win it, and then they take credit away from you. You expect that. But when you get the tough one, and you win it, and you're on your way, and then they come around and take it away from you, and it almost seems like you didn't win it, and they blame you for not winning it, then, then it's murder."

Archie Cox went to Washington, quite cheerfully, to do a dirty job. In a way he was shanghaied, but then he consorts with the kind of people who are addicted to the formation of mugwump press gangs in the public interest, and he might have expected something like that. Elliot Richardson, in need of a suitable hostage, called upon a few federal judges and asked them to step down from lifetime positions during good behavior, to sit in the hot seat for a while, and they thought about that $40,000 a year, and the clerks and the comfortable offices and the secretarial help, and perhaps about Arthur Goldberg, who said: "Sure," when LBJ told him he ought to step down from the Supreme Court of the United States, and they asked themselves why they ought to do a fool thing like that, and said: "No." But Richardson's adenoidal eloquence was not severely taxed in the recruitment of Archie Cox. Mr. Cox is a proud man.

The former Solicitor General of the United States takes no discernible pains to disguise his autocratic assurance of his own impeccable morality and formidable intellect. That combination of attitudes made him pregnable, if not downright receptive, to Richardson's proposition: the nation was in obvious neediness of service from the best of its citizens, a condition amounting to a specific and personal responsibility for Professor Archibald Cox of the Harvard Law School.

A rather sedentary man, Cox looks like he spends much of his time bounding around a tennis court. He embarked upon his first job as prosecutor plainly intent upon satisfying the trust which the Judiciary Committee expressed by accepting him as earnest flesh of Richardson's bona fides as Attorney General of the United States. Being without firsthand experience of the grubby grittiness of making criminal cases — as Solicitor General he had only overseen the kind of Olympian issues of law and policy that Silbert had labored unseen to prepare in the Tax Division — he obtained the likes of Henry Ruth as his Deputy.

Then there was Tom McBride. McBride grew up professionally in OCRS, ramroding the Reading, Pennsylvania, investigation which hooked a large number of crooks and provided a model for Strike Force investigations. McBride's a dour man, appointed by the Nixon junta to a high place in the Law Enforcement Assistance Administration, where he chafed.

Jim Neal joined the team. He worked the *Hoffa* cases for RFK. And there was a number of other mean lawyers, blooded in the Organized Crime and Racketeering Section and used to hard cases, involving hard guys. It was Cox's Army, and it made Nixon nervous. He'd appointed most of them himself, to one post or another, but he was second. The first to appoint them was Kennedy, one Kennedy or the other. They were all the same. Cox was SG under John Fitzgerald Kennedy.

The White House made complaints that Ruth and his pursuivants were a *maquis* for the Kennedy government in exile. Mr. Cox was denounced as *imperious,* the Administration's spokesmen apparently not pausing to consider whether its adversaries might not find a man of imperial mien highly qualified for an embattled post, a certain majesty tending to conduce to fortitude in adherence to principle. Pat Gray, so far as is known, was never termed *imperious.* And, more importantly, the Administration overlooked its own interest, vested in Cox's aloofness and Richardson's principles. Mr. Nixon needed both of them, quite desperately, and the measure of the desperation was his manifest ignorance of the extremity of the need.

Nixon's apparent submission to that need (he had his fingers crossed) mollified all sectors whose reactions could be reliably measured. The trust unjustifiably withdrawn from Silbert was conditionally extended to Cox, because he said he would damn the torpedoes, and thus conferred upon Richardson, who said he would do for Cox what he had pledged and delivered to his Assistants when he was Attorney General of Massachusetts: back him to the end. So from the Richardson-Cox parlay, the Senate and the country got a guarantee of the due bill for justice which had seemed, but was not, doubtful in Silbert's hands.

That should have transferred into Cox's hands, entire, the discretion which anyone would need to get the bag of cats all the way open by luring out one cat at a time. It also left him the option to discriminate among cats, choosing those of grave criminal responsibility for no-holds-barred indictment, going easy upon those more stupid than wicked, and sending those chiefly tainted by association on their way, to sin no more. As long as Cox was photographed walking to the Special Prosecutor's Office early in the morning, and quoted about leaving it late at night, and how holding the job had to his annoyance prevented him from growing vegetables on his farm in Maine; so long as Richardson was quoted as directing Justice employees to log all calls about cases, except those from newsmen (a fairly blunt means of discouraging influence-peddling), the country and the Congress were prepared to reinstate the presumption of regularity in official conduct which, to a degree, undid Silbert when he accepted Dean at face value, trusted Gray, and omitted to dream that a former Attorney General of the United States would lie to a grand jury. The Senators were out to save the country.

It was that sense of urgency which governed the Ervin Committee's exercise of its actual warrant to choose its own mission: a burning desire, which at times became pathetic, to do what the members and the staff believed that the press wanted done.

The Committee proceeded on the notion that what the press (and, presumably, though there was no reliable way, then, to be sure, the public which reads the press) wanted was somebody who could hang it on the President. The Committee was right; when the public hearings began, the press surged into the room with all the seemliness of a lynch mob.

The trouble with that mission was the virtual certainty of its failure. The prosecutors, and the FBI Special Agents working the Watergate investigation under Angelo Lano of the Washington Field Office, were professionals spending full time at their specialty — the investigation and prosecution of criminal offenses — when the Casual Clothes Squad flabbergasted McCord and the Cubans in the DNC.

U.S. Attorney Harold Titus, unlike Sam Ervin, was not obliged to fish

217

Silbert out of the Georgetown University Law School where Sam Dash was teaching when the Committee went hunting for a Chief Counsel. Titus had his men in place.

They worked in confidence, not with the television cameras boring down the throats of the people they interviewed (although it was less confidence than they imagined, far less, because Dean and Gray and Parkinson and O'Brien were snooping on the investigation from June 19 on), and when Silbert put the bricks to McCord about the transmitter, he was not thinking about a vote on the Senate floor on whether to stop the bombing in Cambodia: he was thinking about McCord. Completely concerned about what he would be able to prove, Silbert was consequently undistracted by what, if he had been an official facing partisan political reelection problems, might have tempted him (as it plainly did Senator Lowell Weicker) to settle for any scandalous utterances he could fetch from the witness, or to indulge in a tantrum, well timed for the six o'clock news, when all efforts to get something sensational failed. The Committee, by means of publicity and much huffing and puffing, went out with the intention of squeezing out of people what had stayed inside them under the threat of long terms in jail.

This assumed, of course, that there was somebody, somewhere, who could get the guy good. As, in fact, there was. Not on the actual break-in; nobody seriously envisioned evidence that the President sat in on Liddy's chart-talks about trollops traducing lecherous Democrats in lavishly appointed vessels swinging at anchor off the coast of Florida. The premise was that there was somebody who could be persuaded to nail him on the initiation and management of the cover-up. Someone, in other words, who would confide to the nation how Richard M. Nixon had blown smoke at Earl Silbert.

Fidelity to that premise was various. Ervin sat there, scowling, frowning, and working his mouth, so that one deduced that he wore false teeth that didn't fit him right, but his press officer knocked that down: he explained, with an assurance of credulity in the press that ought by rights to have vanished under the torrent of Watergate examples to the contrary, that Ervin's brain goes much faster than his mouth, and that's why he moves his lips around his own teeth, even when he isn't talking.

Sam mostly contented himself with excoriating the witnesses for disrespect to the Constitution, which earned him renewal of his sobriquet as the Senate's finest constitutional lawyer, notwithstanding the fact that John D. Ehrlichman's foxy old lawyer, John J. Wilson, made mincemeat of

Senator Sam every time they quarreled (representing H. R. Haldeman in a hearing before Judge Sirica, Wilson got feisty with Richard Ben-Veniste of the Special Prosecutor's Office, and received with a smile Sirica's reminder that he was not before the Ervin Committee, and had better subside). Neal, at the Haldeman-Ehrlichman-Mitchell trial, waived Wilson's submission, and devoured him.

Senator Baker discovered, to his joy, that his profile looked good on television, and so did his crinkly smile; he persisted in demanding to know what the President knew, and when he found out. But he never really did anything to develop any circumstantial evidence on those points, and he seriously interfered with the efforts of others to do so.

Senator Herman Talmadge, reputed the brightest man in the Senate, became disgusted in a month by Ervin's evangelism and Baker's bakerism, concluded the whole thing was a waste of time, and attended the sessions mostly, it seemed, to make it clear that he'd been spending his time as Chairman of the Committee on Agriculture, drafting a new farm bill.

Senator Edward Gurney of Florida, perhaps mindful of the explosive potential — realized in December — of his own little slush fund (by July of 1974, he had been indicted for obtaining that fund by means of extortion), plainly hoped that there wasn't anyone who could make the President on the cover-up.

Senator Joseph Montoya of New Mexico had the best questions, probably, of any of the Senators, but seemed to have difficulty listening to the answers; he didn't follow them up. That was because his staff prepared the questions, and the witness delivered the answers, and the staff couldn't wedge itself in between Montoya and the witness to explore the replies, and Montoya didn't know how. He didn't want to, anyway; what he wanted was improving moral advice for the young people of this nation, which he demanded and got from every felon who testified.

Senator Daniel K. Inouye of Hawaii was always ready, and merciless in his questioning, but "the little Jap" — as Mr. Wilson put it, forgetting to mention that Inouye's one-armed, having lost the other as an American soldier in World War II — was balked by the Committee's rule of twenty minutes per Senator (later reduced to ten), and every time he got close to something with Ehrlichman and Haldeman, Wilson started a harangue with Ervin or Dash that reprieved his client from the pressure of the Hawaiian.

Weicker spent much of the time in a rage, it seemed, and it was genuine. He was particularly distraught about what had been done to Pat Gray, and, to his credit, less than enchanted by Gray's servile willingness to have it done to him and then lie about it afterward. But the expression of that rage was calculated; everybody knew by noon when Weicker contemplated a four o'clock tantrum, thoughtfully scheduled to dominate the evening news presumably as popular in Connecticut as elsewhere, and of some potential benefit to a man who got into the Senate with but thirty-eight percent of the vote, opposed as he had been by an Episcopal priest and discredited Tom Dodd, who ran as an Independent. Weicker, like the rest of them, had an understandable interest in his political future, and there was certainly nothing wrong in his determination to secure maximum recognition of the tigerish work which his own staff did to make him look good and to advance the investigation. But that way of effectuating the determination looked contrived.

The Committee's own staff was hastily assembled from that group of lawyers, investigators and researchers who could be spared, and wished to be spared, from what they were doing before. Ervin hired Sam Dash because Dash used to be a prosecutor, and is an authority on electronic surveillance: that, based on the apparent importance of bugging in the Watergate matter, was one of Ervin's ideas that seemed good at the time.

"Well," Dash said, questioning Ehrlichman, "after the Huston plan did not go forward, were you assigned a role to create in the White House a capability for intelligence-gathering at any time?" Nearly fifteen years of teaching and consulting away from his tenure as prosecutor and then public defender in Philadelphia, Dash had forgotten how to put one intelligible question at a time. Witnesses, especially those represented by Wilson, repeatedly took advantage of Dash's multiplicity and muddiness, choosing the least troublesome question from his interrogatory smorgasbord, answering or evading with justified confidence that Dash would fail to go back and take up the discards, one by one.

"I don't know quite what you are getting at," Ehrlichman said. "If you are getting at the special unit and the problems of leaks . . ."

When people sought to take advantage of him, Sam Dash got irked, and became testy. Then he resorted to rudeness, an inadequate substitute for the courteous verbal aggression which he should have practiced. This did not matter very much at the Georgetown University Law Center, where he was a man of eminence whose perquisites included the right to display a little temperament, the recipients of his incivility being dependent upon him, and thus indulgent. It mattered a great deal when the recipient was his adversary, and recognized the tactical advantage available from Dash's petulance.

"I don't know why you have to find out what I am getting at," Dash said, "if you just answer the question as I ask it."

"It's an obscure question," said Ehrlichman, correctly.

"It's a simple question," Dash said, incorrectly. "If the answer is no, say no. If the answer is yes, say yes. Did there come a time when you were asked to develop a capability in the White House for intelligence-gathering?"

"Intelligence-gathering," Ehrlichman said. "The answer would be no."

Ehrlichman had just done what Dash had told him to do. Dash did not like that a bit. "Now you were trying to see what I was getting at." That was incorrect; Ehrlichman saw very clearly what Dash was getting at: he was trying to get at Ehrlichman, and through him, to Nixon. What Ehrlichman was trying to do was prevent him from doing that. "Were you ever asked to set up a special unit in the White House for the purpose of determining whether certain leaks had occurred in major national security areas?"

"In point of fact," Ehrlichman said, "I was." He was asked, in point of fact, to determine where the Joint Chiefs of Staff, inimical to Henry Kissinger's construction of his role as National Security Adviser, were getting their dope about Kissinger's activities. They were getting it from an aide planted on Kissinger's staff. But nobody knew that, then; even Kissinger thought his offices might be bugged, and he had his own staff bugged, too, just to see if they were the sources. And to prove his fraternal loyalty. Kissinger, of course, escaped the pleasure of a stint before the Watergate Committee, and was not indicted for anything. This infuriated Ehrlichman, who gave a secret interview to Seymour Hersh of the *New York Times* about the Plumbers, explaining his action: "Kissinger gets the Nobel Prize, and we go to jail."

"And strictly in terms of your question," Ehrlichman continued to Dash, "I was not asked to set it up. Egil Krogh, Jr., was a member of the Domestic Council staff, and he was asked by the President to form this special unit. I was designated as one to whom Mr. Krogh could come with problems in connection with it, and the President said also that he could come to him with problems."

"Were you in at the beginning of the setting up of this plan?" Dash said.

Ehrlichman said: "Yes."

"What was the unit to do?" Dash asked.

"The unit as originally conceived," Ehrlichman said, "was to stimulate the various departments and agencies to do a better job of controlling leaks and the theft or other exposure of national security secrets from their departments." It was bad enough that somebody had a pipeline into Kissinger's office, worse still, that what came through the pipeline was promptly transmitted to Daniel Schorr, Joseph Kraft and Jack Anderson. "It was a group which was to bring to account, so to speak, the various security offices of the Department of Defense and State and Justice and CIA, to get them to do a better job."

"And therefore," Dash said, more interested in extracting agreement to his concept of the Plumbers than in information about the Plumbers, "this unit was to gather facts, if there was a leak, or to act as a deterrent, I take it, to prevent leaks."

Two questions. "No," Ehrlichman said, "there would have been no need to gather facts under the concept, except to know that there had been an occurrence, but to require vigorous and very active effort on the part of the responsible people in the departments and agencies to find out who was responsible and how it happened and make sure it couldn't happen again."

Dash persisted. "Isn't that getting facts? Would you say some people who go to seek facts in an investigative way can also say they seek intelligence?"

The answer to that question was certain not to add a single cubit to the national understanding of the operations of the Plumbers, no matter what answer was given. That was the kind of question that Watergate witnesses liked best. Ehrlichman was elaborately patient. "Well, but you see what I am trying to say to you in . . . As originally set up and conceived, this was not an investigative unit in the sense that your question implies. It was far more a group that was established for the purpose of getting the security people in the departments and agencies to do a better job of their job."

"Did it ever," Dash said, showing signs of weariness, "was it ever called or was it ever referred to as an investigative unit?" For whatever difference that made.

"Subsequently, it was," Ehrlichman said, "because it became an investigative unit subsequently."

"So," Dash said, with a measure of gratification, "there came a time when you were administering an investigative unit."

"Yes," Ehrlichman said. "In a literal sense, that is true."

"Literal sense?" said Dash, continuing to exalt subjugation of the witness over interrogation.

"Yes, sir," Ehrlichman said, with a faint but unmistakable hint of his determination not to be subjugated.

"Not in an actual sense?" Dash asked.

"Well," Ehrlichman said, "here I am, dueling with a professor over words."

"I'm not dueling with you," Dash said, though he was, "I'm just trying . . ."

Ehrlichman knew what he was trying, and also how to thwart him. "Professor," he said, with limpid arrogance, "if you say it is actual, it is actual."

Dash was now cornered. "I don't want you to take my questions," he said, although he did, if he intended to examine the witness, "and I don't want to put words in your mouth."

"Sure," Ehrlichman said, having accomplished his purpose, which was to discombobulate Dash. "I am trying to give you . . ."

Dash interrupted. "I really want to have your answer to the best of your recollection," he said, having received the answer some time before and having utilized it as a subject for argument with the witness.

"Sure," Ehrlichman said, never having disputed that he started out in charge of the Plumbers, whatever it was that the Plumbers might have constituted in the abstract. "I am trying to give you the real essence of this as we go along, and I don't mean to be fencing over words."

That was the kind of tedious wrangling which took place whenever a stubborn witness appeared before the Committee. It made the press restive. Gleeful on May 17, 1972, when the hearings commenced with the testimony of Robert C. Odle, Jr., former Administrative Director of CREEP (he said he'd been smug when he heard about the burglary at the DNC, knowing it couldn't happen at CREEP because he had Jim McCord in charge of security at 1701 Pennsylvania Avenue), the press didn't grasp the difference between friendly and unfriendly witnesses — and what significance that implied for an unprepared Congress — until Liddy's former secretary, Sally Harmony, appeared on June 5, 1973, and got away clean. And even then, with Rose Mary Woods six months away from protecting her boss, Richard Nixon, before Judge Sirica in the tapes hearings, the press did not fully comprehend what was going to happen when the submissive or ignorant types (Bruce Kherli, a presidential assistant who didn't know anything), the righteous (Leeper, Barrett and Schoffler, the Casual Clothes officers of the Metropolitan Police Department who bagged McCord and the Cubans), the desperate (James McCord and John J. Caulfield), and the contrite (Sloan, Porter, Magruder and Dean) were exhausted, and the hard guys came in.

There was a clue in the two days of testimony by Maurice Stans; proud as Lucifer, he had no regard whatever for Senator Sam, and rebuffed his every effort to force some expression of guilty conscience for destruction of pre–April 7, 1972, campaign contributions. If Congress thought privacy of political contributions was negligible before the new campaign reporting act went into effect, Stans said, Congress should have done something about it.

The Committee was unprepared.

The Committee staff worked under ridiculous conditions; an auditorium in the new Senate Office Building was converted into offices by installation of three-quarter green metal and opaque glass partitions. Investigators sat up on the stage, making telephone calls from a crescent-shaped table last used, it appeared, in a telethon. The noise was considerable, and the equipment was standard Government issue (dreary). Sam Dash early on substantiated the fear that he was working unfamiliar territory; one Senator said that much of Dash's evident floundering was attributable to his inexperience in politics. Only Ervin got any real use out of the majority staff, headed by Dash, and Baker monopolized the minority staff, directed by Fred Thompson. A former Assistant U.S. Attorney in Tennessee, Thompson drew upon his old specialties of prosecuting bootleggers and bankrobbers (and very successful he was at that, too) to help him tackle conspirators, and got nowhere. Initially furious about leaks from the staff, he moderated his reaction when caught, night after night, having drinks at the Carroll Arms and leaking stuff on his own.

The staff worked also, in vain, to meet impossible schedules. The Committee, without any substantial consideration of alternatives, responded to the press's demands for investigation of the Watergate burglary — and those implied by Sirica's actions — all too obediently; it should have cut its staff's teeth on dirty tricks, or something of comparable complexity, and then moved on to Watergate, sitting ten days and taking ten days off to let the staff work up the next series of witnesses, thoroughly. But instead there were five days of hearings in seven working days in May (with easy witnesses); after the Memorial Day recess, the Committee resumed on June 5, sitting three days out of four working days, and on June 12 did the same thing again. There was an interregnum for Leonid Brezhnev's visit to the United States, which the staff used to prepare as best it could for John Dean; he started on June 25, continuing through June 29. The Committee observed the July Fourth recess, and returned July 10 to hear John Mitchell. Mitchell was not friendly. On July 11 and 12, Mitchell testified some more, followed by Richard A. Moore, Special Counsel to the President and a smart man schooled in the uses of ignorance; he used the rest of the week, and part of July 16, when Alexander P. Butterfield was hustled in to disclose that the President had bugged himself and the tapes were in the basement of the White House. Herbert W. Kalmbach testified the same day, and also on the seventeenth, about how he shunted Anthony Ulasewicz about the country, paying people off. Ulasewicz appeared for his second stint on the eighteenth, followed by Fred LaRue, former Special Counsel to the President. LaRue, who was present when Mardian debriefed Liddy about the burglary, finished on the nineteenth, and Mardian followed him the same day. Mardian finished on the twentieth, and Gordon Strachan, Haldeman's staff assistant, took the seat while it was still warm. Strachan ran out of moist-eyed moralisms on the twenty-third, and Ehrlichman sat down. Ehrlichman manhandled the Committee on the twenty-fourth, twenty-fifth, twenty-sixth, twenty-seventh and thirtieth. He was succeeded by H. R. Haldeman.

There were some lies told in that stream of testimony. But that is unimportant, all things considered. What is important is that the Committee allowed itself to be stampeded into attempting the impossible (public investigation of secretive crimes) and thus neglected the feasible (education of the public about how they are persuaded to choose one presidential candidate instead of the other). *John Dean testified in public, on television, on the record, under oath, before Ehrlichman and Haldeman took the stand.*

They didn't have to worry about what Dean was going to say, as they had been obliged to worry when they were privately deposed in civil suits brought by Common Cause and the Democratic National Committee in May. They knew exactly what they were up against. And they were advised by John J. Wilson, who, if he did not have daily copy of Dean's testimony procured for him, certainly had somebody take very good stenographic notes from the televised hearings. He had Dean's story, cast in concrete, before his clients ever testified in public, and he made damned good use of it. Whenever the Committee got close to his clients, or to the President who had some interest in how they did, he juked them. He got into legal arguments with Ervin, and used up Ervin's time. He professed inability to understand Baker's questions, and used up Baker's time. He locked horns with Weicker, and made him very angry, and used up Weicker's time. He had Ehrlichman, the reputed closet liberal of the old Nixon staff, come on like Heinrich Himmler, and then Haldeman, the self-admitted Lord High Executioner, sat down and smiled and smiled and smiled. Wilson was belligerent, insulting (at least to Inouye), formidably well prepared, and a wall-eyed disaster for the Committee. He did what a good lawyer's supposed to do for his client: he ate the opposition alive. It was awful to watch, and it was also grand; one began to understand that it was not entirely devotion to the law that made John Adams defend the British soldiers accused of the Boston Massacre: it was probably also plain love of a good fight that he thought he could win, and he did. The only thing missing, as he waltzed them around, was "Roses from the South." It was a masterful job, and the Committee, out to get an elephant with a flyswatter, was what made it possible. They attacked an offensive-defensive problem with no defense at all. What Neal did to Wilson was the proof of it. The Committee went at it like a man in a raincoat in a subway station, waiting to expose himself to middle-aged matrons; then they were surprised when they got stuffed.

There was an excuse for Silbert. He thought the Counsel to the President, John Dean, in 1972, was probably a man of good repute, whose position entitled him to information about a sensitive case and gave him access to information useful to the investigation of a sensitive case, which he had promised to relay to the prosecutor and the investigators. Silbert, too trusting, had thought the Acting Director of the FBI was on his side, and did not imagine that Pat Gray was engaged in the destruction of evidence. He had no information that the Acting Director for Enforcement, Alcohol, Tobacco & Firearms, Internal Revenue Service, United States Department of the Treasury, was consoling defendant McCord during recesses in the *Liddy* trial, and disgracing a lifetime of police work. Dean's double-agent status was concealed from Silbert, just as Bittman, collecting hush money for Hunt, masqueraded successfully as

Hunt's mere attorney. Until the prosecutors harvested McCord or Hunt, they had no access to the minimum of facts needed to map the territory of the cover-up conspiracy. So they did what they had to do to turn one of those people, and obtained the convictions in *United States* v. *Liddy, et al.*, whereupon their tactical misjudgment of what to do to McCord (to make him collapse before trial) explosively combined with what Dean and Caulfield had done to McCord (to make him stand up before and during the trial), and was ignited by Sirica, who dispatched McCord to the Committee and thus completed the chain reaction which denied the prosecutors the results of what they had won.

The Committee had no such excuse. Its task (which the original prosecutors would cheerfully have performed in the usual course of the criminal justice business, had they been allowed to) was to exhaust what they knew by interrogation, investigate for corroboration or contradiction, reinterrogate, reinvestigate, and by diligent and rigorous collection of certainties, reconstruct what went on after June 17. When Dean wobbled into the fold of sheepish penitents, they had the same obligation with him. Had they carried it out, they would not have been content merely because Dean prefaced his testimony with a 245-page prepared statement. They would have bored in on what he put into that statement, and what he might have left out, reminding him constantly that the oath's in three parts, and thus establishing, *when he testified*, that Gray was not the only fellow who could be counted upon in a pinch to destroy evidence.

Instead, the Committee tested its most important witness to date only in public, Gurney floundering about morosely in his feeble effort to cross-examine Dean into some admission of falsehood, Inouye mousetrapping the White House by putting its so-called "Buzhardt memo's" spiteful questions in a patient tone that left the malice exposed (the memo was not, in fact, drafted by Buzhardt; it was a community enterprise in the White House Counsel's office. But it went to the Committee with some papers carrying Buzhardt's signature, so he got blamed for it).

The Committee thus settled for the truth, and persuaded many onlookers that it got nothing but the truth. Then, late in December of 1973, the Special Prosecutor's Office got the rest of it, perhaps, as far as Dean was concerned, the whole truth, at last. Leon Jaworski's people found out what happened to the Hermès notebooks. The fact was that John Dean kept Hunt's Hermès notebooks himself. Gray never saw them. And Dean destroyed them himself, while Liddy was still on trial, but after Hunt had pleaded. Probably because he thought Hunt had made a deal with Silbert, and didn't want Silbert coming around for those notebooks. Dean was still on the reservation, then.

John Dean, as everyone connected with the Committee knew, was a witness of supreme importance. If the Committee's hypothesis was correct (and it was), Nixon aided, abetted, counseled, commanded, induced and procured the endeavor to prevent communication of information relating to the violation of criminal statutes of the United States, in violation of Title 18, United States Code, Sections 1510 and 2. He was not accustomed to seeing many people. If he had done it (and he had) he did it through Haldeman, Ehrlichman, Colson, Dean or Mitchell, or a combination of them. When Dean took the oath, before the Committee, he was the only prospectively friendly witness in the collection. Mitchell was turning surly, and Ehrlichman later got mad, but Dean was a prime witness in hand.

Such witnesses deserve special care. Not the kind of care that the Committee demonstrated toward all the witnesses, not much care at all, in fact; the kind of care that a prosecutor uses to insure that the witness married by him or his investigators is accurate in his recollections of crucial significance. A mistake of fact, in a pretestimonial interview, is a prior inconsistent statement of minor importance when investigation before testimony shows that the witness was wrong. A mistake of fact, in testimony under oath, is proof of a willingness to lie under oath, and invokes the maxim of *falsus in unum, falsus in omnia* when the witness is caught in his falsehood as he testifies again. The Committee, gratefully accepting John Dean's mammoth statement, failed to exercise special care, to be sure that even so gargantuan a recitativo left nothing important omitted. And Dean left something out: the Hermès notebooks.

Earl Silbert wouldn't have done a dumb thing like that. He would not have jeopardized the credibility of so important a witness by allowing him to set the terms of his own cooperation, and its extent, and he wasn't letting Dean do that when the Committee snatched him away. Nor, for that matter, would the Jaworski staff that began with Archibald Cox have undertaken such a risk; Cox may have had such risks in mind when he moved in May to enjoin public hearings, citing prejudice to future trials. But John J. Sirica denied Cox the injunction, because he thought the publicity was necessary, and the Committee with stars in its eyes did not prepare its witnesses. John Dean put the Mayflower Coffee Shop in the Mayflower Hotel, when it's in the Statler Hilton; that made him look stupid, or forgetful. And he misled people about those notebooks, which obliged him to explain to defense lawyers in actual trials, when it was, really, that he started telling the truth.

The Constitution and the Common Law provide for public trials, not for the titillation of watching another in ultimate peril that drew thousands to the gallows, but to forestall the temptation to whisk innocent citizens off to prison by means of Star Chamber proceedings. Neither provides for show trials, where the issue is not whether the defendant can be proven to have done something, but whether something was done, and who did it. Sirica very nearly made the *Liddy* case into a show trial; he certainly exerted himself as best he could to do so. Then he sent McCord, full of bile, to the Committee, with instructions to tell Sam Ervin whether something was done, and who did it.

The statutes and the Common Law approve of public legislative hearings, to balk the temptation to pass confiscatory or otherwise tyrannical laws in secret, and to give the legislators a chance to consider the effects of new laws. Neither issues any franchise to Congress to conduct show trials, whether to determine who promoted Peress, or to find out who put Liddy up to it, and then paid him off to keep his mouth shut after he got caught doing it. But the Committee members read the *Washington Post* and the *New York Times* as attentively as Sirica did, and, as readily as he had, augmented their lawful obligations with the lawful responsibilities of the press.

Those mandates are not supposed to be transferable. The press, which can probe, hector and denounce as often as it can find somebody willing to share facts that will infuriate, is not allowed to extract information from the unwilling. Powerless to compel testimony, the press is supposed also to lack punitive powers, which are restricted to courts and legislatures and best left there, as the Cleveland papers demonstrated convincingly when they annexed the Cuyahoga County law enforcement machinery to put Sam Sheppard behind bars, notwithstanding the Cleveland osteopath's insistence that his wife, Marilyn, had been done in by a bushy-haired intruder. And the courts and the Congress, vouchsafed the power to get the facts, and to punish the recalcitrant and miscreant, are not supposed to use that power to hector and denounce, or raise the hue and cry. The *Post* and the *Times, Time* and *Newsweek*, NBC, CBS and ABC, worked their side of the street very well; the trouble started when Sirica and Ervin began working it with them.

It was all a matter of motive, as are most bad actions commenced upon what seemed like good ideas at the time. Liddy thought he had good reason to propose his felonious errands, and John Mitchell agreed with him. John Dean was afraid that McGovern would win unless a hush-money network was built, and that was good enough reason for him and Herb Kalmbach, and a lot of other people, to go ahead and do it. John J. Sirica, retired as Chief Judge by statutory age requirement on March 19, 1974, retaining as Senior Judge control of much of the Watergate litigation, was angry about the mendacity which he sensed, and deemed it adequate reason to mount a mini-Inquisition. The Committee, lustful of approval because indulgent of ambition, acknowledged strident public interest in political secrets, deals and crimes, and found that good reason to plunge heedlessly — and harmfully — into matters beyond its competence. Between January 27, 1972, at the very latest, when G. Gordon Liddy proudly showed his charts to the Attorney General of the United States without being promptly arrested, and the end of August 1974, we had, for a country which installs men in government in the good faith expectation of a government of laws, altogether too much government by ungovernable men.

In May of 1973, Secretary of Defense Elliot L. Richardson had been hostage to the Senate Judiciary Committee as Attorney General–designate of the United States, until he should be ransomed by the agreement of Archibald Cox to serve as Special Prosecutor to follow the Watergate truth wherever it led. Richardson was a reluctant hostage; he had tried, in vain, to persuade the President to appoint a successor to Kleindienst from outside the Administration. Richardson perceived the President's problem as one of credibility; he acceded to the President's importunities only when convinced that an outside appointment would not be made, and, being a trifle imperious himself, that his nomination would be at least as unimpeachable as any other prospect's, agreed.

On October 20, 1973, Richardson, who understands the English language, resigned in refusal to dismiss Cox, because he thought a promise to pursue the truth, and to allow the truth to be pursued, declared a pledge that the truth would be determined. Mr. Richardson keeps his word.

Clark Clifford, Secretary of Defense under Lyndon Johnson and general-purpose liberal Democratic sage, heard a report in November that he was under consideration to succeed Cox. He used an intermediary to call the White House. His friend, Clifford said, called "the little soap man, who is he? The little soap man" — Bryce Harlow, former executive vice-president, Proctor & Gamble — "and he laughed and he laughed, and then he said: 'There were five or six of us in the Oval Office, and Mel'" — Laird, former Secretary of Defense under Richard Nixon, recalled to White House Assistant status, over his wife's strenuous objections, to grapple with the President's credibility problems — " 'said: "Mr. President, your real problem here is credibility, and I think you ought to seriously consider Clark Clifford." And the President bolted from his chair and said: "Mel, are you out of your fucking *mind?*" ' "

On January 30, 1974, the President delivered his fifth State of the Union message. He delivered it at bay. Scattered through the well of the House, flanked and outranked by Senators, Cabinet members, ministers and plenipotentiaries of foreign powers, were the members of the House Judiciary Committee, fresh from a briefing by John Doar, the committee's Special Counsel on the issue of the President's possible impeachment. House Administration loyalists, persuaded that the evidence then was insufficient to warrant impeachment, fretful that time might expose a sufficiency, were striving for a go-no-go impeachment resolution decision by April 1. Moderates opposed to the Administration were wavering between April 1, and the May 1 deadline sought by Administration opponents, and the firebrands said privately that it would take until June 1, 1974, to build the impeachment case to overwhelming proportions.

He was in his bunker, clutching the tatters of the greatest elective victory ever accorded an American President, put there by operation of an engine which he and his people had not devised, but had souped up. Mitchell, Jeb Magruder said, approved the third Liddy plan because he "felt that the information would be useful." It was the end of Tom Charles Huston's beginning, and the beginning of Nixon's end. He had thought he had a monopoly on unlawful politics. He had been too confident.

That misjudgment was the source of Elliot Richardson's reprieve. The congeries of pressures, on the President, brought out what Richardson had needed to know, and made him, in his turn, part of them.

# 21

BY TURNS IT was the biggest trial and the greatest theater that the country ever saw. Enthralled, we witnessed Ervin's muddled righteousness, Dash's righteous muddle, Cox's loftiness and Richardson's wrath: the Senate Committee was inclined to accept the view that it had accomplished the greatest civics lesson in history.

That was so, perhaps, though it rather understated what, in the end, had gone on. Without diminishing the educational achievement of the Select Committee on Presidential Campaign Activities, the importance of it was chiefly preliminary and preparatory.

When Sirica accepted the verdict in *United States of America* v. *George Gordon Liddy, et al.*, at the end of January 1973, and Sam J. Ervin, Jr., introduced what would become Resolution 60, few but their fellow tradesmen had ever heard of Henry Ruth, John Doar, Albert Jenner, or Jim Neal. Fewer still had heard of John Dean, and only a half dozen knew that President Nixon had some time before decided that tape recordings of what was said in conferences with him, might be useful when he commenced to ruminate upon his memoirs. There was momentary public diversion when McCord's letter was divulged by Sirica, but there was no widespread or sustained outcry.

That was because Mr. Nixon was the beneficiary of an attitude which, in our system, is supposed to be much more prevalent — invariable, in fact — than it is. Because he was the President of the United States, and generally (though certainly not universally) venerated as such, he actually enjoyed, though informally accused of wrongdoing, the presumption of innocence. Almost nobody else really gets that beneficence, whether he is an ironworker indicted for tax evasion, a governor said to think more highly of lawyers who contribute campaign funds than of those who don't, when judges are to be named, or a cop who refrains from arresting the lunchroom attendant who accepts a numbers bet from somebody else before getting the policeman's cheeseburger.

The President and his loyalists both perceived and employed that advantage, but they performed neither function well. Possibly because they had no precedent (though, of course, none of their opposition had any, either, but overcame the deficiency much more successfully), they failed to consider the nature of the presumption, or else they considered it but mistook it to be conclusive (in the law: a presumption which cannot be overcome, because evidence to the contrary will be automatically excluded), when in fact, like the presumption of innocence which all of us are supposed to enjoy, it was rebuttable. The opposition took the view contrary to the White House, and the opposition turned out to be correct: at some point, even in a presidential case, the evidence accumulates beyond the auditor's ability to disregard it.

Because, with customary arrogance, the Nixon people expected perpetual security from a finite resource of it, they did not husband it. The President, particularly, encouraged the dissipation of his advantage, but neither Haldeman nor Ehrlichman bestirred himself to ration its use. When the only way to preserve the advantage of the presumption was to prevent the increase of evidence which contradicted it, and when the only prudent means of doing that was to avoid conduct which created such evidence, Mr. Nixon demanded, or at least accepted, conduct which proliferated evidence. And then, for reasons that eluded even Leon Jaworski and Jim Neal, he saw to the perpetuation of that evidence, on the tapes.

"Why," Jaworski asked, "didn't he have a fire with those tapes?" Neal, fresh from nailing Haldeman, Ehrlichman, Mitchell and Mardian with those same tapes, asked the same question. Ehrlichman allowed as how, in rueful retrospect, a fire wouldn't've been a bad idea.

But nobody in the White House, before Butterfield testified, seems to have thought either of the honorable thing (to make no obstructions), the practical thing (to make no permanent record of plotting, if plotting was to be done), or even the rational response of a felon frightened that he was about to be caught (to destroy abundant evidence, in his control, that no one knows about).

Even as he bowed to court orders, and grudgingly disgorged a few tapes, endeavored to make a master's counterstroke, and released a whole mess of tapes (transcripts, actually, which he had had, uh, sanitized), and, in August of 1974, at last regurgitated the June 23, 1972, tape that destroyed him, the President with stunningly inappropriate aplomb insisted, at least in front of God and all the people, that the poison he was vomiting up established that he'd done no wrong. The Queen of Hearts, to get that one down before breakfast, would have been obliged to beg off on believing more impossible things, for at least a decade.

What he did not understand was that the Ervin Committee, and Richardson and Cox, had synergistically combined, long since, to make the unthinkable, publicly thinkable. The Committee had successfully communicated the acceptable notion that men ought not to do nasty things, even if those evils that they did lived on long enough after the doing to get themselves elected to the presidency of the United States.

That was not the prodigious feat it was extolled to be, because the presidency does occupy a special place in the political hearts of the country's men, and women too, for that matter; it is probably a lot easier, in the abstract, to arouse a stern insistence upon morality and ethical behavior in the tenant of 1600 Pennsylvania Avenue than it is to persuade a majority that somebody on the level of the job that Spiro Agnew held in Maryland does commit an offense against all the people when he starts hosing down the highway contractors for kickbacks. Still, in all its clumsiness, the Ervin Committee, at times with seeming inadvertence, did produce the result of apprising the nation of its own, pretty strong preference, that candidates for the presidency, and incumbents of the office, eschew funny business in the realization of their ambitions. Not much evidence, maybe, nowhere near enough to rebut the presumption of presidential innocence, but enough to remind us that the presumption was rebuttable, and that, perhaps, there might be evidence enough, somewhere, to do it.

It was that serviceable contribution which Mr. Nixon and his protectors (most of whom, being ignorant of what he had done, acted in good faith, during the Ervin summer, to contradict the remainder, without substantial effect) essayed to disregard. Brooming Cox out, in October of 1973, to leave Richardson cannonading around the country making speeches full of big words and abstract principles (the former

Attorney General did not need to say anything, really, to rouse the rabble, newly informed; all he had to do was show up), was the proof of the miscalculation.

The Ervin Committee had accustomed us to the possibility that the President might, in fact, be a crook. Not this President, necessarily; it was just that watching John Dean, and McCord, and the rest of them, popularized the view theretofore expressed principally by Raoul Berger in his book about impeachment, and also by Robert F. Drinan (D. Mass.) in his 1973 House resolution to take the guy out for failing to ask Congress about bombing Cambodia, and the Constitution of the United States: when the President of the United States indulges in the commission of high crimes and misdemeanors, it is time to roust the bastard out of there, because he isn't fit to serve.

For a majority nurtured in its attitudes toward the presidency by the terms of Franklin Delano Roosevelt, Harry S Truman, Dwight D. Eisenhower, John F. Kennedy, and Lyndon Baines Johnson, that was pretty radical, heady stuff. It is one thing to deny a Herbert Hoover reelection, because people are hungry, unemployed and desperate, and what he has in mind to help them does not seem to be working. It is quite another thing to order the fellow out before his lease expires.

When the President forced Richardson to resignation, and fired Cox, he implicitly affirmed his lack of accurate information about the mood of the country he was supposed to serve; like Japanese soldiers, emerging from Pacific island jungles thirty years after V-J Day, to receive bad news, he was somewhat out of touch.

William L. Hungate (D. Mo.) knew a hawk from a handsaw, and could distinguish an elephant from a mouse with a glandular condition. Before the 1974 off-year elections, he traveled around his small-city, blue-collar, some-farming district, and talked to the people who'd sent him to Congress. Among them there were few regular readers of the *New York Times* or the *Washington Post*. Scant also were partisans of presidential rights divine enough to excuse the commission of felonies. Representative Hungate, of no particular philosophical or affectionate partiality for Richard M. Nixon, was appropriately instructed.

William R. Cohen (R. Me.) discerned no particular reason to embellish a Republicanism nominal at best with a protective coating of strident pro-Nixon advocacy. His constituents seemed reasonably satisfied with his history of voting the way he thought proper, and he decided to persist in that course. The decision did not take very long. Peter Rodino (D. N.J.)

succeeded Emmanuel Cellar (D. N.Y.) as chairman of Judiciary, because Elizabeth Holtzman (D. N.Y.) knocked Cellar off in the primary in 1972. Mr. Rodino enjoyed no reputation as the foremost constitutional lawyer of the House, nor did he covet it; what he did possess, and cherish, was a reputation for doing the right thing, in the right way. Ms. Holtzman, Father Drinan, and other firebrands, while leaving some teeth marks on their tongues, nevertheless restrained themselves. Mr. Rodino saw to it that the majority employed John Doar as Counsel. The minority chose well also: Albert Jenner. Then, in a demonstration of political responsibility bidding fair to affirm by deed all that is best and good in the written ideals of American governmental processes, the Committee, each of whom was up for reelection, practiced self-denial, resisted the temptation to perform with portentous gravity on daily national television, and voted to close its hearings.

There was in that enlightenment not only statesmanship but self-interest. Unlike the Ervin Committee, which had interpreted its grant of terra incognita as a warrant to charge off in many directions, the Rodino Committee, with some internal chafing, restricted its efforts to discharge a limited responsibility, and devoted all of its efforts to that task. It consequently succeeded. John Doar, a large man with an incongruously high voice, and Albert Jenner, a smaller man with little appetite for fruitless partisanship, did much to advance that purpose.

It amounted to multiple acts of self-sacrifice. In substance, the Rodino Committee acknowledged the precedence of the Ervin Committee as ringmasters for the education of the public, and Jaworski's office as foremen of the prosecution. That left the chore of evaluating, as a sort of screening jury, the evidence available, and its persuasiveness in kind and detail, to satisfy the jury of two hundred million that Richard M. Nixon was no longer fit to serve, and ought to be discharged and removed from office.

The Rodino Committee, they decided, would do that chore, leaving to Jaworski the task of wresting further evidence from the White House, ingesting all of the evidence obtained by the Ervin Committee, risking the possibility that the public was not yet convinced, in a working majority, that the President ought to be removed, choosing its ground, doing what nobody else was doing, and trying to do it well.

That decision was not without strife in the making, nor without quarrelsomeness in the implementation. Virtually the only contribution made by the Rodino Committee to the accretion of evidence was mechanical:

the committee spent more money than the prosecutors on audio equipment, and thus got better detail from the White House tapes.

Doar summoned up from the vasty deep few live witnesses, and thus little that was spiritually new, against the White House and its occupants.

From the beginning, Doar to the dismay of the Democratic anti-Nixon *maquis* clung to the position that obstruction of justice was the only charge that would play in Peoria. Enraged about Cambodia, Drinan thought otherwise. The President's shabby cheating on his taxes annoyed others. They complained that Doar was following the Nixon line: unless it could be proven, beyond a reasonable doubt, that the President had covered up the Watergate, the country would not stand for his removal.

The *maquis* were right. That was exactly what Doar was doing, droning on and on to the Committee, without any bright lights or press around, marshaling the evidence.

Jenner equally exasperated his clients among the Republican minority. The pro-Nixon partisans (who at last removed him, just before the release of the June 23 tape, and then dined on crow, in tears) railed at him that he was following Doar's line: if it could be proven, beyond a reasonable doubt, that the President had covered up the Watergate, the country would not stand for his continuation in office.

Jenner's critics were right, too. It was exactly the view that Jenner took. He and Doar, like Richardson and Cox — and later, Jim St. Clair — maintained a very precise cognition of what a lawyer should do for his client: whatever the client wanted done, so long as it was legal, proper, truthful and ethical. John Dean did four months of a one-to-four-year sentence for indulging a more elastic view, and Herb Kalmbach did time too, for the same flexibility, but the country was harmed by their malleability.

The Doar-Jenner ethical and strategic axis failed also to enchant the Jaworski office, which found itself doing all the work to prize evidence out of the White House. There was some snarling at 1425 K Street, N.W., about what Rodino was doing, first issuing congressional subpoenas, then subsiding into stiff notes when the White House ignored them. Yet still they plodded on, until Doar was satisfied that he had collated, compiled, catalogued and fitted into place, every single scrap of available evidence. Then he began, in his reedy voice, telling the members of the committee that Richard M. Nixon should be voted out of office, for obstructing the justice of the United States.

The vote reflected the sense of the country. It came at the end of July,

237

in 1974. It came before the President coughed up the tape of June the twenty-third, 1972. It came before the obstruction trial of Haldeman, Ehrlichman, Mitchell, Mardian and Parkinson (who was acquitted).

There was, in that, some common ground for Rodino, Doar, Jenner, St. Clair and even Nixon: the country would not approve Nixon's removal unless a substantial majority of citizens was convinced beyond a reasonable doubt that the President, instead of seeing to it that the laws were faithfully executed, had labored instead to frustrate them.

The Ervin Committee proposed that premise.

The White House, too confident, did not act to negate it.

The prosecutors accepted it, and so did the Rodino Committee, which created the majority.

For once, in the long nightmare, there was something close to consensus: if it *could* be proved, as it *was* proved, that he had done it, then he had to get out. And if he would not get out, then he would be ejected.

John Doar, and the people he worked for and with, established to general satisfaction that he had done it, and that it was proved that he had done it, and that, if he would not get out, the chances were that he would be ejected.

The President claimed that he was made of sterner stuff than we. When the vote was in, he said that he would fight. In Jaworski's office there was some hardening of attitude. The presumption of innocence was overcome.

# Part VII

*When you are President, and you have done wrong, the trouble with hiring lawyers is that the country is liable to hire some lawyers for itself, and then there is going to be trouble.*

# 22

CHESTERFIELD SMITH, A practical man, in the summer of 1974 perceived no permanent need for a Special Prosecutor. Then president of the American Bar Association (though uncharacteristically pungent in public utterance for a holder of that pontifical office), he exercised its seigneurial prerogative to volunteer his opinions to Leon M. Jaworski, who was hospitable to them because he'd preceded Smith as ABA president. Mr. Smith reminded Mr. Jaworski that his job was required by very special circumstances: "After all," he said, "it's very seldom that you're going to have an unindicted coconspirator as a sitting President."

Mr. Jaworski agreed. And it was not just because his sixty-ninth birthday approached. Nor was it because he had become wistful, after nine months in a very hot seat, for his spacious life as a prosperous Texas lawyer in the fullness of his reputation, which he had interrupted when Mr. Nixon, perceiving not even a transient need for a Special Prosecutor, arranged on October 20, 1973, to remand Archibald Cox to the faculty of the Harvard Law School. It was because Jaworski and his top assistants (Deputy Special Prosecutor Henry S. Ruth, Jr., and Counsel Philip A. Lacovara) had commenced to feel that fatiguing depression which affected all men of good faith who tackled the Watergate: late at night, on days which had begun for them very early in the morning, they found it hard to resist the desperate suspicion that they were being used. By mid-

September, when the former President had been pardoned into publicly subsidized disgraceful splendor, they were sure of it, and similarly assured that what distressed them would survive with their offices to plague succeeding occupants. The certitude was too much for Lacovara; he quit.

They had developed a siege mentality, and they knew it. They had seen the siege mentality in the Nixon White House, and they found it hateful there, but they feared that theirs, for the future, might be worse. They thought so because they thought it to be the inescapable lot of anyone who might come after them.

When Haldeman and Ehrlichman and their master departed 1600 Pennsylvania Avenue, there remained in the Executive Mansion no indigenous sinister force certain to transmute a Jerry terHorst into a Ron Ziegler. The Nixon White House paranoia, like Daisy Buchanan's love for Tom, was only personal in its causation. But Henry Ruth thought any Deputy Special Prosecutor would incur the same afflictions of morale that saddened him, and he feared the consequences to such a person, and to his work, if the affliction were to be endured for an entire career.

Ruth had accepted his post, under Cox, and in October 1974, agreed to succeed Jaworski, because his extraordinary sense of personal obligation to public service did not permit him to act upon advice which I, and many others more prudent and less courageous than he, received and obeyed.

When Elliot L. Richardson, in May of 1973, set up shop to recruit staff prosecutors to restore public trust in American justice, prosecutors across the country experienced a great excitement, and had to be conversationally restrained from rushing off to join him in his lofty enterprise. Less excitable men, whose advice some sought, counseled discretion as preferable to valor, if one was thoughtful of his future. They had a dark proposition, which Ruth did not seriously dispute: "Watergate is tar-baby, and anyone who hits it will get stuck." The difference between him and us was that he declined to let the premise overcome his view that someone, whatever the enormity of the risk, had to hit it nevertheless.

For Henry Ruth, whose dedication to the common weal abided through ten uprootings of his family in thirteen years, a hard job which someone must do is a hard job which he must do. When he declares, from empirical studies, that the job is impossible, he is probably correct. Then, when he reasons from that to the conclusion that results of an impossible job should not be promised to a populace which yearns to trust again, because its trust has been defiled before, he is indisputably right.

"Prosecution," said Henry Ruth, who with promethean exertion preserved intact the Special Prosecution Force staggered by Cox's dismissal, "doesn't solve anything." And be damned if he will be party to *tableaux vivants*, staged to gull a public eager to be trustful, into believing that it solves everything.

(On the weekend of September 21, 1974, President Gerald R. Ford addressed the International Association of Chiefs of Police, in convention arrayed at the L'Enfant Plaza Hotel in Washington — and accompanied by squadrons of motorcycle cops and shiny prowl cars which went charging about the District in formation for the next week, lights flashing and Wilson's Warbler sirens howling, running red lights and disrupting pedestrian traffic to the service of no emergency but the urgent adolescent desire to show off. The President, to the satisfaction of his audience, affirmed his certitude that law enforcement officers must not rest until every person who commits a crime is sent to jail. Excluding, presumably, those individuals who conspire to obstruct justice while serving as Presidents of the United States. Henry Ruth, approximating the percentage of those jailed, among those apprehended at all, at 1.3 percent, suggested that the President's sincerity would have been more apparent if Mr. Ford had chided the cops severely for malfeasance.)

Henry Ruth's skepticism — approaching a limited nihilism — about the solvent properties of prosecution, originates not in a starry-eyed notion that people will always be good, but in a skein of practical and theoretical experience obtained in thirteen years of diligent work. In 1961 he commenced three years as a prosecutor in the Organized Crime and Racketeering Section at Justice, under Henry Petersen. Then, for a year, he was an attorney in the Office of Criminal Justice, under the Deputy Attorney General (where Earl Silbert and John Dean would later serve under Richard G. Kleindienst, en route to their Watergate appointments in professional Samarra). He spent two years as Deputy Director of LBJ's Commission on Law Enforcement and Administration of Justice. There were two more years on the faculty of the University of Pennsylvania Law School. In 1969, Richard M. Nixon appointed him Director of the National Institute of Law Enforcement Assistance Administration. Then Ruth served for three years as Mayor John V. Lindsay's Director of the Criminal Justice Coordinating Council in New York. And he served the Pennsylvania Governor's Commission on Crime, the Pennsylvania

Prison Society, the Philadelphia District Attorney's Committee on Alcoholism and Drug Addiction, the New Jersey Joint Legislative Committee for the Study of Crime and Criminal Justice, the Pennsylvania Council on Crime and Delinquency, OEO Legal Services, the National Commission on the Causes and Prevention of Violence, the National Advisory Commission on Civil Disorder, the ABA Advisory Committee to the Special Committee on Crime Prevention and Control, the New York Governor's Crime Control Planning Board, and the Visiting Committee of the School of Criminal Justice, SUNY, at Albany. Prosecution punishes, he thinks, and that is all. It may have a cathartic effect upon the vengeful observer, and it may frighten the offender so he doesn't do it again, but it doesn't solve anything: it just acknowledges realities, and deals with them, as they occur. It does not, as a matter of fact, accomplish very much by way of insuring that the same realities, disagreeable as they are, will not crop up again tomorrow.

When he took his job, Henry Ruth had in mind to see to the imposition of all the punishments which could be fairly imposed upon Watergaters, consistently with the provisions of the Constitution and the laws of the United States. In 1973, that was a fairly tall order, and he was content with its scope when he was not concerned about its magnitude. He thought one of the problems of this Republic, arising out of G. Gordon Liddy's damned and foolish plans, and the Nixon Administration's self-indulgent appetite for them, was the widespread public suspicion that felonies performed in high places go regularly unpunished. Mr. Ruth does not think that felonies should go unpunished, even though he has those serious reservations about the long-term curative and preventive effects of such punishments, so he took the job.

What he did not do (or did not intend to do, at least) was volunteer to discharge also the various corrective responsibilities which he considered rightfully the provinces of the congressional and presidential areas of government. He was not at all sure that they could solve the problem, either; any democratic system of government, after all, presumes the good faith of the people who get to run it, and if people of bad faith grab it, there is going to be trouble; he was not aware of any way to insure that those who seek to run the government would be, invariably, people of good faith. But that was someone else's problem, somebody else's impossible job. His job, while plainly difficult in prospect — to introduce men of bad faith to surroundings enclosed by four gray walls, with visitors limited most of the time to guards and sad old padres — was, he thought, finite. Not finite enough, maybe, but he would do the best he could.

Very shortly he began to realize that he'd been only dreaming. For a Congress and a White House (and, when Elliot Richardson was gone, a Department of Justice led, if that is the word, by William Saxbe), the Special Prosecution Force, in a desert of indecision created by politically arid uncertainty of what the American people knew, wanted, and would stand for, was the green, green grass of home.

In perfect harmony, Senators, Congressmen — including Peter Rodino of New Jersey, of the House Judiciary Committee — and those faceless White House spokesmen who arrive, in times of trouble, not in single numbers but at battalion strength, solemnly averred their mutual creeds: the whole matter was in the hands of the Special Prosecution Task Force, and they had every confidence that it would shortly be resolved. Right there, and no place else.

Mr. Rodino would of course be happy to receive the tapes and other stuff which the Force had dredged out of the White House at the most excruciating expense of time and commotion.

The White House, perforce, was determined that the Force leave no stone unturned in its drive for all the facts, but equally firm in its assurance that a substantial number of the larger stones must be left undisturbed in deference to executive privilege.

The Senate, which extracted a few lies out of Richard G. Kleindienst, up for confirmation as Attorney General of the United States, was pleased to refrain from citing him for contempt of Congress, inasmuch as the Special Prosecution Force could be depended upon to carry out all the old coffee grounds and orange peels left behind in the Administration's garbage collection on the Hill.

Mr. Saxbe took the position that the President was entitled to charge the Government for his lawyers, until he got hooked, at least, and that, of course, was important among his motives for hiring lawyers — escaping unhooked.

Henry Ruth is a modest man, in the best sense of the word; he did not think that Cox's Army, under his leadership or that of Mr. Jaworski, could, by itself, save the Republic. Nor did he think that the people who talked as though they thought so, really thought so, either. To him the idea was a lot of rubbish, sanctimonious if proposed out of cynical desire to escape accusations of malfeasance which would be leveled publicly, if some of the suspects got away, childish if propounded sincerely.

There was nothing unique about the nature of the public pressure which the Special Prosecutors felt. When an investigation commences to give off the scent of hunters on the track of important rascals, reporters foregather to inquire of its progress.

Field investigators remember their training, and refer all questions to the prosecutor. The prosecutor, if he has any sense, looks up the local rules, reminds himself of the bag of argumentative cats which he will open to claw at his case with subsequent complaints of prejudicial pre-trial publicity, and with as much courtesy as possible, keeps his mouth shut.

The reporters, miffed by this taciturnity, obtain what they can from public records (the names of witnesses subpoenaed to testify before the grand jury, for example), and eke it out with clandestine calls to lawyers and private investigators who represent the suspects. Then they write stories attributed to informed sources, being as careful as possible to cull from those utterances (made out of profound self-interest of discrediting the investigation, and faithfully reflecting that interest) whatever information was simultaneously imparted.

The reporters' effort seldom meets with more than indifferent success, so that prosecutor and investigators, rising early and retiring late, laboring mightily to guard against destruction of good evidence and manufacture of false evidence by sneaking up on prospective defendants, suffer at the same time the indignity of finding their names, abilities, manners, intentions, and motives misrepresented, occasionally impugned, and sometimes proposed for ridicule in the morning papers. For this discomfort, their only emollient is the intramural exchange of sympathies expressing the view that their critics don't know what they are talking about, and are biased to boot.

At the beginning of their crusade, back in June and July of 1973, the Special Prosecutors had safe passage in the public press, and perhaps became a little spoiled. Media pulpits and sources, influentially speedy in the nomination and election of prosecutors as villains for their harshness in the Chicago Seven, Catonsville Nine, Ellsberg, Black Panther, Harrisburg Five, and Dr. Spock cases, by some unaccountable means had acrobatically contrived to include Earl Silbert and the rest of the original Watergate prosecutors in the same tribe of pariahs, not for being too harsh but for being too easy.

# 23

THE SPECIAL PROSECUTORS were resolute in their determination to refuse public adoration any influence upon their investigative and prosecutive decisions, just as their brethren had sternly tried, in unpopular cases, to develop strategy and tactics without reference to public disapproval. Still the fact remained, in the summer of 1973, that it was a hell of a lot nicer, personally, to be the guy who was chasing John Ehrlichman than it was to be the guy who was arguing the Government's side in pretrial motions filed by defendants indicted for offenses allegedly committed at Wounded Knee.

Richard Ben-Veniste was "aggressive" and "self-assured" when he leered at the press in the jury box while harrying Rose Mary Woods about the gaps in the tapes which Jaworski had extracted, at long last, from the White House; the same behavior, from Ellsberg prosecutor David Nesson, was arrogant, openly contemptuous and obnoxious.

The rule of prediction (and any prosecutor knows this) is to examine the subject ox carefully for identifying marks of ownership; if you gore a good guy's ox, your nastiness will be nastiness, but if you gore a bad guy's ox, your nastiness will be a principled refusal to knuckle under to intimidation by high-priced defense lawyers.

The best prosecutors do their utmost to take no heed of the rule of prediction, to select those to be gored by separating them from those against whom the evidence, necessary for goring, does not rise to the point at which it passes beyond a reasonable doubt.

The Special Prosecutors were among the best. But it is still legitimate to wonder if their utmost was sufficient. That legitimacy, in large part, arises out of the case of *United States of America* v. *Richard G. Kleindienst*, 74–256. It is implied also in the prosecution of John Connally, who, with the coruscating counsel of Edward Bennett Williams, beat a very questionable bribery case in 1975.

Kleindienst, to his sorrowful amazement, carried the bad guy's mark. Connally carried it also, to his considerable indignation, but he's another matter, because he got away.

Ruth and Jaworski, conferring with Kleindienst's lawyer, without any joy of their own in the fact, had convinced him of it. Counsel for the Government, and counsel for the defendant: each perceived the case as difficult, but it was more than that. Out of all proportion to the gravity of the offense, to the malevolence (scant, if any) of the man who had committed it, and the issues of fact and law (few) which it embodied, No. 74–256 was a microcosmic exemplar of most of the explosive questions contained in the plea-bargaining system of contemporary American justice. Kleindienst did not lack for remorse, and the prosecutors — the ones in charge — were not devoid of compassion. But there were public expectations, and political suspicions, and things built into the criminal justice system, and all of them conduced to make a comparatively trivial matter into a disaster for nearly everyone who had anything to do with it.

On March 8, 1972, Senator Edward M. Kennedy, for the Senate Judiciary Committee, inquired of Attorney General–designate Richard G. Kleindienst whether, in his capacity as Deputy Attorney General, he had remarked any White House inquisitiveness about, or intrusiveness into, the matter in which Assistant Attorney General Richard McLaren was conducting antitrust matters involving ITT. It was stronger than that, really: Senator Kennedy wanted to know if the President or his men had meddled in the affair.

Kleindienst was under oath. "I was not," he said, "interfered with by anybody in the White House. I was not importuned, I was not pressured, I was not directed, I did not have conferences with respect to what I should or should not do."

On April 19, 1971, John D. Ehrlichman had called Kleindienst at the Department, and ordered him to drop the Government's appeal in the case involving ITT's acquisition of the Grinnell Corporation. Kleindienst refused. In the afternoon, the President conferred with Ehrlichman, who reported that the Department was not complying with the President's wishes that the Government drop the appeal by failing to file a statement of jurisdiction with the Supreme Court.

"They're not going to file," Nixon said, but Ehrlichman was not so sure: "they've been horsing us pretty steadily." The President then spoke to Kleindienst on the telephone: "I want something clearly understood, and, if it is not understood, McLaren's ass is to be out within one hour. The IT and T thing — stay the hell out of it, is that clear? That's an order. The order is to leave the goddamned thing alone. Now, I've said this, Dick, a number of times, and you fellows apparently don't get the . . . message over there. I do not want McLaren to run around prosecuting people, raising hell about conglomerates, stirring things up at this point. Now, you keep him the hell out of that, is that clear? Or either he resigns. I'd rather have him out anyway. I don't like the son of a bitch." The President concluded: "You're, my order is to drop the goddamned thing. Is that clear? Okay."

Kleindienst did not drop the goddamned thing. Instead he went to his boss, John Mitchell, and informed the then–Attorney General that he would resign unless the President rescinded his order. Mitchell went to Ehrlichman and admonished him that Kleindienst would do as he promised, probably taking McLaren with him, with staggering public effect, unless McLaren was allowed to proceed. Ehrlichman went to the President, and the President backed down.

For this lèse majesté the Deputy Attorney General was accorded by the White House no measurable increase of a fondness that had been minimal at the outset. His clout was derivative anyway: on the positive side, John Mitchell could live with him, and Mitchell was then still in good odor at 1600 Pennsylvania Avenue; on the negative side, he was a protégé of Senator Barry Goldwater, and the Administration, fashioning foreign policies very liberal for a conservative outfit, preferred not to offend the Arizona Tory by ejecting his man from Justice. It took the personal threat of Goldwater wrath, in 1972, to budge the reluctant President into appointing Kleindienst Attorney General; Nixon would have liked it better if he had remained Acting Attorney General, and acceded to formal nomination only on the understanding that Kleindienst would shortly depart into private practice, once he had the full office.

Called before Judiciary, not quite a year later, lodged at last by hard work, loyalty and fortune within tantalizing proximity to the position of first lawyer of the United States of America, content (and trying not to be smug) about having backed the President and Ehrlichman down, responding to interrogation by the most influential of politicians opposed to that same President, Kleindienst, ignorant of the tape recorders hitched to the President's phone, resolved a quandary. As he saw it, the thrust of the Kennedy questioning was whether he had gone into the bag on the ITT cases. He had not. He had not, in fact, gone into the bag in November of 1970, when Robert T. Carson, shortly to be investigated himself, offered the Nixon reelection effort as much as $100,000, in consideration of certain courtesies to a gentleman then under federal indictment in New York; Kleindienst refused. He knew, after checkered experience of fourteen years in Arizona politics, and six more in national efforts, that the bag existed, but he had never been inside.

Still in all, what Kennedy was after would, if he got it, support the awkward inference that President Nixon had held the bag open for Kleindienst. His own view was that the President's April 19 instruction had been ill conceived, improper and impulsive. But Kleindienst, himself impulsive, and inclined to install questionable intuition in management of matters probably better handled by his considerable intellect, was by habit and long practice disposed to overlook such excesses, deeming them appropriate for absolution so long as no action was based upon them. The President had retreated. No damage had been done. But to divulge the President's effort, however misconceived, to do that harm, would be to arm the Administration's most hated foe — Kennedy — with information which would be promptly exploited to calamitous effect in the press. Interfered with, importuned, pressured and directed by the White House, Kleindienst had stood firm, and the result was an ITT settlement fully favorable to the Government. He therefore denied, under oath, that he had been abused, and had successfully resisted. When the truth would have done him credit (though infuriating his President), he chose to lie instead. To his subsequent sorrow, Richard G. Kleindienst was a stand-up guy.

The statute says that a person under oath before a competent tribunal (such as, for example, the Committee on the Judiciary of the United States Senate) had better not, willfully and contrary to such oath, state or subscribe any material matter which he does not believe to be true, and if he does, he is guilty of perjury and good for a fine of $2,000 and five years in the can, or both. Experience in prosecution or defense says that if the Government can prove that he did it, *and that he got something for it* — such as money or no indictment for committing some other felony, or something which he otherwise would not have had — and that he knew he was doing it, and doing it for that reason, *beyond a reasonable doubt*, then he will be convicted of doing it, branded a felon, and, if he is a lawyer, disbarred. Generally the courts — which revoke licenses to practice law — are pretty severe on lawyers who lie under oath. The United States Senate doesn't go for that behavior either.

When the story came out, the press sided with the Senate. That, for the Special Prosecutors, was a four-by-eight straw in a very high wind. It signaled the considerable importance which the public would be likely to attach to the case of Richard G. Kleindienst; as Gerald Ford would later fail to perceive, the publicly unacceptable resolution of a case become symbolic can stimulate a blanket rejection of the manner in which all cases are resolved, and the Special Prosecutors were sensible of that danger. They were also determined to avoid it, because they had a sober understanding of the grave responsibility which they carried: restoration of public trust in the operation of the criminal justice system.

It was that motive which led them also to rely upon Jake Jacobsen, too, when the public found out that Jake said he'd paid off Connally from the milk fund: they thought they had to prosecute.

That made them mirror images of the ordinary American prosecutor. Where the local, state or federal prosecutor enjoys, resents or misuses his greatest freedom, that of prosecutorial discretion, they were securely hemmed in. And at least in the view of defense counsel who represented clients under Special Prosecution investigation, where the ordinary prosecutor is most burdened, the Special Prosecutors were by circumstances permitted to run all but at large.

Under American law, the prosecutor has absolute discretion in his choice of cases to prosecute. It is virtually impossible to make him bring a case if he does not want to. Murderous Klansmen for decades mounted their night rides, shielded from prosecution by the likemindedness or timidity of contemporary bigots in charge of state and local law enforcement; that evil was tolerated. The kids who smoked pot and took pills and performed certain rites of fertility at the 1969 Woodstock Rock Festival were neither arrested nor charged, because the prosecutors had approved police reasoning that official intervention would catalyze more trouble than it would enforce propriety; that self-restraint was not reversible by pronouncement of middle-class, middle-aged disapproval of the goings-on.

It is equally impossible to prevent a prosecutor, in ordinary circumstances, from carrying out his decision that a case will be brought. Clay Shaw was literally at the mercy of James Garrison, the New Orleans District Attorney who had no mercy, but who did have an obsessive delusion about a conspiracy to assassinate JFK and an urgent need for a legal circus to distract attention (and perhaps even to head off investigation) from a scabrous and festering network of corruption over which he presided when he was not yelling about the imagined plots of others. James Riddle Hoffa's legions of Teamsters could not save him from imprisonment at the hands of Kennedy Justice. John N. Mitchell and Maurice Stans were forced to trial in the Vesco case, notwithstanding strong suspicions (harbored by people who felt little personal affection for either defendant), borne out by acquittal, that there was at least as much of Whitney North Seymour's egotistical desire to leave office as United States Attorney, for the Southern District of New York, with a couple of big scalps up for scissoring, as there was solid evidence against the two men. But nothing could be done about that case, either, except go to trial on it.

For well or for ill, depending on your point of view, the Special Prosecutors commenced their work with the subjective view that they were denied by their peculiar circumstances much of that raw decisional power. Some of them thought that they were fettered not to start cases, which in less urgent situations would have been brought (because a marginal case, ending in a not-guilty, might initiate erosion of public confidence in their judgment). Some felt themselves constrained to bring cases, which in less volatile atmospheres would have been rejected (because a safe-conduct to a person notoriously suspected might provoke a popular conclusion that the fix was in, still, or again).

Objectively, the prosecutors may have been wrong, or less correct than they thought they were. Ten years from now, assuming the whole mess has been resolved by 1985, the consensus may be that the Special Prosecutors in fact enjoyed exactly the same decisional prerogatives as any American prosecutor of this decade. Still the line prosecutors (typified by Ben-Veniste, his sidekick on the Plumbers Task Force, Jill Vollner, and

Joe Connolly, who headed the ITT Task Force) worked from the premise in its positive articulation: all possible cases, weak or strong, must be brought, to satisfy the public. The staff prosecutors (Henry Ruth chief among them) asserted the negative aspect: that rigorous quality control be exercised, so that weak cases — losers — not crop up to the public depreciation of the Special Prosecutor's wisdom and integrity.

This led to more than simple philosophical differences in the offices at 1425 K Street, N.W., where the only sign visible to a visitor emerging from the ninth-floor elevator read: "Suite 900. Grocery Manufacturers of America." It led to considerable pulling and hauling between "the Southern District guys" (as the partisans of aggressiveness became known, in acknowledgment of Ben-Veniste's preeminence as disciple of Mike Seymour's attitude of getting everybody) and the cooler heads who followed Ruth.

The Southern District guys, all things considered, got the better of the quarrel, and thus by implication propounded for public consumption the opposite of Ruth's hypothesis. At least seeming desperate for a solvent universal enough to remove Watergate stains, the public was invited to believe that the Special Prosecutors thought that prosecution solves everything.

There is a potentially iterative effect in the operation of a prosecutor's office, any prosecutor's office. It looks like the product of the interpretation which the prosecutors in the office put upon public reaction to the investigations and prosecutions which receive public notice. But its causation is much nearer to hand: in most instances it depends not at all upon the intercession of the press as middleman (communicating to the public those facts and attitudes which prompt public reaction); its source is the members of the judiciary who preside at the trials of the prosecutor's cases.

If the judge — or the judges — like the sort of cases which the prosecutors bring, there will be more cases of that kind prosecuted. If the judges display animosity toward the kind of cases which the prosecutors bring, there will be fewer of them. If the judges complain about shortages of certain types of cases, the prosecutors will be more strenuous in the investigation and prosecution of that kind of case.

The press only reports, in ordinary circumstances, the studied reactions of judges to the varieties and sufficiencies of the cases which are brought. The media reaction takes on independent significance only when it contradicts the judicial reaction; otherwise it merely serves to reinforce that response from the bench. The judge who dismissed the Wounded Knee cases got good notices for doing it, but bad notices for complaining that the dismissal was necessitated by the refusal of the defendants to proceed to a verdict with a jury of less than twelve. The Department of Justice responded by giving merit awards to the prosecutors, which displeased the press and had the effect of vindicating the judge.

Judges derive veto power over prosecutions, and prosecution policies, from a convention of American criminal justice which resembles, but supersedes, the convention which accords the prosecutor absolute authority to choose the cases that shall be brought to indictment. Once the case has been indicted, in ordinary circumstances, the prosecutor is stuck with it. The indictment is rather like a large crow, indifferently cooked and served insolently: if there is proof enough, the Government will make the defendant choke it down, and if there is not, the prosecutor gets to eat it. In public, with attendant embarrassment.

The trial judge determines who eats the bird. His discretion — to suppress evidence, to dismiss indictments, to refuse to admit evidence, to question witnesses, to comment on evidence when instructing the jury, and to grant judgments of acquittal notwithstanding jury verdicts of conviction — is reversible, on appeal, only where error of law, or egregious abuse of discretion, can be demonstrated to the appellate judges. A clever trial judge does not commit errors of law, nor does he trespass beyond (if that is possible) the use of discretion into its abuse.

While there were several judges of the United States District Court, for the District of Columbia, who handled Watergate cases, one, in later 1973 and early 1974, loomed over the rest: John J. Sirica.

*Time's* Man of the Year of '73, former Chief Judge Sirica at seventy is a nice guy if you like martinets, a useful man if you dislike perjurers in power, a fearless man by any account, and a powerful man whose power proceeds from the fact that he holds his job for life. In other words, he is not accountable to the electorate or anybody else, unless his tenure "during good behavior" is curtailed by a construction of attending Falangist cocktail parties as "bad behavior." If it isn't, and it won't be, he is at all but perfect liberty to be as lawless as he likes in the defense of what he deems to be ordered liberty. It was that condition, of course, which Messrs. Haldeman and Ehrlichman, Mitchell, Colson, Dean, Liddy, et al., erroneously believed themselves to share.

Judge Sirica's definition of the bounds of his discretion would have comported nicely with Louis XVI's view of himself as the French State. Having extracted what he thought to be the truth from James McCord, E. Howard Hunt, and others (by the imposition of long prison terms, or the threat thereof) in 1973, Judge Sirica was blandly reassuring when John Ehrlichman, H. R. Haldeman, John N. Mitchell and the rest protested, in 1974, that, really, he shouldn't sit on the trial of their cases on charges of conspiring to effect the cover-up, because he had his mind made up. Sirica found himself to be without bias or prejudice, and six judges of the nine-judge Court of Appeals for the District of Columbia, preferring not to identify themselves, upheld him.

"Somebody," said a man in the Special Prosecutor's Office, "should tell Judge Sirica that he's not going to make Man of the Year two years in a row."

Nobody did, because nobody with anything to lose dared the mission, and there wasn't anyone with something to gain. As he was required to do, by law, Judge Sirica on his seventieth birthday relinquished his post as Chief Judge of the United States District Court for the District of Columbia. But he had by then established a tonal norm for federal judges dealing with Watergate matters. It affected his colleague Judge Gerhard Gesell one way: it made him almost recklessly aggressive in management of pretrial motions brought in the Ellsberg burglary case by John Ehrlichman, Gordon Liddy, and the miserable Cuban Americans, and he was downright intemperate in his lectures, rebukes and admonitions to White House Special Counsel James D. St. Clair. So much so that he had to back down, on a couple of occasions. Sirica's example affected another colleague — his successor as Chief Judge, George Hart — in the opposite fashion: evidently not enamored of the Sirica policy of stern measures for the fallen mighty, he tempered a modicum of justice with a lavish amount of sympathy when he sentenced Richard G. Kleindienst.

For the Special Prosecutors, there was an influential educational effect in that combination of judicial responses.

Sirica, in the process of creating himself as the definitive Judge-as-Avenger during the Liddy-McCord trial during January of 1973, was a regular handful for then–Assistant U.S. Attorney Earl J. Silbert. Silbert did not relish the prospect of suffering so much assistance from the bench that probable convictions would be probably overturned. But by the time Archie Cox went into business, Sirica had become a one-man gang, having polished his role to the same point at which Hal Holbrook all but became Mark Twain.

Privately, the staff Special Prosecutors and the line prosecutors, agreeing that the Ehrlichman-Haldeman-Mitchell-Parkinson-Mardian case (in the early summer of 1974) would certainly constitute the second-brightest jewel in their crown of public service, maybe the brightest, viewed Sirica's control of it with varying enthusiasm.

The line prosecutors were pleased, because they believed, correctly, that he would be strict with the defendants during trial, and severe with them after the foreseeable result was obtained.

The staff prosecutors felt some trepidation, similar to Silbert's: Sirica might be so prosecution-oriented that he would bitch the thing up and make a defense record for appeal.

With Mr. Nixon still defiant in the White House redoubts, that prospect was worrisome in the extreme: if then-pending subpoenas wrenched from him conclusively incriminating tapes, and if the House and Senate combined to impeach him, then the Special Prosecutors would be caught between a very large rock and a very hard place, paralyzed in their striking arm and rendered mute to explain why.

If Haldeman and Ehrlichman and Mitchell successfully appealed a Sirica conviction in the cover-up case, they would have to be retried. A retrial is always a tedious, messy, delicate matter: the evidence is never as impressive on second presentation, and the lawyers for each side are simultaneously bored, and afraid of contributing to new errors — or a repetition of previous errors — that will lead to still another reversal. In the usual course of such things, a new judge, irritably uninformed of all the preliminary matters, issues and questions of law, must be designated to insure as much fairness as possible, and he makes the retrial worse.

The first trial in the cover-up case was certain to be protracted, and to receive considerable public scrutiny. That circumstance would militate against a speedy second trial because it would stimulate publicity which would prejudice the rights of the defendants. If Mr. Nixon, out of office, became an added starter for the second trial, the publicity issue would be magnified a thousand times, making an early trial impossible.

That, in turn, would put resolution of the cover-up issue at least into 1975, and perhaps into 1976, when it would be further and hideously distorted by its simultaneity with a presidential election. It would be threatened in consequence with public repudiation of its intended purpose as a restorative of trust in the criminal justice system, reduced by campaign rhetoric from an inspiring demonstration of evenhanded justice to a seedy political adventure. The Special Prosecutors resembled the mystical religious in their personal commitments to achieving not only justice, and the appearance of justice, but also public acceptance of the appearance as faithfully representative of the substance of justice.

They were also pragmatic about the necessities of people seeking elective office; they knew very well that a GOP slate, hemorrhaging voter support through hundreds of Watergate wounds, would be driven to attempt to staunch the flow by attacking the prosecutions, at least by innuendo. The Democrats would have to reply, in one way or the other.

The result would be additional publicity, potentially destructive of the fairness of the retrial, endangering further the likelihood of getting it started in the first place, thus delaying justice — justice deferred is justice denied — still longer.

As a practical matter, if that happened the Special Prosecutors would be: blocked from seeking an indictment of Mr. Nixon; defenseless against the vituperative criticism that would attend what would look like their shifty and corrupt decision to perpetuate the cover-up; gagged by the rule that prosecutors may not explain why they do and don't indict people; and crushed by the realistic knowledge that such complex matters could never be intelligibly explained to laymen anyway.

All that was needed, to wreck everything that the Special Prosecutors had tried to do, was some explosion from John J. Sirica, who had, late in life, made a zestful career in the detonation of judicial munitions. He had the best and most important case, to date, in his hands, and because he did, he had the power to destroy the ultimate case, if it ever could be made. (Gerald Ford would take care of that matter in September 1974. But in June and July, the Special Prosecutors had no way of knowing that.) The staff Special Prosecutors had but one protective device, and that was to keep Sirica happy. To that end, they had but one means, and that was to pursue the defendants with undeniable aggressiveness.

The line Special Prosecutors knew this, and built the fact into their arguments about other cases. Judge Sirica read the papers, talked to clerks, had been known to glance at a newsmagazine, and had demonstrated, to universal acceptance, his essentially proprietary attitude about all Watergate matters. So his influence on the Special Prosecutors, by reason of his control of the cover-up case, was not limited to Jim Neal, who would try the issue; it also conduced to the behavioral modification of Richard Ben-Veniste on the Plumbers Task Force, and Joseph Connolly on the ITT Task Force, and in turn affected their relationships with Henry Ruth and Phil Lacovara and Leon Jaworski. It made the line prosecutors more aggressive, more righteous, and consequently more vulnerable to frustration. That is a dangerous condition for a prosecutor, special or ordinary.

# 24

THE CRUNCH WAS threatened when Judge Gesell started shouting about all the dire things he had mind to do if the White House persisted in its refusal to regurgitate tapes which John Ehrlichman said he needed for his defense in the Ellsberg burglary case. Jim St. Clair took more flak than a B-24 Liberator over Dresden ("You tell your client, Mister St. Clair . . ."), but while it was disagreeable, it was also meaningless: Gesell was better at hollering than he was at choosing things to holler about. Here was a plain instance of a man, who acknowledged limits, trying in vain to imitate, convincingly, a man who acknowledged no limits. He failed. Judge Gesell backed down, deferring his confrontation with Nixon, as he would have it, to the Sirica tapes decision then awaiting argument before the Supreme Court.

The crunch came when Judge Hart disposed of the Kleindienst case. It came to his court, for disposition, in substantial part because of the effect that the conduct of Sirica and Gesell had had upon the Special Prosecutors. It was a disaster for all parties.

Peers of the realm, under British tradition, were formerly accorded a melancholy perquisite: in deference to their rank, conviction of a capital offense entitled them to be hanged with ropes of silk; yeomen twisted humbly in the wind in nooses of scratchy hemp.

In the exercise of a cognate privilege, Richard G. Kleindienst, on May

16, 1974, was allowed to describe his own direct falsehood, categorically pronounced in direct contradiction of the truth, as mere intemperate reticence. He thus acquired the unenviable status of the first former Attorney General of the United States to attain subsequent recognition as a common misdemeanant.

The alternative, he feared, would be description as the first such common felon; if later generations should find the distinction substantially insignificant, there yet remained to him the forlorn hope that the ethics committees of contemporary bar associations would not, and would rest content with reprimanding him instead of lifting his ticket to practice law, as is the usual fate of lawyers found out in felonious enterprises.

He made his choice in tears, as he had received the news, more than a year before, of John Mitchell's cover-up involvement. There is a good chance (not a certain chance, but a good one) that he made the wrong choice.

Excruciatingly, he and his lawyer, Herbert ("Jack") Miller, who would later represent Mr. Nixon, apprehended that chance of misjudgment, with all that it implied, when they were agonizing over the decision. It was a matter of cutting losses while cornered. It was a matter of extricating a former Attorney General (very big game for a roving band of fierce young prosecutors, and thus assured of hot pursuit for acts which might have gone unnoticed, or at least have been forgiven, in, say, a Customs collector) from a trap which he had entered in order to become Attorney General in the first place.

If he had not lied, in all likelihood, he would not have been senatorially confirmed as Attorney General; if President Nixon had not possessed a comfortable and justified expectation that he would lie, if it seemed exigent, he would not have been appointed, and thus confided the opportunity to lie. And if his lies had not achieved their purpose, if the Senate had rejected him as Mitchell's successor notwithstanding his lies, he would not, in all probability, have so consumingly engaged the attention of Joe Connolly and the rest of the ITT Task Force. For Kleindienst, the cost of getting what he wanted was the disastrous loss of that very thing, and virtually everything else besides; for the brakeman's son, the price of becoming Attorney General of the United States turned out to be complete disgrace, accomplished by a self-inflicted wound.

He accepted the silken rope because he morbidly concluded that its rejection would bring prompt indictment, and trial before a jury in the District of Columbia, and conviction, and imprisonment. He was certainly correct about the probability of indictment. There is much to be said in support of his calculation of conviction.

The probability of a Kleindienst indictment evolved in part from the fact that he had lied, in part from the fact that he had lied to the United States Senate, in part from the fact that it was public knowledge that he had lied to the United States Senate, and in substantial part from the fact that John J. Sirica sat beetlebrowed in the courthouse, reinforcing by his very manner of existence a set of personal dispositions, and structural influences upon those dispositions, in the office of the Special Prosecutor.

Take the structural influences first: Archie Cox, setting up the office as Richardson's hostage to the United States Senate, had never before been a prosecutor; his countervailing advantage was his clear understanding, from which he did not flinch, that he lacked practical experience in the job. He therefore hired people who did.

The course of human events being what it is, the people who knew how to prosecute, in 1973, were people conditioned (directly or at second hand) by the Kennedy Justice methodology. Imperfectly articulated as it was, that methodology was developed upon the premise that law enforcement should not be passive, but aggressive. The governing hypothesis was that there is an ineradicable difference between good guys and bad guys, apparent to, and actionable by, the good guys. Out of that came target law enforcement: upon identification as a bad guy, the suspect may resign himself to merciless investigation, reinvestigation, indictment and reindictment, trial and retrial, until at last the Government secures a verdict which ratifies its prosecutors' assessment of the defendant as a bad guy. That is what happened to Jimmy Hoffa. He may have deserved it. He may not have, too.

Traditional American law enforcement, somnolent until report of a crime, left unprosecuted the most egregious frauds, and thriving organized criminal commerce, because no one complained. The defect of reactive law enforcement was contained in its operational theory: that the gravity of the offense — and thus its merit as a prosecutable crime — varies directly with the efficacy of the commission of the offense as a stimulus to outrage.

The effect of that theory was to grant safe-conduct to a great many recipients of bribes, loansharks and major bookmakers: since few, doing business in such contexts, were angered enough by the commerce to complain, nobody was prosecuted. Whole syndicates burgeoned by accretion on the legitimate economy.

Nevertheless, the targets — people — of the alternative process are selected on an ad hoc basis. It is terribly personal. It is not monitored by a disinterested custodian of the due process of law.

When Vito Genovese was the target of prosecution, I was not distressed, because I was sure that, if he was not the *capo di tutti capo* of the Mafia, he was at least in contention for the title, and that was good enough: *mafiosi* are evil, and I was sure of that. So was Richard Ben-Veniste: his résumé recites, under "Significant Cases Prosecuted," the trials of Carmine Lombardozzi "(Income tax fraud)," Salvatore Granello "a/k/a Sally Burns (Union kickbacks — income tax)" and James Plumieri, "a/k/a Jimmy Doyle (Union kickbacks)."

The trouble is that Charles W. Colson was similarly assured about Morton Halperin, who left Henry Kissinger's National Security Council staff to join the Brookings Institution. Chuck Colson isn't stupid. John D. Ehrlichman knew Daniel Ellsberg was a bad guy; he isn't stupid either. John Dean had a whole list of enemies of the President, and plans on how to screw them ("What an exciting idea"), and the President himself harbored special hatred for Edward Bennett Williams, together with dark unspecified plans for his destruction. I suppose it is easy to see a quantum difference between the hazard posed the Republic by the murderous business of the Mob, and the decision of a Washington lawyer to represent the *Washington Post*, but the distinction eluded the Nixon Administration, and it is precisely that sort of error which due process of law is supposed to render harmless.

Cox, with Ruth's assistance, arranged the Special Prosecution Force on the aggressive model of law enforcement, which evolved from the development of the Organized Crime and Racketeering Section.

The passive model, customarily found in state and local prosecutors' offices, makes the prosecutor a processor of finished cases. When the police have finished their investigations, they deliver the cases to the lawyers, and the lawyers feed them into the grand juries, which spit out indictments which the lawyers then process in the courts. The only substantial designation of an area of responsibility is the territorial factor: if the crime occurs in his district, the prosecutor will handle it. For the management of crimes involving breaches of the peace, the passive model is quite acceptable. For conspiracies, frauds, rackets and suchlike, it is not so good.

It was the recognition of this, brought on when the Mob intensified its labor-racketeering and incursions upon white middle-class commerce (thus angering voters with clout who had serenely tolerated its pillaging of the poor), which led to the establishment of OCRS, and the development of the active model. Mating the investigative and prosecutive functions, it adds to the territorial designation two further letters of marque and reprisal: designation of prospective suspects (no longer does the prosecutor decide whether to prosecute by asking: "Can we prove he did it?"; he begins with the decision to prosecute at least half made, and reasons: "We know he did something, and as soon as we can prove it, we indict the bastard"), and designation of likely subjects which, when investigated exhaustively (income tax returns, for example) may prove fruitful of evidence.

William Merrill, Assistant Special Prosecutor in charge of the Plumbers Task Force, was for five years Chief Assistant United States Attorney in the Eastern District of Michigan, where, as his résumé recited, he was "personally responsible for directing investigation and conducting trial of major federal criminal violations in areas of mail fraud, organized crime, labor racketeering and tax evasion."

Ben-Veniste listed a year spent in the Special Prosecutions Section of the United States Attorney's Office in Manhattan, and another year as Chief of the Official Corruption Section.

Mr. Cox and his subordinates, by designating five operational Task Forces in the Special Prosecutor's Office (Watergate, Plumbers, Campaign Contributions [headed, at the outset, by James Neal, the prosecutor who got Hoffa], Political Espionage, and ITT), impliedly specified, as to each force, its own discrete list of suspects.

Ben-Veniste's Watergate Task Force, and Merrill's Plumbers Task Force, started out with permits for most of the impressive trophy heads. Neal's Campaign Contributions Task Force (having once resigned from the force, he would return to prosecute the Ehrlichman-Haldeman cover-up case) was gunning for John Connally, George Steinbrenner, and abundant major corporations and their officers who had succumbed to polite extortion, denominated as contributions to the President's reelection campaign. The Political Espionage Task Force, headed by Richard J. Davis, twenty-seven, was pretty much pro forma: Donald Segretti had lost all heart for resistance, and pleaded guilty promptly, regurgitating what he knew. Joe Connolly's ITT group was after Kleindienst. Who the hell else did they have? Dita Beard? Had they come to Washington to sit on their hands? Or had they leaped to Cox's banner to make sure the country got even? They had come to prosecute.

That attitude, among the line prosecutors, had its utility for the Republic. It was about time some of the bastards got scared, and they did. Suspects habituated by high office to confidence in the perpetration of felonies, and thus to immoderate serenity in the face of accusations constituted pretty much of truth, made more complacent still by the aimlessness of their investigation by the Ervin Committee (and heartened, simultaneously, by the ease with which their lawyers diverted the Senators), became discomfited when they thought about the harriers in Cox's office.

William O. Bittman, deserted by his professional sangfroid in his representation of E. Howard Hunt, eschewed the opportunity to discuss his hush-money messenger service with Sam Ervin. But he cooperated fully with the Special Prosecutors, and thus escaped indictment and (he hoped) disbarment.

Oil company representatives, initially overbearing when contacted about illegal campaign contributions (one prosecutor, temporarily lulled by the speedy contrition of airline executives and other corporate officers, gained an inkling of petroleum arrogance when he declared to one mogul that he could prove an unlawful six-figure contribution to the Nixon Finance Committee, and received the reply: "It's our money. Fuck you"), accepted instruction from convictions soon accomplished, and became more governable.

Chuck Colson, whose public accounts of events leading up to his plea of guilty to a felony did not wholly square with the prosecutor's recollection (he claimed newfound religious faith had moved him in conscience to spurn Jaworski's humble offer to let him plead to some misdemeanors, but Jaworski remembered advising Dave Shapiro, Colson's lawyer, that the President's former Special Counsel would either admit to a felony, or get convicted of one), took a three-year sentence, with a minimum of one year to be served before parole, in demonstration of his assessment of the office.

Similarly dissenting from Ron Ziegler's dictum that "contrition is bullshit," Egil ("Bud") Krogh cited renascent virtue as the proximate cause of his plea, without explicit animadversion to the probability, as he saw it, that he would be tried and convicted of complicity in the Ellsberg break-in if he declined to acknowledge it voluntarily, and would get more time in reward for his efforts. With the others, he saw more than the powerhouse of legislative and public wrath arrayed behind the dire promises of the Special Prosecutors: he saw also, in his tormentors, a sublime aplomb derived in part from their nearly mystical dedication to their cause, and in part from their broad warrant to achieve it. It was then that he began to develop his firm purpose of amendment, as had Jeb Magruder and John Dean before him.

Alert to the startling consequences of the ill-bred near-disdain visited by Ben-Veniste upon the parade of the President's lawyers laboring without respite or success to keep him out of White House archives — the nastier Ben-Veniste got, the greater his access to tapes — they estimated their positions as bad, and deteriorating rapidly, and so they capitulated.

Nobody, in circumstances such as theirs, wakes up in the morning and decides, for lack of anything better to do, to go to jail for the next six months or a year. Nobody, having risen so high in the company of confederates personally amiable, elects for random reasons to implicate them in felonies before courts and grand juries. Contrition, when experienced during investigation and prosecution, is perhaps not diminished in excellence for the soul, but carries with it nevertheless some heavy and disagreeable earthly burdens: you have to turn fink, which is undignified, and you still must go to jail.

There is only one source of motivation colossal enough to subjugate a man to acceptance of that hideous impost: the rational fear that his pursuers have the will and the means to enforce an alternative which is worse. John Ehrlichman expressed his confidence that the prosecutors lacked at least one: the means. William Merrill tried him for lying about the Ellsberg burglary, for participating in the Ellsberg burglary, and for obstructing justice in its investigation of the Ellsberg burglary; Ehrlichman got five years, a minimum of twenty months to be served. Dwight Chapin stood his ground and refused to admit to comparatively innocuous acts which were prohibited by the United States Code: he got six months when convicted; he might have hit the street if he had pleaded. The voice of the walrus is not often heard, but when it commences to rumble about cabbages and kings, the kings had done well to listen.

Against the benefits of zealousness must be weighed its detriments. Henry Ruth knew those; he disapproves of fuss (when he gets angry — to make him do that, one must impugn his integrity, to his face, and then, as one friend says, "He raises his voice to our normal speaking level") and, with his late 1950s ties, shirts of unquestionable mediocrity (he doesn't care about clothes, or his white-sidewall haircuts, but he likes his white '67 Valiant: "It's in great shape. It'll last another ten years"), prefers to underplay everything. Henry Ruth underplayed the Saturday

Night Massacre, for God's sake, and when Jimmy Doyle, the Special Prosecutor's public information officer, commenced to wax wroth about Cox's firing, clamped down on him, with unexceptionable courtesy. Doyle said then, and says now, that Ruth was right. Just as he was right, also, to give Ben-Veniste free rein in the tapes controversy between October 7, when Cox was sacked, and November 5, 1973, when Jaworski was sworn in to take Cox's place: Ben-Veniste's feistiness was a standing rebuke to any critic who might suggest that the fight had gone out of the office with Cox, and it worked. Excited utterances to the press were not needed, Ruth said, and borrowed a phrase from Cox: what was needed, he said, was to tend to business and "chop wood." He thought there was a lot of wood to be chopped in the Kleindienst case.

Jaworski agreed. He succeeded Cox with the burden of a rebuttable presumption that he was in the wrapper. Sixty-eight years old, full of honors, holder of the Legion of Merit, a former prosecutor of Nazi war criminals, Jaworski was viewed with suspicion on Capitol Hill. One Senator called a Washington lawyer who had roots in Texas and requested a quick summation of the man's character. From three judges and two members of the Texas bar came this assessment: "goes where the money is," "won't rock the boat," "his respect for power's too great to permit him to be aggressive." So advised, the Senator said: "Oh, Jesus."

Jaworski either confirmed or demolished the truth of those estimates, depending on the point of view. Having accepted appointment to Cox's job, he flew into Dulles International Airport, there to be collected by Doyle, who got the transportation detail from Henry Ruth because, in Doyle's opinion, the lawyers in the gloomy office thought themselves too fine for such duty. Jaworski, confining himself to monosyllabic conversation, retrieved his luggage; Doyle, made cautious by a *Wall Street Journal* story published that day, and detailing Jaworski's long association with John Connally, did not attempt to draw the new man out. In the car, out on the highway, Doyle drove in comparative silence, thinking about Cox, whom he had revered, while considering the fact that Jaworski had brought no one with him. No personal aide. No personal secretary. No trusted associate. No family, no friend, no dog.

Then, abruptly, Jaworski said, "Now, as for John Connally: I haven't seen or talked to him for over a year." And Doyle, who cared about the probity of the Special Prosecutor's Office, began to feel a little better. To him, and to the majority of the staff, further experience with Jaworski established either that he knew that the power had passed from the

President to the opposition, or else that he planned to do his job and did not care where the power was; either way, he was entirely satisfactory. He had not, he said, come to Washington to debase a lifetime of professional distinction, and he didn't.

Joe Connolly of the Special Prosecutor's Office did not agree. He imbibed the Southern District view and did not approve of silken ropes. He understood, but disliked, the Jaworski concept of the prosecutor's function in such matters as the Kleindienst case, disliked it enough to resign when Jaworski sorrowfully arrived at a bargain which Jack Miller sadly accepted. It was a classic compromise: it left both sides dissatisfied.

Jaworski, not in the habit of supplicating predecessors for guidance in direction of his performance, from the first assayed the Kleindienst matter as demanding of consultation. He called Cox, and called him often. Cox was as short of answers as Jaworski.

# 25

JAWORSKI HAD INHERITED, from Cox, an inchoate plea-bargaining policy which faithfully — and thus confusingly — reflected the puzzling transient phase of policy in the Office of the United States Attorney, and the United States District Court, for the District of Columbia. Which, in turn, exaggerated (because Sirica was there) trends in courts and prosecution offices across the country. It was rather like a bunch of old whores getting converted, one by one: for years we belted out the cases, and made a modest living at it, and thought no more about it. Then, evangelized by idealists who said that what we did (because, we thought, we had to do it) was wicked, we were filled with remorse.

Those deals were condemned as usurping the powers of the judges (who were, of course, complaisant accessories before, during and after the fact of the arrogation, because it meant they didn't have to try about eighty-five percent of the cases brought and they had all they could do as it was to try the fifteen percent that could not be bargained).

Bargains were denounced as productive of offensive disparities in lengths of time served for similar offenses (which, in fact they were, because the severity of the deal which the prosecutor can make depends as much upon the net tonnage of his evidence as it does upon the gravity of the crime which it proves; thus a car thief up against a strong case in the Middle District of Tennessee is not about to get as merciful a recommendation on a Change of Plea as a car thief with a similar record, up against a weak case in the Northern District of Illinois).

And, it was said by those vouchsafed by some angel or another the guardianship of our civil liberties, the practice of plea-bargaining promoted among those entering the pleas a most unseemly cynicism about the majesty of the law which rules us, which position demanded the pious but nevertheless acrobatic feat of overlooking how in fact it was that the pleader found himself in the position of striking his deal (by acting conformably to a cynical attitude about the majestic law, and getting caught at it). Like others recently sworn off cakes and ale (non-smokers, drunks and professional ladies), we effected a chafing compromise between what had to be done, and what, it seemed, ought to be done: we kept on doing it, but we were now ashamed of it, and we called it by different names, endeavored to sanitize it, and did it nowhere near as well. Then we apologized for doing it.

The method of this madness was to assert, with wondrous solemnity, that the judge — whose job it is to put the pleader in the slammer — is perfectly unaware of the fact that the pleader appears in sackcloth and ashes because the prosecutor has convinced his lawyer that the alternative is the Iron Maiden. This was supposed to insure that the pleader acted purely from repentance, with no mean thought whatever that copping out would get him three to five (the prosecutor, under the old, discredited system, having agreed to recommend that to a judge who could do as he damned pleased anyway) instead of the seven to ten he could probably get if he tried the thing, and lost.

The judges, having promulgated decrees that they would no longer accept recommendations when changes of plea were entered (to be consistent, in most jurisdictions, they also refused further recommendations in sentencings after trial), were consequently assumed actual beneficiaries of a most prodigious feat of retroactive intellectual virginity, and by fiat certificated as fully capable of believing at least three impossible things before breakfast each day, and a great many more before lunch. Then by attempted clairaudience, they attempted to sentence as they would have sentenced if they had not foreclosed themselves from hearing what the prosecutor thought was about right for whatever the defendant did, and admitted to having done because he figured he'd get convicted of doing it if he went to trial.

This did not work nearly as well, but it made everyone well removed from it — appellate judges, watchdogs of civil liberties, mugwumps, bleeding-hearts and others who never tried a case, belted one out, or had anything to do with the blood sport of keeping people out of jail and putting them in — feel much better. Those involved, primary among them being the defendant anxious to carve a little off his term by submitting as gracefully as possible to its imposition, found it productive of great uncertainty, which is the goddamnedest thing to manage when the issue about which all are uncertain is an indeterminate chunk of a man's life, unconvincingly ill fitted with a red wig and declaimed in pious tones to be but a few irreplaceable years of his liberty. For all those years we rolled up our sleeves and traded human futures as though they had been Hudson Super-jets and Studebakers, with questionable rings and valves, bad rubber and transmissions that went bang in the night, and then we went up to see the judge, and he took the plea, and the defendant heard us say what we had promised we would say. He didn't always get what he had gotten us to say, but we all had a pretty good idea of what the judge would go along with, and when you got a ball-park figure, you could rest pretty much assured that you had, at least, a moderately dependable estimate of the size of the ball park.

Archie Cox inquired about the practice in the District in 1973, and found that it was utterly confused. Some judges in the federal court would take recommendations from the United States Attorney's Office. Some would not. Some heard recommendations, but with resentment, and Harold Titus handled the delicate situation by throwing up his hands: recommendations were made only in cases of such vicious offenses that the accused was certain to go to jail anyway, and for a good long time, too.

Cox decided that the Special Prosecutors would not trifle with recommendations, which was the kind of decision that might have been expected from a former Solicitor General of the United States: principled, pristine and the very dickens to deal with when you had a specific felon teetering on the verge of pleading guilty, and venturing, somewhat timidly, to inquire whether it might be possible to barter a portion of his own skin for those of others. It worked fine, as most such policies do, until it was applied in the crunch. Whereupon it failed, miserably. Cox was gone, by then, but Jaworski, intent upon continuity of policy as preservative of both integrity and its appearance, was just as perplexed as his predecessor would have been. He felt he had to prosecute Kleindienst. If the man would not plead, he would have to be tried.

Jack Miller, Kleindienst's lawyer, knows a trap when he sees one. If the

Special Prosecutors were determined to bring a case against Kleindienst, the former Attorney General would be all but compelled to plead guilty; Miller saw no chance whatsoever of getting an acquittal from a District of Columbia jury for a former member of the Nixon Administration. Miller thus began by striving to persuade the prosecutors to leave his man alone, quickly perceived that he could not prevail, and shifted his ground to talk them down from a felony charge (which would probably put Kleindienst in jail and out of the bar association even if he did plead, given Sirica's pervasive influence at the courthouse) to a misdemeanor (which would give the man a fighting chance to stay on the street). There was another reason, too, to lobby strenuously for a misdemeanor complaint instead of a felony indictment, and it was surpassingly important.

Felony indictments (and those charging misdemeanors, as well) issue from the grand jury and are distributed among the judges by the clerks. In some districts, the parceling is entirely random: if six judges sit in the court, Judge Number One will not get his second case until Judges Two through Six have received their first cases. But in most districts, there is a catch to that: the processing forms, appended to indictments by the prosecutors, invite the Government's lawyers to say whether this new case appears to be related to earlier cases, and if it is, it goes to the judge who has those prosecutions, on the theory that there is no use wasting time teaching two different judges about the same set of facts.

In Washington, Judge Sirica brooded over Watergate-related cases, and lawyers representing prospective defendants in prosecutions not yet begun were very nervous about what he would do to their people when they got to court.

A misdemeanor does not require grand jury indictment. A misdemeanor, if the prosecutor so elects, can be charged by an Information (so can a felony, for that matter, if the defendant waives indictment, but Miller didn't want Kleindienst owning up to any felonies, so that was out).

Informations are not ordinarily mixed in with indictments for the clerk to draw to the judges, particularly when they accuse defendants who are prepared to plead guilty on the date of arraignment. Such Informations, in Washington, are handled right off by the Chief Judge. In May 1974, Chief Judge Hart had succeeded Sirica to that duty. It therefore followed that a misdemeanant who waited until May to capitulate to a Watergate-related offense would have a pretty decent chance of ducking John Sirica.

From the defendant's view that was a very fine thing indeed, and getting his case disposed of by Judge Hart was an even better thing. There is nothing quite like the relief which surges through a man when he thinks he's found a way to swap an all-but-certain chance of going to jail for an equally certain chance of getting off with being told to go and sin no more.

The Special Prosecutors, except for Connolly and those under him, were not averse to Miller's gambit. Ruth and Jaworski had substantial reservations about prosecuting Kleindienst at all, at least did not dispute with violence Miller's prognostication of the likelihood that a D.C. jury would hook Kleindienst if he were tried, and dissented from Connolly's firebreathing position that Kleindienst deserved to go to jail for what he'd done.

Unlike Connolly, Jaworski and Ruth and Lacovara worked in a continuum. They had to be mindful of the effect of a Kleindienst prosecution upon the evolutionary development of cases in the Plumbers Task Force, in the Campaign Contributions Task Force, and throughout the rest of the office. And of the impeachment hearings on the Hill.

Kleindienst, treated with moderation, produced very valuable information about Richard M. Nixon, leads that took the prosecutors (then not precluded, by Gerald Ford's spasm of charity, from indicting him, and having little reason to anticipate that they would be so prevented), and thus the House Judiciary Committee, to potentially important evidence against the President. Lashed with the full power of a felony charge, or hustled off to jail, Kleindienst would have been embittered, and said nothing.

His destruction would in turn strongly discourage other potential informers, and cause a ripple effect adverse to other prosecutions, among them the one that John Doar was running for Peter Rodino.

"It was important," Jaworski said, "that we weren't unloading on anyone." It was important, too, that it not seem that they were unloading on anyone. At least as significant as convictions, in the Jaworski view, was "bringing out the facts. There's history being written here," he said in the early summer of 1974. "The House Judiciary Committee would be in a vastly different situation without the information we developed." Unquestionably: what Doar was doing was the enormous task of marshaling the evidence collected by the Special Prosecutors, the Ervin Committee, and the FBI. He was not investigating. The House Committee was not enforcing subpoenas. Those chores were left to Jaworski. And there was the obligation to keep a tight grip on birds in hand: "We didn't want to end up with somebody getting off after a trial and then have people saying: 'Well, what were you doing down there? Sitting on your ass when you could've been taking guilty pleas?'"

For all of those reasons, Jaworski and Ruth acceded to Jack Miller's maneuvering to get Kleindienst off with a scolding, probably a fine, and maybe a suspended jail sentence. The statute allowed for a year, a hundred-dollar fine, and required thirty days to be spent in jail. Jaworski called Judge Hart and asked if the Court wanted a recommendation from the Special Prosecutor. The Court did not.

Kleindienst had pleaded on May 16. The Judge, a former Republican National Committeeman with a local reputation as a fairly stupid man, continued the case to June 7 for sentencing. He did not, if he had by then experienced its pangs, confide his extravagant sympathy for a former United States Attorney General who stood in the dock to admit to much less than he had in fact done. On June 6, Jaworski called the Judge and offered to cancel an out-of-town speaking engagement (set for June 8), if the Judge thought his presence would be useful at the sentencing. No need of that, the Judge said, and Jaworski went.

Friday, the seventh, was also the day Gesell picked to go after St. Clair, which showed how taken Gesell was with Sirica's example. Of course Gesell went too far, and had to back down the next week, but his tantrum was a nice counterpoint to Hart's maudlin eulogy of Kleindienst, extolling his loyalty without any real, explicit cognition of the fact that it had impelled him to do something which he certainly should not have done, and the fact that he was getting off pretty easy for having done it even before Hart's absolution. Hart put Kleindienst on the street, suspended his fine, and patted him on the head. And he seemed to say that the Special Prosecutors agreed with him. That would put Hank Ruth in a corner with the John Connally investigation (Jaworski had disqualified himself from that decision), or at least he thought it did. If Connally wasn't prosecuted, there would be cries that the fix was in.

The commotion about Kleindienst was something fierce. The Special Prosecutors — Connolly quit in high dudgeon over the Jaworski resolution of the Kleindienst problem — had a new experience: now they were the targets of the abuse, no longer public darlings. Prosecution had demonstrably failed to solve the Kleindienst case, which should not have been brought in the first place, and was accordingly and noisily denounced as probably unsatisfactory to solve the Nixon case. Never having promised anyone a rose garden, expressly rebuffing, without success, sundry requests for and expectations of a rose garden, the Special Prosecutors had fallen short of delivering a rose garden, and the press and public were thereupon enraged.

The experience made the Special Prosecutors very cautious, and they had been far from reckless before. It confirmed Jaworski in his creed that occupation of the presidency by a coconspirator put a political shield between the felon and the criminal process, assuming that the conspiracy was one with political ends. Jaworski was willing to speculate about whether a President who hit his wife with an ax would require impeachment before indictment for murder; the discussion was a diverting intellectual exercise. But he was not confronting such a case. He was steering the best course he could in a case which was clearly political, directly involving suspected malfeasance in the discharge of the presidential obligation to take care that the laws should be faithfully executed.

The political system, as far as Jaworski was concerned, had to remove the political shield before the suspect could be so much as considered for the criminal process. Rodino's committee was doing that. Jaworski was happy to be of whatever help he could (though he was quietly dismayed to discover that he was plainly expected to do all the dirty work, with his subpoenas, while the Committee refused to enforce the tapes demands it made upon the White House, and rested content with sending firm little notes). But he was very reluctant indeed to trespass upon what he believed to be the separate political hegemony of that committee. As long as Richard Nixon was the President of the United States, and Leon Jaworski was the Special Prosecutor, there would be no criminal case in United States District Court alleging that Richard M. Nixon had broken the law in connection with Watergate. Prosecution, he was certain, would not solve the political problems that President Nixon had created.

He is taciturn, now, about what might have happened. But everything in the office, after September 8, 1974, points to the deduction that Richard M. Nixon would probably have been indicted for conspiracy to obstruct justice, and probably for obstruction of justice, in the Watergate cover-up. Title 18, United States Code, Section 2, provides: (a) Whoever commits an offense against the United States or aids, abets, counsels, commands, induces or procures its commission, is punishable as a principal. (b) Whoever willfully causes an act to be done which if directly performed by him or another would be an offense against the United States, is punishable as a principal. Section 1510(a) provides: Whoever willfully endeavors by means of bribery, misrepresentation, intimidation, or force or threats thereof to obstruct, delay, or prevent the communication of information relating to a violation of any criminal statute of the United States by any person to a criminal investigator . . . shall be fined not more than $5,000, or imprisoned not more than five years, or both.

On September 3, 1974, Henry Ruth reported to Jaworski that ten other investigative areas of possible criminal activity by the by-then former President were being explored. "None of these matters," Ruth wrote, with characteristic self-restraint, "at the moment rises to the level of our ability to prove even a probable criminal violation by Mr. Nixon, but I thought you ought to know which of the pending investigations were even remotely connected to Mr. Nixon. Of course, the Watergate cover-up is the subject of a separate memorandum." Lacovara was copied in.

On September 4, 1974, Jaworski wrote to Philip W. Buchen, Counsel to President Ford. He gave, as requested by Buchen, his opinion that it would be a long time before Mr. Nixon could get a fair trial in the United States. You can't get a fair trial until you've been accused. His predicament would be worse than that of the defendants in *United States* v. *Mitchell, et al.*: "The defendants in the Mitchell case were indicted by the grand jury operating in secret session. They will be called to trial, unlike Richard Nixon, if indicted, without any previous adverse finding by an investigatory body holding public hearings on its conclusion." Then he nailed it down: "It is precisely the condemnation of Richard M. Nixon already made in the impeachment process, that would make it unfair to the defendants in the case of *United States* v. *Mitchell, et al.*, for Richard M. Nixon now to be joined as a coconspirator, should it be concluded that an indictment of him was proper." They were after him, forestalled only by the fact that their sensitivity to the prior claims of the political sphere had engendered the responsibility to be similarly mindful of the rules of fairness imposed by the criminal justice system.

Mr. Buchen reads pretty well. He also releases portions of correspondence carefully, and chose not to quote those parts of Jaworski's letter which firmly indicated, to President Ford, that his predecessor was a candidate for indictment, and maybe pretty soon, too. President Ford consulted his conscience. On the eighth, he pardoned Mr. Nixon, and thus, at last, did Hank Ruth find an ally in his advocacy of the premise that prosecution solves nothing.

# 26

THE HUMAN COST of the adventure was appalling. It should be reckoned two ways: in what there was, in hand, that was lost, and in what there might have been, that was not realized.

In what there was: he had good friends; they were disgraced. He had loyal henchmen: they were incarcerated. He had had, as a matter of fact, some good ideas, but they were vitiated. He had earned a place in history, more than modest: his entitlement was revoked (in early 1975, the trustees of the Nixon Library went public with the dismal fact: there was no longer any support for such a project, and the man who had broken through the bamboo curtain, arranged at least the beginnings of relaxation with the USSR, and gotten us out of Vietnam — while he raged against the people who wanted him to get us out of Vietnam — agreed).

In what there might have been: in the spring of 1972, when the cherry blossoms came out around the Tidal Basin, and the buses full of seniors started to arrive from the Middle West, so that the people bent on marrying young, and for the rest of their lives destined to support, the values that he said he held, the liar, could see the masonry and the pillars that symbolize those values, we were not in altogether bad shape. But we were headed for it, if we were not careful.

Too many people had rising expectations that were rising too fast, and too far. The cars were too fat, and they used too much gas. There was an increasing disparity between the value of the products that workers made, and the costs of the products that all workers had come to expect as their rewards. The talk was about a four-day work week, for the same or better pay. Nobody said anything, that was audible, at least, about a no-day work week, for increasing numbers of the unemployed.

He was not careful, and because he represented us, and we elected him, again, to represent us, we were not careful. So what a man with the luxury of his last election behind him might have done to instruct the elevator operators of this Republic that what they do is simply, if unfortunately, not worth $28,000 a year, in 1972 dollars, was not done. For two years, while the veracity of John Dean, and what it might portend, occupied the nation, we drifted into a recession, combined with rampaging inflation, which abused the poor while it straitened the middle class, and made the wealthy, rightly, fearful.

It could happen again. There is a risk built into that short document that Sam J. Ervin, Jr., was so fond of quoting, and it is a big one. It is part of the judicial system that puts a John J. Sirica in control of a case of surpassing importance. It is part of a legislative system that puts a Joseph Montoya in place to question witnesses, who may design to lie to him. It is part of an executive system that lodges a John Dean in a place where he can demand to know, and get to know, what the Chief of the Criminal Division of the United States Department of Justice, and the Acting Director of the FBI, have in mind to do, tomorrow. It is what makes a John Doar, and a Jim Neal, and a Henry Ruth, such exhilarating exemplars of what is best, and noblest, in ourselves. It is what abashes all of us, when the mortification of a Henry Petersen, the disgrace of a Herbert Kalmbach, the tardy virtue of a John Dean and the avarice of a William Bittman, come to light. It goes back to Original Sin, that risk, and there is probably no tolerable way to get rid of it. It's the risk of bad faith, of credulity, of awe, of stupidity, of greed and crookedness and, in the end, of too much trusting.

Now and then, having taken that risk repeatedly, because we prefer not to shift to the sort of totalitarian government which allows for the risk by assuming that it will certainly be resolved, against the risk-takers, we will find that we have lost the gamble, and that we have another scoundrel, running things. Another bunch of crooks.

When and if that happens again (and it shouldn't be too soon, because there ought to be at least a decade or two of deterrent effect, from this agony), we will have to go through it again. We have this odd notion —

that we are a government of laws, not of men — when in fact we are a nation, like every other, which is governed by men who either obey the laws in its governance, or do not. And we are wedded to it. It's unrealistic, naïve, impractical, and it contravenes every aspect of human experience that we know about.

It works. It worked. Not because it had to, or because, like an internal combustion engine in good tune, turning over when the ignition switch was hit, it was certain to do so, but because we insisted (just as Richard Nixon and his friends asserted that what they subjectively declared to be the truth, was the truth) that what we were entitled to insist upon being done, was to be goddamned *done*. But we were right, and they were wrong.

The law, which is only good for the punishment of totally abhorrent violations of the social contract, functioned quite adequately to reprove, and then to remove, and ultimately to punish (not as harshly as was merited, but to punish nonetheless), those who had willfully departed from the spirit of the contract. John J. Sirica, presiding at the Haldeman-Ehrlichman-Mitchell-Mardian-Parkinson trial, behaved quite well, in fact, calmed, perhaps, into a more judicious deportment by satisfaction that the end of the adventure was in sight, and that what, so proudly, he had hailed, had endured.

The place, the Jefferson Memorial, is clean, well lighted, and open all night. After midnight there are plenty of parking spaces. In the soft darkness now, as before, the security guard sits at his desk next to the column on the left, as you enter the rotunda, and he does not look up unless you are boisterous. You are free to go in now, as before, and be as awed by the great bronze figure as its model would have been embarrassed by it, and, if you please, to start to read again, about liberty.

We are a pretty tough people. Giving us the swerve is unproductive.

# Index

Beard, Dita, 263
Ben-Veniste, Richard, 247, 252,
253, 258, 262, 263, 265
and tapes, 266
Berger, Raoul, 235
Berrigans, the, 213
Bicentennial, 80
Bimini, 170
Bingham, Dana & Gould, 207
Bittman, William O., 135, 141,
145, 146, 263
as Hunt's attorney, 61–63, 66,
70–76
re Hunt's money, 226
re Hunt's notebooks, 62–63
Black Panther case, 246
Boudin, Leonard, 135
Bremer, Arthur, 110
Breslin, Jimmy, 170
Brezhnev, Leonid, 225
Brookings Institution, 110, 262
Brown, Pat, 10, 196
*Buagents*, 105
Buchen, Philip W., 275
Burger Court, 4
Burns, Sally, 262
Butterfield, Alexander, 213, 225,
233
Buzhardt, J. Fred, 206, 227
Byrne, Matt, 130

**C**

Calley, William, 87
Cambodia bombing, 235
campaign contributions, 20, 264
Campaign Contributions Task
Force, 263, 272
Campbell, Donald, 33, 176
and Liddy indictment, 94
Camp David, 169, 172, 175, 176,
179, 207, 208, 209, 210, 212
Cardozo, Benjamin N., 4
Carson, Robert T., 250
Castro, Fidel, 91

Catonsville Nine case, 246
Caulfield, John J., 214
Dean and, xiv, 159
McCord and, 80, 133–140,
144–155, 227
New York Police experience, 139
Senate Select Committee
testimony, 224
Ulasewicz and, 52–58
CBS, 171, 229
Cellar, Emmanuel, 235
Chapin, Dwight, 265
Chappaquiddick, 53, 110
Chicago Seven case, 246
Chilean Embassy wiretap, 111
CIA, xi, 87
and the Cubans, 92–93
and Ellsberg profile, 123
gambit to divert FBI
investigation, 125–128, 131,
165, 183
Gray's theories about, 21
as Hunt's employer, 60, 91
Nixon's instructions to Dean
about, 17, 21, 22–24
Clark, Ramsey, 6, 12, 105
Clark, Tom, 105
Clifford, Clark, 230–231
Cohen, William R., 235
Colombo, Joseph, 12
Colson, Charles W., Jr., 116, 254,
262
and Ehrlichman-Dean meeting
about Hunt, 60
and Ellsberg's psychiatrist's
break-in, 112
and guilty plea, 264
Hunt pardon and, 23
and Hunt's safe robbery, 61
Liddy and, 117–118
Mitchell and, 183
Nixon Administration and,
109–110, 159
Nixon cover-up and, 228
sentencing of, 130–131
and White House office, 101

and prior knowledge of break-in,
171–172
and Senate Select Committee
testimony, 170, 224
Sloan and, 38–39
U.S. Attorney disclosures, 186
*Mapp* case, 4, 104
Mardian, Robert:
Dean and, 57
debriefs Liddy, 225
Mitchell and, 15
Nixon tapes and, 233
and *Pentagon Papers*
investigation, 111
Senate Select Committee
testimony, 225
trial of, 238, 278
and Watergate cover-up, 125
Maroulis, Peter, 33, 199; *Liddy
et al.* trial, 83–84, 151
Martinez, Eugenio R.:
burglar, xviii
and *Liddy et al.* trial, 85, 87,
90–93, 142
*See also* Cuban Americans
Massachusetts trial practice, 69
May Day antiwar protest, 178
Merrill, William, 263, 265
Mexican money, 125, 126. *See
also* Dahlberg, Kenneth
Miami convention: call girls, 113
Miller, Herbert ("Jack"), 260, 267,
270
*Miranda* case, 4
Mitchell, John N., 132, 254, 255
appeal of conviction of, 256
and cover-up involvement, 125,
128–130, 259
Cuban Americans and, 91
Dean and, xii, xiv, 9, 57, 165
Gemstone and, 112–114
and grand jury perjury, 29–30
Hunt and, 147
ITT and, 249
Kleindienst and, 186–187, 193,
205

and knowledge of Watergate
break-in, 17, 115
LaRue and, 42
legal practice of, 10
Liddy and, 101, 117, 198,
approval of, 56
DNC wiretap plan, 14
plan of, 13–14, 119, 173, 230,
231
trial of, 69
McCord and, 58,
clemency for, 137, 148
Magruder and, 42
Muskie and, 115
Nixon and:
as a cause, 133
knowledge of cover-up,
172–173
loyalty to, 14
sacrificed by, 15
and tapes, 233
perjury of, xv, 32, 174, 190
prosecution of, 104
as scapegoat, 22, 182–185, 187
unwillingness to take rap, 169
Senate Select Committee and,
14
Liddy plan testimony, 119
preparing testimony for, 42
testimony, 225
witness, 228
trial of, 238, 275, 278
and Vesco case, 252
as whipping boy, 173–176
wife of, 174
Mob, the, 26–27, 147, 194,
262–263; discipline of,
xiii–xiv. *See also* Mafia, the;
organized crime
Montoya, Joseph, 120–121, 219,
277
Moore, Richard A., 167, 184, 225;
Dean's Senate Select
Committee testimony and,
171–172
Moynihan, Daniel Patrick, 110